Architectural
Programming

Architectural Programming

Creative Techniques for Design Professionals

Robert R. Kumlin

McGraw-Hill, Inc.

New York   San Francisco   Washington, D.C.   Auckland   Bogotá
Caracas   Lisbon   London   Madrid   Mexico City   Milan
Montreal   New Delhi   San Juan   Singapore
Sydney   Tokyo   Toronto

Library of Congress Cataloging-in-Publication Data

Kumlin, Robert R.
    Architectural programming : creative techniques for design
professionals / Robert R. Kumlin.
        p.   cm.
    Includes bibliographical references and index.
    ISBN 0-07-035972-5 (hardcover)
    1. Architectural design—Data processing. 2. Computer-aided
design. I. Title.
    NA2728.K86 1995
    720′.68′4—dc20   95-15116
                                                       CIP

1 2 3 4 5 6 7 8 9 0 AGM/AGM 9 0 0 9 8 7 6 5

ISBN 0-07-035972-5

*The sponsoring editor for this book was Joel Stein, the editing supervisor was
Joseph Bertuna, the production supervisor was Pamela Pelton. It was set in
Century Schoolbook by Priscilla Beer of McGraw-Hill's Professional Book Group
composition unit.*

Printed and bound by Quebecor/Martinsburg.

McGraw-Hill books are available at special quantity discounts to use as premiums and sales promotions or for use in corporate training programs. For more
information, please write to the Director of Special Sales, McGraw-Hill, Inc.,
11 West 19th Street, New York, NY 10011; or contact your local bookstore.

Contents

Preface

Since the late 1960s, the methods of facility programming have evolved to a more or less agreed upon mainstream of methodology and thought for practicing professionals, albeit with many subtle and sometimes unique variations. There is no similar consensus, however, among the academics and behavioral scientists. As a result, a review of the literature reveals a wide range of thought both theoretical and pragmatic, most of which is of only marginal value to the practical needs of a person charged with preparing a facility program. In addition, since most of the literature devoted to the subject is written by academics and social scientists, much of it is devoted to research and evaluation techniques and the behavioral sciences. There is much to be learned by the study of this literature, and the results of this research are valuable tools for the programmer and design professional, but they are only a small part of the picture.

Programming, although it has a significant impact due to its seminal nature, is only a small part of the entire design and construction effort. Indeed, it usually represents less than 5 percent of the billing for the design professional and, for the client, only one-half of 1 percent of the construction cost of a building.[1] There is no debate, however, that a well-crafted program is the best foundation for both an effective design process and a satisfied client. Therefore, most professionals are interested in programming both effectively and efficiently.

[1]Preiser (1993) reports the results of an American Institute of Architects (AIA) survey on programming that was published in the July 1991 issue of the *AIA Memo* that one half of the respondents reported that 2 to 5 percent of billable time is devoted to programming. This is the only survey related to the topic that I am aware of and since only 83 firms responded, its conclusions are suspect. Having said that, however, some of the responses seem to be consistent with my experience and bear repeating. To support the perception that the client does not perceive the importance of the program and is not thereby willing to consider it as a separate and billable service, one-fourth of the firms said that 90 percent of their programming was not billed at all and only 11 percent of the firms bill their programming over one-half the time as a separate

The principal objective of this book is to review the best contemporary thinking and practical field experience related to facility programming and to propose a system upon which the facility programmer can build a simple and effective methodology. In addition, to gain perspective and reveal what has and has not worked, the text reviews the evolution of the programming art, evaluates current practice and theory both common and idiosyncratic, and looks at present practice and future development in the light of new technology and management concepts.

Secondary objectives include the codification of the language of programming, especially in the calculation and definitions of terms for area to generate a reliable and commonly understood data base. In addition, advances in management concepts and the ideas of allied disciplines such as lateral and nonlinear thinking, small group sociology, and problem solving techniques are reviewed in terms of their application to the art.

To be answered in any preface are the reader's questions: To whom is the book addressed? Should I read it? In response, the book is basically a manual on how to program effectively in the real world; the author is an architect and programming professional and therefore the focus is on the experience of what does and does not work and what is and is not important in the context of the entire planning and building process. Although research and the behavioral sciences are addressed, the student of these disciplines will find little new broken ground within these pages and is directed to the bibliography to find resources for a more complete treatment of both these subjects.

---

service. The survey also indicated that few firms offer programming services separate from design. Yet, my experience has been that the sophisticated institutional client perceives the facility program as a document of great value and will normally not proceed into design without it. This is especially true if the project is large and complex and there is much at risk. There are, I believe, two principal reasons for this inconsistency: (1) many programs are now done by facilities groups within corporations and institutions and (2) the competitive nature of the architectural profession and the ignorance on the part of the client as to the effort involved (and benefit received) in the preparation of a facility program force most consultants to swallow the costs of programming within their fee. Most often the problem is not that of not having a program but that of having a badly prepared or inadequate one; no professional can compete by telling the potential client how bad the program is when the competitors are not complaining either because they are naive, essentially willing to do the necessary repairs free or proceed into design without the advantages or constraints of a well-crafted program. This attitude is not likely to change until the design professionals educate their clients on the value of a comprehensive program.

Among facility administrators and managers, both the seasoned specialist and novice in the large institution should benefit, as the book is both a primer and catalog of advanced techniques. Since the main thrust is pragmatic, the administrator who may only program one or two projects in an entire career will find within the text the necessary directions and sample forms to get the job done. The veteran programmer of the large institution with a codified system in place should benefit from the diverse selection of tools and techniques and find the bibliography and examples useful. Both groups should benefit from the checklist of common errors and the standard forms.

Most contemporary facility programming is done by the design professionals: architects, engineers, planners, and designers, as a part of the overall design services for a project. Much of it is done badly, especially among the smaller design firms in which the perception exists that programming is not a critical issue because the projects are usually less complex. This is not true, however, as exposure to the programming methodologies used by the more sophisticated larger organizations and programming consultants will help the smaller firm practice on a higher level of sophistication and overall efficiency. In addition, the programming methodology suggested in this text breaks a project down into manageable issues before the very beginning of the design process and thereby allows a small firm to handle a larger or new building type credibly and thereby expand their practice. The experienced individual in the large design service organization will benefit from some of the experiences of other large firms that are related here and should find, at the very least, a few proven techniques and tools that can be applied to their everyday practice.

This text is designed as a reference to be read in layers of detail as your skills and interests increase or, alternatively, to offer help on a particular aspect of programming when needed. When reading this book, the professional with at least some experience in the art and an urgent project in hand should skip the introduction (Chap. 1) and start with Chaps. 2 and 3, "The Program Team" and "Program Strategy." If generating a program budget is the problem in hand, Chap. 7 will give you an appropriate direction and format. Chapter 4, "Program Document," has an appropriate format and list of typical contents for most programs and should help your determination as to what is and is not relevant. A checklist of common errors in Appendix B serves as a useful guide for avoiding the most common and costly mistakes. A review of the sample forms included in the Appendixes will give the reader either a quick way to get a program done for the project at hand or serve as a springboard to develop similar documents for the future project intelligently and effectively.

For the novice, it is best to start with Chap. 1, to get a proper perspective and review alternative thinking on the subject. Chapter 6, "Programming Theory," explores the rationale behind the proposed methodology. To sharpen kills for both process and documentation, the reader should explore Chap. 5, "Tools and Techniques of Information Gathering," this chapter also contains some suggestions on how to resolve an impasse should you encounter difficult people or problems. Chapter 8, "Language of Area" is a handy reference that should be read once to acquire an appropriate programming language, later it can be used as a appended reference to your program.

Lastly, programming is about common sense and good judgment; the methodology described here, along with its techniques, tools, checklists, and insights are merely methods to organize both process and communication (1) to help you sort and handle large amounts of information effectively, (2) to incorporate both qualitative and quantitative attributes in your process and documentation, (3) to achieve consensus and support from your clients for the project design process to follow and (4) thus to help your client get the best possible facility achievable with the available resources.

Acknowledgments

As an architect and designer working for large architectural firms in the 1970s and early 1980s, I muddled my way through the programming process as did many of my colleagues without giving it much thought. It was not until I joined CRS as a director in 1981 that I came to realize the value of the facility program both as a process and a product, and took my first steps towards treating facility programming as a serious and demanding art. By the early 1980s, CRS (now CRSS) had codified their process and had a separate programming group; for the uninitiated there was much to learn. Mentors included both Willy Peña and Steve Parshall, but it was Kevin Kelly whose plain good leadership and sense of perspective helped get many of my projects off to the right start. I am indebted also to Fred Lindquist, former CEO of TKLP in Philadelphia, for giving support to my programming efforts and advice on how to make programming work better for the really large and complex research facility.

But you cannot program in the real world without clients. Among the many great and understanding ones I have been privileged to work with over the years, Dick Murtland of ARCO, David Lunde of the University of Georgia, and Michel Diot of Diot Conseil stand out—together we advanced the art of programming and had fun along the way. In addition, my thanks is extended to the many clients that allowed me to use their projects as examples in this text. Special thanks goes to Therese Sampson and Mark Streckenbein of Atlantic Community College for allowing me to use their project at the Mays Landing Campus as an example of top-down and bottom-up retrofit programming.

Both Ben Graves of Educational Planning Consultants and Ray Ovresat of the University of Illinois at Chicago were kind enough to read preliminary drafts of this text; many of their comments and suggestions are incorporated in this final version.

Lastly, my appreciation is extended to my daughter, Loralyn Kumlin, a talented young architectural designer practicing in Chicago, for doing many of the drawings in this text. I could never have met the deadlines without her.

Robert R. Kumlin

1

Introduction

Contemporary Design and Programming

The jury is still out. We are still too close in time to gain full historical perspective, but there is a growing consensus that 1945–1975 will be remembered as a brief period when some of the worst architecture and planning in history were created. Regrettably, almost 80 percent of the built environment in the United States was completed during this period, and every city still bears twisted gold anodized aluminum scars wallpapered over what used to be some of its best architecture. Neither the schoolhouse nor the campus were spared. Every college campus has at least a few buildings designed during this period that are oblivious to the context and character of the institution, and windowless or near windowless school boxes dot the landscape from coast to coast.

Communities, cities, and the landscape perhaps suffered worst of all with the commercial strip, the malling of America, the ghettoization of the inner city, and the bedroom suburb, all of which metastasized explosively during this period. It is no coincidence that the emergence of facility programming as a functional discipline closely followed the emerging post-war embrace of this uniquely American version of Modern Architecture and justified some of its worst excesses.[1] Programming's

---

[1] The lesson is still being learned. All over the United States, discount chain stores selling general merchandise have had the policy of buying land cheaply in the outskirts of small communities and waiting for the expansion of the population to come to the location. When and if the population density becomes high enough, the store is built, and since it offers almost all the commodities of Main Street at a lower price, the immediate result is that Main Street becomes a hollow shell and the very charm that caused

contribution to the contemporary condition lay in the strictly quantitative approach of its earliest manifestations: its attraction lay in its image as a systematic approach to design.

The promotion and acceptance of facility programming in the narrowest quantitative sense were driven by many architects' naive belief and their clients' mostly unspoken agreement on a fundamentalist interpretation of the modern movement's dictum "form follows function."[2] A cost-effective and bottom-line approach to programming was only part of the continuum of the accepted function only, systematic design process, and it fit well with most administrators' needs for simplification, easy understanding, and justification: if form follows function, why do you need anything more than a description of the function? For the commercial developer and speculator this approach greased the skids to maximum profitability, especially when competing against older structures with the excess baggage of nonfunctional attributes. "Soft" issues such as environmental quality, esthetics, cultural continuity, context, and historical value are difficult to evaluate and communicate and were generally ignored. For the few who thought differently, the wide acceptance of the system often gave the design professional little platform from which to plead for qualities that had historically contributed to the delight of the man-made environment. As a result, the concept of the facility program as only a list of functional spaces was perpetuated well into the late 1960s when programming as a discipline first began to be addressed by the design professions. Only in 1976 as

---

many of the people to move there in the first place disappears, replaced by vacant and boarded storefronts. Only now are communities beginning to recognize and resist this kind of urban guerrilla warfare by rezoning land and denying building permits.

[2]Most readers will recognize this statement by Louis Sullivan. It has been used so often as to be properly called a cliché. It is difficult to believe today that this naive interpretation was a widely held opinion in the architectural profession until the middle 1970s, but people who were there will remember the popular reality. For those of you who are not familiar with the history, I will offer the following brief historical synopsis of an extremely complex idea. During the last few decades of the nineteenth century popular American architecture was revival architecture, its principal home was New York City, and its principal material expression was layers upon layers of terracotta gingerbread. Critics such as Montgomery Schuyler and James Jackson Jarves rightly railed these encrusted derivatives, and Louis Sullivan with his architecture, his books, and his partner Dankmar Adler and others captured the spirit of a new American architecture by adopting a new functionally related style of architecture (later called *The Chicago Style*) around the turn of the century. Ayn Rand's *The Fountainhead* is an enjoyable fictionalized and compressed version of the battle; a better overview is Mumford, *The Brown Decades* (1955). Today, I think most people would agree that the cure was needed, but that, for the most part, it has been worse than the disease—there are many more loved terracotta revival relics than "modern" concrete buildings of the 1960s and 1970s.

Pruitt Igoe collapsed beneath the wrecker's ball[3] was there a ground swell for a more holistic approach to architectural design and only now is it beginning to be realized.

A Brief History of Programming

Every human physical construction has only commenced after some need has been formulated, and instructions to the builder are as old as human civilization. God's specifications for Noah's ark has left every Sunday-school child wondering about the size of a cubit (a measure of the human arm from the end of the middle finger to the elbow—somewhere between 18 and 22 inches). As ancient texts are discovered and unraveled, mixed among them are instructions on how to build this granary and that palace, etc. The instructions are usually brief and, with rare exception, strictly functional; they specify what was needed and leave the how (the design) to the architect and builder who, until the beginning of the Renaissance, was usually the same person. This brevity was usually sufficient, for even large and monumental buildings had simple functions, technology changed slowly, and the evolving design response was mostly conventional and predictable in its basic attributes. When poetry was created, it was due to the creativity of the architect or builder, who added vision and detail in much the same way that the baroque musician was expected to embroider the work of the composer, who traditionally scored only the skeleton of the composition.

Until the eighteenth century, building types remained simple and, except for the occasional royal palace, civic building, or religious complex, there was little need for elaborate instructions to the architect. The rise thereafter of the large national state and its central government generated buildings of more complex and specialized function to accom-

---

[3]Pruitt Igoe was a housing project for the poor in East St. Louis that was built in accord with a rough interpretation of Le Corbusier's model of urban planning, which utilized multistory urban blocks of apartments in an open landscaped setting. By the late 1960s it had become obvious that the multistory apartment blocks were completely dysfunctional in any sense except the modern architecture imagery in which they were designed. In the end, crime, vandalism, and the lack of caring by the residents overwhelmed the project, and the buildings were simply torn down. The occasion of their demolition has since been considered the watershed of fundamentalist modern architecture in America. Chicago has since bravely struggled on with Cabrini–Green, a similar project. After many initiatives, including locating a police station in one of the towers and the proposed suspension of civil rights to accomplish search and seizure, to mention only two, the best that can be said is that the situation has been neutralized and the sniper fire has been eliminated.

modate the burgeoning bureaucracy required to run them. During this period, a few large industrial complexes were created to move and process basic commodities, such as food and cement, but it was not until the industrial revolution at the beginning of the nineteenth century that an explosion of specialized building types occurred. This, when added to the ever enlarging and multiplying government functions, created the initial need for a program that was more than an informal and simple verbal statement of requirements from one individual to another. Also, about this time, many major civic buildings throughout Western Europe were awarded by competition based on a simplified written program. After some early failures with this approach at the beginning of the century, competition programs became more elaborate and specific and as a result, by the end of the century, the architectural response became more successful. The Paris Opera House by Garnier (1861–74) and The Amsterdam Stock Exchange by H. P. Berlage (1898–1903) are two familiar, successful, and later examples of buildings awarded by competition.

Birth and Development of Programming as a Separate Discipline

Contemporary interest in facility programming as a separate discipline worthy of study was signaled in 1966 by the American Institute of Architects (AIA) publication of a booklet called *Emerging Techniques of Architectural Practice,* which contained references to the scheduling of the programming phase, space analysis and analytical diagrams, questionnaires, and "other planning techniques." This was closely followed in 1969 by another AIA booklet, *Emerging Techniques 2: Architectural Programming,* and the near simultaneous, but unrelated, publication of the book *Problem Seeking: An Architectural Programming Primer,* by Peña and Focke of Caudill Rowlett Scott (afterwards CRS and now CRSS). The 1969, 70-page AIA booklet was generally a catalog of programming techniques and reflected that programming was clearly a responsibility of the client, except that the architect was to take the client's program from which "the architect then can develop his program instrument from which the designs are produced."[4] *Problem Seeking*

---

[4]This approach is clearly designed to designate complete programming services as an additional service for which the architect was to be compensated. Programming is still listed as an additional service in the current AIA B141—the AIA's most commonly utilized form contract. The fault of this approach is that it alludes to, but does not differentiate between, what I call a functional program and a facilities program (see the Glossary). It then goes on to say that the owner will be required to provide a program if the architect is not paid to do it. This fuzzy thinking—is the owner required to provide a facilities program or a functional program?—confuses the issue.

was the first (although idiosyncratic) approach to programming that was conceived as a complete system; the book was revised and reissued in 1975 and again in 1987, and describes the successful and widely emulated methodology still employed by HOK (who purchased the professional service business of CRSS) in their day-to-day practice.

From these beginnings many approaches have been developed and much research has been done, although publications describing them have been few and generally inaccessible to a wide audience. More recent comprehensive works include the AIA publication *The Architect's Guide to Facility Programming,* Palmer (1981), a comprehensive overview of the subject (which is now, regrettably, out of print), and *Methods of Architectural Programming,* Sanoff (1977). The papers contained in the annual proceedings of The Environmental Design Research Association (EDRA) have always been a rich source of related material: since their first conference in 1969, this organization has been on the forefront of research in this discipline. These and other resources are referred to throughout the text and included in the bibliography.

Who programs? Wolfgang Preiser (1993) reports that although there is a diversity of educational background among people who program, most individuals who assume the role have been trained as architects. Most of them are employed in large architectural or engineering firms and many of the remainder are employed in larger institutions or companies as part of a facilities group. A few are employed in consulting firms that specialize in programming and predesign services.

It seems that these programmers are trained mostly on the job. At the university, training in programming is typically offered by the school of architecture and is either buried in the studio process or treated as part of the curricula devoted to theory or professional practice. In the studio the stated goals for the program's inclusion are related to consideration

---

In effect, it has actually forced most architects to offer programming services at no cost to the client (see footnote 1 to the Preface for more on this). This may have been the first unwitting example of the AIA's instructions to architects to retreat from the leadership position of all aspects of the construction process to the present day position of just one of the participants—rather than discovering a new and needed service and telling architects to do it, the discovery results in the denial of the service. Shortly thereafter, Chuck Thompsen of CRSS invented the concept of the separately paid construction manager, chipping away at the architect's services at the opposite end of the spectrum. This latter initiative was a reaction to the similar identify-as-separate-service, then-deny-as-standard-service approach related to programming but this time related to additional construction administration services. Now, most construction managers are what everyone used to call general contractors and the architect has lost primary control during construction, much to the detriment of the building's quality and the client's actual received value.

of the effect of outside influences and client requirements on the design outcome. These programs, if created as part of a design problem, are just as likely, however, to be a justification of the design as a consideration of the site condition, budget, and client's needs. In addition, even if programming is taught as an individual subject, the emphasis is on the theory and arrangement of the program as a document with little emphasis on the process needed to create it.

Programming as Part of the Design Process

From the very beginning of contemporary thought about programming as a separate discipline, the question of programming's relationship to design was a central issue for the design professional, and the successful resolution of this issue was viewed as one key to developing a successful methodology. The key question then was: How should programming be done to achieve architectural excellence? A contemporary addition to this concern would be: How can programming help the built environment be more responsive to the users' needs and the needs of the environment? Questions related to these issues include the following:

When should programming be done?

Who should program?

What is a successful facility program and what does it contain?

Each of these questions needs to be addressed in turn by looking at the various approaches that have been proposed, evaluating them in the light of experience when possible, and then based on this evaluation giving the reader some recommendations from which his or her own approach can then be formulated.

When Should Programming Be Done?

The first thought gives the obvious answer—programming should be done as a prelude to design and completed prior to its beginning. It is an answer that I agree with, for the most part, as it is simple and appeals to common sense. There is some merit, however, in looking at the rationale of a number of approaches that integrate programming more closely with design to discover why they do not work as well, especially when viewed in the context of the entire design process.

Programming responds to the level of detail required by the task at hand, and there are various and conventional categories of programs designed to respond to each of these needs: the *master plan program,* which treats a project in only its largest dimension, the *schematic design program,* which is a prelude to the design of a building, the *component program,* which is devoted to one specific aspect of a project such as maintenance, furniture, equipment, and specialized engineering systems. All of these program types and their contents are described in more detail in Chaps. 3 and 4. Both the master plan and component programs are easily accomplished in the simple and segregated, program-then-design sequence, as these programs are usually more simple, have narrowly focused objectives, and are considered at a single level of detail. However, the design process of the individual building or complex of buildings suggests that programming may be considered continuously and simultaneously with design.

The rationale for this approach lies in the reality of design as a heuristic process that proceeds from the general to the specific, and that along the way written criteria of various types accompany the drawings to determine the project development fully for the succeeding design phase. I am aware of three principal variations to the continuous approach: programming *is* design, programming as prescriptive management, and programming as iterative process. There may be others.

The approach that programming is design immerses the program completely in the design process of the project; the facility program ceases to exist as a separate document or series of documents and might, for example, in its most extreme expression, be reduced to a series of marginal notes on drawings. This approach assumes that the programmer is the professional who is designing the project and that the programming happens simultaneously with design.

Programming as prescriptive management assumes that the programmer first creates the schematic design program prior to the beginning of design and then continues in a steadily diminishing and reciprocal role with the design team throughout the entire design and documentation process, creating along the way more detailed programs to describe and circumscribe the design response. In effect, after the inception of design, the "programs" become management tools and the programmer a monitor of the design and documentation process.

Programming as iterative process integrates programming with design into repetitive loops of program–design–evaluation–feedback, which occur throughout the design process. The pattern is familiar to the reader as elementary management theory and its rationale addresses the reality of the design process as a series of hierarchal decisions: each loop responds to a different level of detail. This system is similar to programming as prescriptive management except for the implication that the design response continuously revises the program(s) as it reveals more detail.

There are both strengths and weaknesses in these concepts that integrate programming into the design process, but on balance, the weaknesses prevail. Both the iterative process and the prescriptive management approach encourage continuous involvement by everyone throughout the design process. They are characterized by their advocates as more responsive than the segregated, program-then-design approach. Their weakness, however, lies in the subjection of the entire design and documentation process to a new language and process that, in this context, are strange to both the design professional and client. If done by the design professional, integrating these concepts into the commonly understood and fine-tuned process of design and construction documents adds an additional burden of review and management. If done by the client, it is a management process, not programming, and should only be necessary for the largest projects.

In addition, these latter two approaches suffer from trying to reach too far and assume that every action requires a program (or statement) when, in fact, this is not always true. For example, both systems suggest that when the evaluation of the schematic design phase documentation is fed back to the design team the proper response would be a design development program as the restatement that starts another loop. Following the logic, both the prescriptive management and iterative approaches also postulate a construction document program as the beginning of another (third) loop. In reality, neither the design development program nor the construction document program exists in conventional practice. The closest approximations might be some of the written documents given in the next paragraph, and these documents are descriptive rather than prescriptive. In reality, if this methodology was applied to the written program alone, it suggests multiple iterations as ever more detail is created and the design responds. Experience has shown that this process of program multiplication and revision is not useful, as the new development itself (in both written and graphic form, called design development, construction documents, etc.) is sufficient.

On balance, I believe that the integration of the programming process into the design process is more of a problem than an advantage for the average project. In regard to the iterative and prescriptive approaches, the reality of the programming and design process for a building suggests only a few traditionally identifiable documents that could be called "programs": the schematic design program, the site program, architectural and engineering criteria (AEC), the furniture, fixtures, and equipment program (FFE), and the specifications. Certainly these are not sufficient to build a universally applicable system, and of these only the FFE program and the specifications need be done during the design phase of the project. In addition, the participative process, one of the unique advantages claimed for this approach, routinely occurs within the traditional design process and is not dependent on the integration of the concept of design as programming or the concept of design and program integration. I believe that both these approaches are attempts by people involved exclusively in management and programming to expand their role and control more of the design process. By expending resources that could more properly be allocated to the design professional (or for that matter not expended at all) and by having the design process controlled by people who are probably not designers, this approach will neither encourage creative architecture nor give the client enhanced value.

With respect to the concept that programming is design and should therefore be completely integrated, I believe that this works on only the least complicated projects. It assumes that the programmer is the design professional who is designing the project and that the programming happens simultaneously with design. It works especially well if both the client and design professional are completely familiar with the building type and have worked together before. This methodology intertwines the design so thoroughly with the program that it becomes impossible to determine whether the design responds to the program or vice versa, and for the more complex structure the process can easily become a risky voyage with few landmarks for all participants. In addition, this concept as a universal approach is of little use when the criteria for a project need to be developed prior to the engagement of the design professional. This approach, which places the program completely in control of the design professional, is at the opposite end of the spectrum from the two programmer-controlled design processes described above.

Based on the above considerations, I believe that any consistent and effective methodology of programming must be based on the segregated program-then-design approach applied at the beginning of any defined task and completed more or less prior to the commencement of design. It is a more balanced and simple approach, applicable over a wide range of situations and levels of detail, and, as such, is a system responsive to continuous improvement and refinement. It is the basis of the approach advocated and described in this text.

Programs (if they can be called that) related to special components such as laboratory layouts and furniture schedules should be done as separate tasks at a time in the design process when it makes sense to do them, and these tasks should be done on a program-then-design basis specifically tailored to the requirements. Chapter 3 addresses some approaches to special component programs.

Who Should Program?

To determine who programs, there first needs to be a distinction made between a functional program and a facility program. The functional program provides raw data, usually as a justification for funding, that demonstrates the need for a physical facility related to the mission of the organization. For the educational institution this often takes the form of a described curriculum with required contact hours and projected student population. In other instances, the program may relate to a population change or new function, both of which require increased accommodation. For the public institution it is often in a standard format mandated by a higher authority. Often, when related to teaching, it is referred to as an educational program or specification.

For the corporate facility, the functional program usually describes the number of personnel, their functions, and basic organization: this program is often in the form of an organization chart and personnel by function list. There are many variations of functional programs, but they all share the attributes of justification, raw quantitative data related to people or functional description, and a description of the relationship of these to the basic mission of the organization. They are not facility programs.

These functional programs are always prepared by the owner, user, or client, sometimes with the help of an outside specialty consultant. They are an essential source of the raw data required to prepare the facility program. It is important to recognize that a functional program *always* exists although sometimes in an unexpected and unconventional form. It may, for instance, be a series of documents or memoranda: I have programmed major projects in which it was discovered to be only an unspoken agreement among senior management. The functional program (or lack of it) should always be addressed as part of the initial global decision makers' meeting (see Chap. 3 for more details).

As to who does the facility program, for the owner, user, or client there is a selection of strategies from which to choose: the in-house facilities group, an in-house task force or committee, the design architect or engineer, or a separate programming consultant who may or may not be an architect or engineer. For the facility manager, the choice to go outside depends partly on the capabilities of his or her organization and availability of qualified in-house individuals (easy to determine) and partly on the chosen strategy (more difficult). Cost is usually not an issue because programming is such a small part of the total project cost, but the availability of funding at the proper time may be a determining factor. Consideration of the teaming strategy is treated in detail in Chap. 2, and this should help you make a final determination. In addition, *when* a program is required often determines *who* should do it, and a full discussion of the factors related to timing is also given in Chap. 2.

If the facility programming is to be done by the professional who will design the project, there are a number of staffing strategies that may be considered. For the small project and small firm, the individual architect who designs the project and who is also the principal in charge is a natural choice because of the advantage of the acquired project familiarity. The advantage of continuity, however, is offset by the danger of consciously or unconsciously introducing programming bias (the danger of having the program slanted toward a preconceived design solution). For the larger project, the time demands on the principal are too great and another staffing strategy is indicated.

In firms of architects, engineers, and interior designers who do larger and more complex projects and are large enough to be departmentalized or divided into studios, it is advised that the architects' programming team be led by a person experienced in the art of programming. Since programming is the first working contact with the client and requires the addressing of key issues, the principal in charge usually develops the strategy, manages the process overall, is present to initiate the programming, and presides at key meetings. If the principal in charge is also the designer, there is the added benefit of continuity (but, as noted earlier, the danger of programming bias exists).

Experience suggests that the best results are achieved, however, when the principal designer does not lead the programming team, but rather when the team is led by a management principal or project manager and a lead programmer. This approach is the one advocated herein if the programming is to be done by the same consultant that will design the project. It has many positive attributes for both the design professional and the client. In this strategy the programming team is staffed by junior designers who will later assist the design principal in the development of the project. This approach generates a continuity of information, gives junior staff early exposure to clients, and creates a wide reservoir of programming experience within the firm. It avoids the problem of programming as an early specialized career focus (an anathema to most young architects), allowing the firm to use their best and brightest, and avoids the problem of having a strong designer bludgeon the program into agreement with a preconceived design solution. Sufficient numbers of individuals will choose programming as a career path to staff the senior lead programmer positions. A variation of this strategy that also works well is to train project managers to assume the role of lead programmer as part of their duties. This approach is often utilized by the midsize (20 to 30 persons) firm because of staff limitations, by the engineering/architecture firm because of management orientation, organization, and staff distribution, or by the firm specializing in a complex building type such as laboratories or hospitals because the detailed knowledge required only comes after many years of experience.

A third and now more frequently used strategy is to have the program developed by either an architect or engineer specializing in the building type or a programming consultant. The program would then be handed off to the architect who would design the project. This process omits the programming bias but eliminates some of the opportunities for continuity. A complete analysis of the pluses and minuses of all these options for the facility manager can be found in Chap. 2.

What Is a Successful Facility Program?

The successful facility program can only be measured by the results of its application that are revealed when the project is completed. There are some criteria, however, by which both the process and the document can be measured along the way:

- Were the program predictions regarding scope and cost achievable and accurate?
- Was the predicted efficiency (net to gross) achieved and did the final design meet the expectations of the client regarding the quality of the spaces and finishes within the structure?
- Did the program allow the widest latitude for creative design and simultaneously keep the final result within the quantitative parameters?
- Was there enough information, and was it organized and expressed in a manner to minimize information overload and be easily accessible?
- Were the client's requirements, visions, dreams, intentions, and priorities clearly and immediately apparent to the design team and manifest in the final solution?
- Did the program have the enthusiastic support of the users, stakeholders, and decision makers?

The purpose of this text is to give you the tools so that the answers to these questions can be an unequivocal "yes."

2

The Program Team

In the widest sense, the program team is everyone that participates in the creation of the program. Contributions come from many sources; some of these are obvious and found close at hand while others, such as regulatory agency officials and their requirements and public records, will need to be identified, sought out, and brought to light to ensure that a full picture is obtained.

It is useful, however, to define the team more narrowly than this and, based on the members' role in the process, I use three common sense appellations to describe the participants: the program team, the program participants, and resources. They are defined as follows.

The program team includes the people directly responsible for creating the program. It is comprised of key members of the program participants, defined below. When an outside consultant is chosen to lead the program team there is, in a sense, two teams, the consultant's team and the owner's team, which must be combined into one.

The program participants include all people that directly participate in the creation of the document, that have a stake (is a "stakeholder") in the outcome of the program, and that have the power to effect change either by fiat or influence. The program participants include all members of the program team.

Resources include everyone else involved in the process that can contribute information.

Determining who is part of the program team and identifying the contributing participants are key elements of the programming strategy. Since the size of the project and the complexity of the organization parallel the complexity of the programming task, for the larger project it is often not an easy task to make this determination. Current theories of organizational analysis suggest four different perspectives: the formal or structural approach (usually represented by the organization chart), the informal approach (who works with whom and who really does the work?), the technological approach (what does the organization produce, how does it produce, and how does it interact with the outside world?), and the value system approach (how does the organization make decisions and what are its values and style?). See Farbstein (1993) and Pugh (1971) for a more detailed treatment of organizational analysis and the impact of client organization on programming. A consideration of each of these perspectives will help in making your choices.

In addition, one of the reasons for a new or remodeled facility may be the reorganization or reconfiguration of the whole or parts of the company or institution. Universities, for example, become collections of colleges and corporations become collections of product- or project-oriented, multidisciplined teams, both strategies often replacing former departmental structures. Management theories, educational strategies, research methods, and technology are constantly changing, and in an age in which global economic competition and the education of the work force have replaced war as the ultimate tool of diplomacy, this kind of change is accelerating. With these reorganizations come the loss or addition of departments, functions, prestige, power, and jobs. Since the facility program can be the vehicle that makes these changes concrete, choosing the programming team and the participants may be a high-stakes game.

In these circumstances, the team is often restricted to fewer individuals, often at a higher management level. Revised organization charts are often extremely confidential documents in this environment, and the added dimension of information security must be added to the programmer's task. All of these issues affect the choice of the team and the participants. If you are an outside consultant, this selection process along with how the information is handled should be done with the client as part of an initial strategy meeting (see Chap. 3).

The program participants finally selected for a university chemistry building might look like this (program team members are denoted with an asterisk):

President of the university

Executive vice president

Campus architect*

Department chairperson*

Scientists* and scientific staff

Building administrator* and staff

Director of the physical plant

Campus parking representative

Student representatives*

Faculty representatives*

Representative of the donor/funding agency*

The programming consultants*

Building type specialty consultant*

Other specialty consultants for special problems

Representatives of other special interests, etc.

Resources might include building code officials, representatives of utility companies, and specialty consultants such as geophysical, vibration, or acoustical consultants.

The program participants for a corporate office building may include the following:

CEO

CFO

Division vice president of the group that will occupy the building*

Director of corporate facilities*

Department heads* and staff

Representatives of special interest groups (management information services, maintenance, etc.)

Programming consultant*

Specialty consultants for special problems

As above, others with the power to affect the outcome but without a stake should be thought of as resources only.

The in-house components of the team should designate an alternate for each participant during the programming process, as the process is intense and the people with the authority to make decisions usually have limited availability. It is desirable, but not absolutely necessary, that the alternate have the authority to make decisions on behalf of his or her leader. If the alternate's authority is lacking in certain areas it is only necessary that the leader be available to render the decision in a timely manner after a conference with the alternate, who will then return with the response to the programming team.

Most people charged with the execution of the facility program are reluctant to risk reaching to the very top of the organization for input. You need reach no higher in the organization than the decision maker with the final authority regarding the program, but reach him or her you must if the program is to have the full support it requires. Experience has shown that the participation of the high-level decision makers can be brief to fit their schedule and that the issues addressed can be consistent with their interests (see the section titled "The Global Decision Makers' Meeting" in Chap. 3).

The dramatis personae for each organization and each project will be different, and their selection is usually a matter of common sense. Some decision makers will be committees and not individuals; very often influence bears little resemblance to the position on the organization chart. The only criteria are the three stipulated: participation, stake in the outcome, and the power to effect change.

In the matter of participation it is usually wiser to be inclusive instead of exclusive rather than risk major modification, which may cause the team to revisit issues that have already been laid to rest. The objective is to get the widest support and consensus. The charge is to find all the decision makers. It is not unusual, especially in small companies that are closely held, to have presidents or CEOs limit their component of the program team to one or two individuals. It is also typical to have the highest-level decision maker decide to whom the program team should talk and how far down into the organization to reach for information; their counsel on this should be one of the agenda items for the global decision makers' meeting.

Creating the Program Team

To create the program, we must first create the program team and its leadership. There are three basic options:

1. Have the architect selected to design the project, as a specialist in the building type, program the facility as a part of the design process. The architect becomes the leader of the program team.

2. Have an in-house committee program the facility with or without the use of outside assistance. The team leader is designated from within the company or institution.

3. Have the program prepared by a programming consultant, architect, or engineer as a separate contractual task. The team leader is the consultant.

All of these options have in common the requirement for single point responsibility and strong leadership, and all of them require an inhouse committee or individual with the power to make decisions and with the charge to produce the document *and* (most importantly) secure the support for it within the organization. There are advantages and disadvantages to each approach:

Option 1: Programming by the Architect or Engineer as Part of the Design Process

There are some strong arguments supporting this choice. In complex and specialized (but not extraordinary) building types, such as children's hospitals or pharmaceutical pilot plants, the architect or engineer is often the only source for state-of-the-art current practice and regulatory data. In addition, the architect or engineer brings to the table information such as historical building costs, reasonable efficiencies, and a knowledge of the entire process and required program elements. Many architects practicing in these specialized building types have excellent abilities and broad experience in programming (but some do not). This methodology is often most successfully adopted when the facility to be programmed is very similar to another project that is to be used as a model and that was also designed by the same architect or engineer.

Another compelling reason for this approach is that when the selected architect leads the program effort and produces the document he or she "owns" it along with the construction cost and schedule. All other approaches risk the rejection of the program by the architect or engineer chosen to design the project. (This risk can be eliminated, however, by requiring either acceptance of the program or acceptance with proposals for modification as part of the proposal process prior to selection of the consultant.) There are, however, some other difficulties with this approach:

- For major projects it is usually not difficult to find a consultant who possesses both design and programming skills, but on smaller projects for which the choices are limited because of geographical preferences or other criteria, the preferred architect or engineer may not have both skills.

- The architect or engineer may consciously or unconsciously build bias into the program in the form of skewed priorities. These typically relate to design issues and usually take the form of lowered efficiencies and higher contingencies, quality, and cost. Contrary to the desire by the architect to separate the design from programming conceptually,[1] programming, as a prescriptive process, is in a sense design because it defines the boundaries of successful solutions.

It may make sense to consider the program document as client-created independent criteria prepared separately to serve as the basis for creating and evaluating the design. This is especially true if the client does not feel qualified or does not have the time and resources to monitor the possible bias.

- Often this methodology is utilized as a perceived economical alternative when funds, time, or resources have not been made available to do the program as an identified task or service. This is not a good reason to use this approach unless the fee is increased to compensate the architect or engineer, as it will result in either an initially good program and the consequent reduction of services elsewhere in the project or an inadequate program. Programming when adequately done requires a separate effort and focus.[2]

- Finally, there are additional difficulties involved in programming with the same architect or engineer that designs the facility; these are timing and the resulting necessary assumptions and risks that the facilities manager must make defining the project. Selection of the architect most often occurs after the project has been identified as to both scope of work and cost. Hardly anyone hires an architect or engineer and signs a contract for services without defining a project in some way, albeit roughly. Indeed, it is usually impossible to develop defensible criteria for selection before the rough parameters are known.

  Assuming that the architect will program the facility as part of the design contract, usually no funds are allocated previous to the award of the contract for services. Therefore, the basic parameters are usually defined beforehand without the benefit of the necessary effort, resources, and time (but usually with great risk and anguish on the part of the creator). Most often it is done as part of the heated rush to

---

[1]In Peña, et al., (1987), for example, programming is called *analysis* as opposed to design, which is called *synthesis*.

[2]The most typical form contract utilized by architects, the AIA B141-1987, recognizes programming as an *optional additional service* and additionally requires the owner to provide a program under *basic services* should this additional service not be authorized. The Preface and the Introduction discuss this in more detail.

create an annual capital budget. A common and costly mistake (often requiring a revised application for additional funding) is assuming that a functional or educational program with the addition of some assumed area requirements and a budget assessment is a skeleton facility program. It is not.

■ An obvious and alternative solution to circumvent some of these problems is to hire the architect or engineer under a separate contract to program the facility and then decide later whether or not to extend the contract to include design services. This approach includes many of the advantages of retaining a separate programming consultant and is, on balance, one of the better strategies for retaining an architect or engineer for programming services; it brings with it, however, some other problems.

There are two separate difficulties generated by this approach, depending on whether you intend to hire programming architects or engineers and allow them to compete for the design project, or whether you will not consider them as a precondition to the award of the contract for programming services. If you choose to let the programming architects compete, you will be accused of bias if they win the project, and it is likely that some of the best qualified architects or engineers will decline to compete based on the perception that the job is "wired" (an impression that the programming architects may try to encourage). Should you decide to disqualify the programming team from competing, you may find it difficult to get qualified architects to program or, if once obtained, perhaps regret that you will not be able to use them for the design.

It is recommended that if you choose an architect to do the programming and have the monitoring capability to omit bias, hire the architect that you want to use for design to do the programming under an early separate contract. Should the architect prove unsatisfactory during the programming process, he or she can be excluded from later consideration. Since the architect knows that future contracts depend on programming performance, there is considerable incentive to do it right.

Option 2: Programming in House

Because of the increasing awareness of the importance of the physical plant and its effect on the mission of the organization, most large institutions and companies now have people or departments devoted to physical facilities. Many of these individuals are highly qualified, and the existence of organizations such as The Society for College and

University Planning (SCUP) and International Facility Management Association (IFMA) has provided the necessary literature and forums for the exchange of information to keep these individuals up to date. Having qualified people mitigates some of the disadvantages of this approach, but even then the fact remains that most institutions have limits to their resources and even those with assigned staff members often find them overcommitted with little time for additional projects.

The owner's rationale for this approach is that "no one knows our facilities' needs as well as we do and that all of the expertise we need is under this roof." This argument continues, "Why should we bring in outside experts...our scientists, animal handlers, faculty, office managers, etc., do not need a competing outside voice...they are the experts."

There are some strong merits to this approach in limited circumstances. It works well (and in some situations it is the only methodology possible) when the facility under consideration is driven by technology or process to the extent that the building or created enclosure and environment is an afterthought. Examples would include refineries, particle accelerators, automobile factories, and food-processing plants. For most other projects there are two types of weaknesses to be overcome with this in-house approach—knowledge and organizational.

- Knowledge of the building type and typical space standards is lacking within the organization. Although records of existing facilities within the organization are available, often it is difficult to find standards outside the organization. It is therefore difficult to project not only space standards but also efficiencies that are reasonable and defensible.

- The omission of spaces that are both required and ancillary to the primary functional spaces such as storage, vending machines, and copy rooms is a common occurrence using this methodology. Indeed, even when these spaces are included, it is common to make mistakes about appropriate size and number. Food-service facilities, shipping/receiving, and the number and distribution of conference rooms, to name a few, are common problems.

- Knowledge of construction costs and realistic project schedules for both structures and site improvements is often lacking, resulting in unrealistic cost projections, unacceptable contingencies, or both. Construction cost is also dependent on schedule and often the schedule is another critical factor of the project.

- Knowledge of regulatory requirements and the means of obtaining them are not known. As regulatory requirements steadily increase in number and complexity, this becomes increasingly critical regarding the program. This is especially true if the site analysis is to be accomplished as part of the effort.

- Knowledge of the appropriate language, content, and format of a good and sufficient building program is lacking. Reference to this text, its bibliography (which contains references to many other helpful texts), and references to other building programs will overcome these handicaps.

- The availability of leadership time within the organization is often a primary constraint mitigating against this approach. Of the various strategies proposed, this one will make the most demand on the resources of the organization.

- Having the program created within the organization eliminates the advantages of the outside voice and vantage point. It is almost impossible for the inside team to ignore the culture, structure, and political realities of the existing organization (which many times have actually been created by the existing physical facilities), and the resulting bias towards perpetuating the status quo may leave many opportunities for functional improvements and cost savings undiscovered. Indeed, one of the basic purposes of many programming efforts is the discovery of alternative means of organization, operation, and human interaction to facilitate the mission of the organization. In addition, should restructuring and/or reorganization of the company or institution be a possible result of the effort, it may be prudent to keep the programming confidential until the appropriate moment in order to minimize harmful disruption and speculation.

Should you decide to choose this alternative and lead the program from within the organization, it is recommended that you have the program team leader obtain outside assistance in those matters for which it is felt that expertise is lacking.

Option 3: Utilizing the Independent Programming Consultant

Utilizing the independent consultant who specializes in programming is similar in many ways to having the architect or engineer lead the programming under a separate and early contract, as previously expanded upon in option 1, but without the design contract/program bias conflict of interest difficulties.

The disadvantages with the specialist in programming is, in many instances, the lack of in-depth knowledge of the specific building type or function that is to be programmed. This may only be a small difficulty if the project is simple and/or unique but may prove to be an insurmountable problem if a high plateau of knowledge related to a specialized building and the state of the art is needed. Indeed, most of the firms that specialize in programming exclusively devote their practice primarily to space planning for the corporate office.

To suggest that for a specialized building a short period of "research" devoted to the building type as part of the information gathering process is sufficient is at best naive. It does not reflect either the complexity or recognize the knowledge required to generate a process and program that reflects the state of the art for any but the most elementary programs. This approach seems most akin to the aristocratic gentleman's approach of "muddling your way through," high on prestige and self-esteem for the consultant, low in efficiency and respect for the owner's time and resources.

Often, the way to resolve this difficulty is to include in the program team for the complex building an expert in the discipline or building type. This individual could be an independent consultant or an engineer or architect experienced in the building type, acting as a team member. Other specialty consultants may be added: construction managers or independent estimators for building costs; local civil engineers for site improvement evaluation and regulatory requirements; laboratory, acoustical, or vibration consultants, etc. The objective for each program is to determine the need and get the best people available. The program consultant should initially select the principal members of the team and supplement the team as additional needs are identified. For the retrofit or remodeling project, it is essential that the consultant be an architect or other design professional conversant with the wide range of technical details and issues that are part of these projects. For this kind of project all the traditional engineering disciplines will need to be engaged and coordinated in addition to the specialty fields. To accommodate a wide range of programming projects, the ideal programming consultant would have the following attributes:

- Having a system established to identify, gather, organize and display data so it may be efficiently analyzed and recorded.

- Having the ability to use the appropriate tools, including computers, graphical display devices, questionnaire forms, cost evaluation forms, room data sheets, and engineering criteria forms which are available and have been tested and refined over many projects.

- Using programming team members that are trained in the discipline including the allied disciplines of information theory, group dynamics, team building, brainstorming, lateral thinking, and other creative problem-solving methodologies.

- Having the experience to evaluate what is important and what is not, integrating building construction and cost data into the program, and balancing this in relationship to the qualitative data expressed in the program.

- Having direct experience with the facility type or utilizing a specialty consultant allows the programming consultant's team to bring specialized industry experience to the table and compare the proposed program elements with current state-of-the-art practice.

- Having the advantage of the independent perspective and the ability to maintain confidentiality as needed.

One consultant may not possess all of these abilities; as always, the challenge is to choose a team that comes closest to your needs and whose members have the chemistry to work intimately with the owner's team.

3

Programming Strategy

The process of programming creates both a document and the environment in which it is to be received. The objective is not only to produce a document, but to produce a document that has the support of those with a stake in the project outcome. This chapter provides an overview of an orchestration of events that have proven effective in achieving both of these objectives. Chapter 5 contains additional refinements and details of both the tools and operational mechanics, some alternative techniques, and some ideas on what to do should you encounter difficulties.

Most of the information for a facility program is gathered in group settings from people who will own, control, or occupy the facility.[1] This interactive interviewing and its related activities are called in this text a *program workshop.*[2] It is the centerpiece of the programming process described here. The strategy described in this chapter focuses principally on the structure of this workshop process and describes other activities—the gathering of site and environmental information and the

---

[1]In the results of the 1991 survey on programming published in the July issue of *The AIA Memo,* as reported by Preiser (1993), interviewing was given first place ranking as a method for data gathering, followed by surveys and document analysis. In addition to this, one quarter of the responses were in the "other" category in which interactive work sessions were the most prevalent source of information. This corresponds well with my personal experience with a number of large firms and suggests that by far this is the best and most prevalent method of gathering and verifying program information.

[2]Peña et al. (1987) of CRSS use the term *squatters*; other common appellations by consultants include *work sessions, charettes, consensus building, design forums, interactive discussions,* and *multiple channel communication.* The term *workshop* is used in this text because it is the most commonly recognized term for this kind of group process across a wide spectrum of disciplines.

gathering of written and graphic documentation in the context of the schedule of the overall workshop activities.

The process described here is not a precise algorithm but rather a uniquely shuffled sequence of recurring events that need to be fine-tuned to the specific project and organization. When devising the particular strategy, it is not possible to determine the exact amount of focus that should be devoted to each issue, as the process of discovery will determine what is appropriate and necessary. It is helpful, however, to have a general idea of the completed result, and a list of the usual contents of a program are described for your reference in Chap. 4.

There are three principal types of programs: the master plan program, the facility schematic design program, and the detailed fitout program. For the first two, there are significant additions to be made to both the process and documentation if the program involves the retention and/or renovation of existing facilities. The difference between these three program types is the level of detail. Each requires a different strategy.

The master plan program looks at a project only at the largest scale. It is most often used to determine the feasibility of a project, to analyze a site for a potential use, or to determine the gross characteristics and patterns of growth of a large or complex project with many buildings or component parts. It is most often a "top-down" process, involving fewer individuals on the client side of the team, and these individuals are usually at a senior level. When, as is often the case, there are existing facilities that must be woven into the plan, these must be assessed as part of the program (I call this a top-down and bottom-up program). Usually site analysis plays a large part in the development of all these programs and unless the project involves planning on an urban or regional scale and/or a detailed existing facilities audit, the process and documentation are often much abbreviated compared to the facility schematic design program. Often a graphical master plan is prepared by an architect or planner based on this program and site analysis. Other documents that accompany the master plan program or follow it for the really large or long range building program may include site analyses, environmental and geological surveys, landscape guidelines, architectural and engineering guidelines, phasing plans, a master site plan, project management and administrative plans, and cost projections. Many times the program alone may be the final document if it demonstrates that the project is not feasible.

The facility schematic design program is the most common and most familiar program; it is usually what we mean when we refer to a building program. It is the program required by the architect/engineer to begin design of a project. Since there are usually many stakeholders or interested parties in the creation, utilization, and occupancy of a physical facility, the process usually becomes more immediate and of more interest to a wider audience than the master plan program. The process is further complicated when the program relates to a new use for an existing facility.

The detailed fitout program usually follows the completion of the preliminary or schematic design of the project and addresses the finer details of what goes into the building. It is most often done by the architect/engineer or a specialty consultant who is part of the consultant team. This program has different names depending on the building type and convention:

Laboratories—laboratory fitout program

Office buildings—interior, work order, or tenant fitout program, or furniture, fixtures, and equipment (FFE) program

Factories and industrial buildings—equipment fitout program

Others—FFE program

Often this kind of program is executed as part of the equipment or furnishings layout. For the hospital, laboratory, or facility with complex physical attributes, detailed environmental and utility requirements are determined for each space if they have not been done as part of the schematic design. Often in simpler buildings this detailed fitout program is omitted and the ability of spaces to accept the required furniture and fixed equipment is either assumed or tested by trial layout during schematic design. If the detailed fitout program is omitted, then it is necessary that all major fixed equipment that will go into the facility be otherwise identified and described so that electrical power, cooling loads, utilities, and the environment can be accommodated.[3] This information can be included in the facility schematic design program or executed later as a separate document package.

As the facility design program is the most common of the three program types, I will initially describe the strategy for this program type and then expand on the differences for the others with references to this process. Additional requirements, related to the slightly more complex programming when existing facilities are involved, are noted for each step.

---

[3]See Appendix C for a sample equipment data form that should be distributed to the user to obtain the required data.

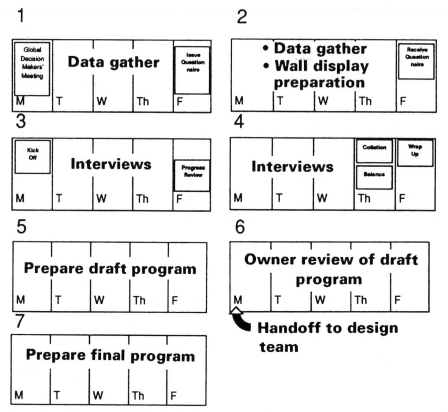

1

Global Decision Makers' Meeting	**Data gather**			Issue Question naire
M	T	W	Th	F

2

• **Data gather** • **Wall display preparation**				Receive Question naire
M	T	W	Th	F

3

Kick Off	**Interviews**			Progress Review
M	T	W	Th	F

4

Interviews			Collation / Balance	Wrap Up
M	T	W	Th	F

5

Prepare draft program				
M	T	W	Th	F

6

Owner review of draft program				
M	T	W	Th	F

Handoff to design team

7

Prepare final program				
M	T	W	Th	F

Figure 3.1 The seven week schedule. The typical sequence of events for a schematic design program for a building. *Note*: initial strategy meeting described in the text may precede the first week of activities and is not illustrated here.

The strategy for the facility schematic design program in its most usual form has a sequence of events and schedule as illustrated in Fig. 3.1. The program confirmation interview and the discovery of like facilities (models) are events that are not always necessary; they are discussed below but not included in the schedule figure. For an average size project of up to 200,000 sq ft in gross area and of average complexity, the programming should require from 7 to 9 weeks without confirmation interviews. This may be extended if detailed questionnaires need to be prepared or delays are required because of the unavailability of key members of the client's team or key decision makers.

Initial Strategy Meeting

This meeting should include the leadership of the program team, and its purpose is to delineate the strategy and sequence of events for the entire programming process. For projects of limited scope this meeting may be combined with the global decision makers' meeting. The agenda should include the following subjects:

- Determination of the schedule, including the rough blocking out of the interview schedule (for the interviews, there should be at least three to five blocks more than the number of interviews anticipated to allow for the unexpected).

- Identification of the groups and interests to be considered and the determination of the individuals who should lead and represent them.

- Identification of all resources and data available and the means to obtain them. This might include organization charts, plans of existing facilities, reports, and site surveys. Often there exists a previous iteration of a program document for a project; this might be a functional program, which was prepared earlier to determine the scope of the project or its capital cost for budget purposes. This program is often brief and incomplete, but if it is the basis for the project, it needs to be addressed at this meeting. A list of typical data follows in the section titled "Data Gathering."

- Discussion of any known difficulties or hurdles that need to be overcome; this could include sensitive issues and issues related to working with specific groups or people.

- Determination of logistics, including physical spaces to house the team (discussed later in detail); telephone service; after-hours access to the facilities (usually the process extends well into the night); availability of secretarial help for typing, contacting individuals, or making travel arrangements; and other logistical issues that may be unique to the project.

- Compilation of the project directory. This should include the name and phone number of all the key team members, including additional consultants and emergency numbers.

- Scheduling the visitation of the existing facilities or trips to visit other "model" facilities.

- Determination of the agenda for the global decision makers' meeting.

- Preliminary determination if additional specialty consultants or specialists from within the owner's organization are required to address specific issues. Determination of the method of selection and who will engage the consultants if they are required.

In addition to all of the above, the issue of whether to have meeting notes prepared for all the interviews needs to be addressed in this meeting. One school of thought suggests that the program document itself is the record of the meetings and that therefore no additional record is required. There is some merit in this approach, as the notes do, in large part, repeat the same information and tend to be bulky and difficult to access, especially for large projects. In addition, the practice of transmission and confirmation of meeting notes by all attendees should then be followed so that an appropriate paper trail is created; this may require adding some time to the schedule. My recommendation would be to prepare meeting notes for only the more complex project for which hierarchical or multiple reviews are required and omit them for all others. If bulky, the notes should be bound in a separate reference document. It is essential, however, for the program reader to know who made the decisions. Therefore, even for the simple program document without meeting notes, a list of the meetings and the attendees should be added as an appendix to the program document.

Global Decision Makers' Meeting

This meeting includes the most senior decision makers in the company or institution who have the power to affect the program. It is ideally scheduled prior to any other interviews, as the decisions made in this meeting delineate the boundaries in which all other decisions must be made. Because of the limited time availability of senior decision makers, the session is usually abbreviated (an hour is the most you can expect and a half hour more likely); therefore, the agenda must be carefully prepared to address only those issues that drive the program at the largest scale.

The meeting need not necessarily be formal; it is the time to have the leadership wax philosophical and the team evoke visions and goals. The challenge to the meeting leader is to direct the questions and elicit responses to only the greater issues. Most often, the problem is one of insufficient abstraction. If the president suggests "a brick building," the appropriate response should be to determine the objectives behind the concept by asking more questions. "The building should use natural materials and have warmth" may be a better answer, as it allows the design team more creative latitude. On the other hand, "the building must be clad predominantly in red brick to match the rest of the campus" may indeed be a legitimate constraint and no further abstraction is required. The agenda for this meeting may include the following topics:

- The mission statement—a description of the purpose of the project and a summation of how it fits into the overall context of the organization's purpose.

- Confirmation of the strategy and interviews.

- Review of the assumptions upon which the program will be based (e.g., overall cost, occupancy, site characteristics, and schedule). This can be summarized in a graphical wall display (discussed later in more detail) or reduced to a printed page.

- Evocation of the decision makers' thoughts related to the issues, objectives, data, criteria, and concepts of the project. For a list of some of these evocative topics, see Appendix A. Some issues that are commonly addressed in this meeting include the following:

  Image—grand, modest, natural, landscape, spartan

  Image fulfillment—use of materials, relationship to the environment, mass of buildings, use of site, views

  Working environment—natural daylight, natural ventilation versus mechanical ventilation, interior space without windows utilization, security

  Employee amenities—lounge, vending machines, food service, parking

  Visitor amenities—lobby, reception, exhibit, parking

  Organization of program elements—to achieve benefits of organization or productivity, to encourage interaction and communication

  Change and growth—projections and their validity, flexibility (expandability, versatility, or convertibility), loose fit, occupancy of the facility at completion, capacity for future increases

  Schedule—confirmation of the timetable for programming, design, construction, occupancy date

The directives received from this meeting along with other confirmed data will form the basis of the information for the initiation meeting that precedes the individual group and department interviews. If there is a questionnaire to be distributed, and there is a purpose to be achieved by doing so, some of this information may be encapsulated in the introductory letter with which it is accompanied.

If the architect or engineer who will design the project is leading the program effort, it is wise to have the designer for the project attend this meeting also, both to get the most important information firsthand and also to develop a rapport that will be useful during the design phase of the project.

Data Gathering

The time between the initial strategy meeting and the interviews is the period for gathering, organizing, and analyzing the data that will generate the parameters and information for the interviews and the final document. The objective is to get all the data that is available relevant to the program. A list of the data required for a typical project may include (the most important are noted with an asterisk):

All available client data*	Utilities service*
All available program data*	Climatological data
Historical growth patterns	Present adjacent land use*
Staff and employee projections*	Future adjacent land use*
Organization charts	Traffic reports and analysis
Growth projections*	Assessments for improvements
Organization culture	Permit fees
Current occupancy data*	Statistical data
Comparable building data	Area parameters
Existing site improvements*	User characteristics
Space standards*	Community characteristics
Personnel space standards	Site amenities and restrictions*
Industry standards	Easements*
Economic and financial parameters	Proposed off-site improvements*
Schedule and time constraints*	Site access
Site survey*	Site topography
Government and regulatory agency approvals and schedule	Site geophysical report

If the project involves existing structures that will become part of the equation, an assessment is required. This should be initiated at this time and done simultaneously with the other programming efforts. This effort will require a completely separate team comprised of architects and individuals from all the engineering disciplines. If there is little information available on the condition of the structure, a facilities audit may be required. At the program level, the audit does not need to be complete, just complete enough to assess what needs to be done to have the structure meet the new program requirements (although this should be done in a format that can be completed during the later design phases by either the client's physical plant staff or the consultant).[4]

---

[4]A good format for a complete audit is contained in *The Facilities Audit* by Harvey H. Kaiser (1993), which is available through IFMA or your bookseller.

Questionnaire

During the period of data gathering and prior to the programming workshop, it is useful for all but the simplest projects to issue a questionnaire. Much of the questionnaire related to quantitative issues can be put into a standard format. There are some parts of the questionnaire, however, that need to be specifically tailored to the project type, and there are usually some questions that relate to the unique aspects of the particular project that must be freshly generated. Most consultants have standard formats related to the specialty building types upon which they most often focus, and, for projects of average complexity, these generic questions and forms can be readily assembled and distributed in a week or so after the strategy meeting. In the illustrated seven week schedule, Fig. 3.1, a week is allowed for the completion of the forms, which are then used as the basis for much of the agenda at the departmental interviews. Having much of the quantitative data in hand prior to the workshop permits a more productive session and reduces the probability of time overruns. If time is available, it is usually productive to allow the programming team a few days prior to the workshop interviews to organize the data.

On many complex projects, such as hospitals or animal holding facilities, the questionnaires may be lengthy and detailed and thus may require more than the single week suggested; no matter how detailed, however, no more than two weeks should be allocated for the completion of the questionnaire. If you believe it likely that more time is required, it might be wise to consider simplification. Because of the time required by the respondent to address the issues properly, it is best to have the questionnaires distributed under the signature of the most senior authority available within the organization with a specific time and hour for return indicated.

Although each type of questionnaire will be specialized and different, there are some ingredients common to many of them. Questionnaires most often include the following information:

- *A space list format* that includes columns for personnel tabulations and projections for both space and occupancy.
- *An adjacency matrix* or similar format to describe both interdepartmental relationships and intradepartmental relationships of spaces quantitatively.
- *A relationship diagram request* to illustrate graphically the departmental organization, the relationship of groups to other groups, and the flow of people and goods.

- *A list of questions* specifically tailored to the type of facility to be programmed, and a list of questions specific and unique to the facility. The more generic questions typically relate to flow patterns, ancillary spaces, and support spaces. Unique and custom-tailored questions usually relate to qualitative issues, inquiries regarding possible design alternatives (e.g., "would you rather have roof parking next door or basement parking in the building and pay $2.00 a day?"), and evaluation of their presently occupied facilities.[5]

- *A series of diagrams or prompts* designed to evoke decisions related to layout preferences, diagrams of special facilities, or preferred standards or modules.

- *Equipment data sheets* that are to be completed for which such fixed equipment will be a primary determinant of the space size or layout or have a significant impact on mechanical loads.

- *Room data sheets* are often utilized to illustrate the requirements of each room, usually on a single page.

- *Architectural and engineering criteria* (AEC) are often included as a part of the questionnaire when there is likely to be a large number of diverse and critical requirements (e.g., a research laboratory or hospital). These can be included on the room data sheet or in a separate form.

On occasion, multiple questionnaires are prepared for a complex project to reflect the level of input that is requested and the fact that certain decisions should be confined to the global decision makers or senior staff. Experience suggests, however, that the detailed questionnaire with the widest distribution (usually this is at the department or group level) should be carefully edited to exclude those decisions outside the respondents' power to answer and that the larger and more global issues be addressed as a simple list at the global decision makers' meeting or at a senior staff meeting held prior to the detailed interviews.

Whatever the final approach, the importance of simplifying and editing the questionnaire to only the issues that are critical and meaningful cannot be emphasized too strongly. Almost without exception, the

---

[5]Henry Sanoff, in *Methods of Architectural Programming* (1977), starting on p. 31, gives a brief overview on how to formulate questions for behavioral science issues. Formulating questions to get reliable answers is an art with many hazards; many volumes have been written on the subject and for many people it is their lifework. If the answer to a question will have a significant effect on the design of a facility, it is best to hire someone who can do it correctly.

program questionnaire is an additional task thrust upon the respondent; having repetitive questions, questions of doubtful value, or questions outside the power or interest of the respondent shows a lack of respect for the respondent's time. In addition, as the reader knows, the longer the questionnaire, the less likely it will be answered carefully, if at all.

Program Workshop: Preparation

Preparation for the program workshop includes the evaluation of data that has been gathered and the division of it into three groups: (1) data that needs to be communicated during the workshop process, (2) data that will go into the final program document but that does not need to be addressed during the workshop, and (3) data that is not relevant to the program and needs to be returned, filed for future use, or discarded. The data that needs to be communicated during the workshop process will have to be prepared into packages for each of the events and decisions made as to the method of presentation. Suggestions for presentation are included under each of the separate events detailed below.

For the outside consultant, the logistics related to the workshop are similar to setting up a remote office, and some of these issues have already been treated in the section titled "The Initial Strategy Meeting." The exact tools to be used to prepare the final document will drive the staffing and methodology for the program workshop team. It is only common sense, because of the intense nature of the activity, to have tools that are compatible. If for example, you are utilizing an IBM compatible computer system with Lotus 123 and WordPerfect for the final document, it is advantageous to use a laptop personal computer and portable printer for the workshop that can be used in the final system. For more discussion of the merits of the various techniques and hardware suggestions see Chap. 5.

As much preparation as time allows should be completed prior to the interviews. If responses to the questionnaires are in hand, space lists should be prepared in the final format (for example, if the final document is to be on the computer, discs should be taken to the workshop along with generated hard copy).

Program Workshop: Initiation Meeting

This is the opening event of the workshop and everyone who will participate in the programming process should be invited to attend. The purpose of the meeting is threefold: (1) to introduce the programming team, (2) to acquaint everyone with the process, objectives, and schedule, and (3) to communicate the necessary data and program parameters that have already been established, including those established at the global decision makers' meeting and other events.

The methodology of presenting this information depends on the size of the group. For really large groups, a completely outfitted lecture hall or auditorium is best; slides, opaque or transparent projectors, and projected television are the media of choice. For most groups, however, a wall display combined with slides and boards in a large conference room is appropriate. For the very small group, a meeting room with a hand-drawn graphical wall display might be enough. The objective is to communicate a large amount of information effectively. It is recommended that the session be introduced by the highest ranking individual available in the organization so that the programming of this facility can be placed in the context of the overall mission of the company or institution. Usually a time slot is allowed for questions and responses at the completion of the presentation, and often the participants will convene after the meeting to make additions or adjustments to the interview schedule. The entire meeting should not exceed an hour and a half, and its contents should be previewed by the leader of the client's programming team.

Program Workshop: Interviews

How to prepare for and conduct a departmental interview session is treated in great detail in Chap. 5; here only the highlights and basic structure are presented. The program interviews should be structured in two hour blocks of time. Each interview should last about an hour and a half, with the balance of the time utilized for overruns, preparation for the next interview by the programming team, and maintenance items such as secretarial liaison for travel arrangements, schedule adjustments, and telephone calls. If the content of the interview suggests that the time required will exceed a two hour block, then another can be added. If this second interview is scheduled serially after the first, it is recommended that the half hour break be maintained. Experience has shown that the intensity of the work sessions limit productive concentration to about a one and one-half hour period. As recommended previously, it is advisable to have three or four blocks of time left open in the initial schedule for the unexpected additional interview or uncompleted agenda. If this period is not used for interviews, team members will find it a welcome breathing space to devise strategy, organize data, and collect their thoughts.

If possible, it is best to have all of the interviewing done by a single team. On large projects, however, multiple teams may be required for concurrent interviews, and these teams will need to be briefed beforehand to assure the overall team leader that all of the interviews are conducted with a consistent format and methodology. When multiple teams are required, it is recommended that the leader sit in on a few sessions of each team to ensure this consistency.

The interviewing team should consist of no fewer than two: the leader to ask the questions and facilitate the meeting and an assistant programmer to record the information. If the creation of a graphical wall display is part of the strategy (see Chap. 5) a third team member may be employed to do this. Ideally, there should be another team member who is not present at the interview and who serves as an alternate for the assistant programmer on a rotating basis. The creation of this leapfrogging arrangement allows for the processing of the information immediately after the meeting when the information is fresh; the information can then be fed back to the participants for immediate confirmation shortly after the interview. In addition to the programming team members, specialty consultants may be needed if expertise outside the team is required to identify the issues and reach a conclusion (mechanical engineers and food service consultants come first to mind).

The number of people to be interviewed at one session may be only one individual and should rarely exceed eight; more than eight has proven not to be productive. If the group represented is very large, then the interests of the constituents will have to be gathered beforehand by the leader of the group, who will then speak on their behalf.

Common sense dictates that, if possible, interviews of a more comprehensive scope precede those that are more specific. It is best, for example, to first meet with the interdepartmental committee or heads of departments to set overall parameters such as the laboratory or office module, departmental relationships, and space standards before meeting with the chemistry department members to determine their space list. If this hierarchical schedule can be accomplished, changes to the program and surprises for the users can be minimized.

The physical accommodations required for the program team depend on the interviewing strategy. It is usually best to have a large conference room on the user's premises dedicated for the duration of the programming interviews to serve as the workshop. With this strategy, all interviews are conducted in this room, except for the global decision makers' meeting and meetings with single high-level executives, which are usually held elsewhere. If the programming team intends to use a graphical wall display as a communication device it is essential that this single room strategy be utilized.[6]

The alternative to the single workshop strategy, although not nearly as effective, is to visit each group individually on its own turf. Indeed, for many programs with the objective of consolidating separate and remote activities, this is the only possible approach. If this methodology is utilized, a way must be found to communicate the global parameters already established. If a wall display is utilized, it can be packed up and transported. More convenient are slides and overhead projectors, but there is usually not enough time to create the material. If the global material can be reduced to printed pages, this is probably the most convenient, although the ability to grasp the project as a whole is lost and repetitive additional effort must be made to explain the project anew each time.

Whether the single workshop approach is utilized or not, the program team will require additional office space to act as headquarters for the operation. The space will be utilized as workrooms to evaluate and process data and serve as a secure repository for the programming team's equipment, files, and supplies. If there is no dedicated single room in which to conduct the workshop, then there must be at least one large space (or a conference room made available) for program team meetings; all other spaces can be broken up into office sizes, but if there are many, the spaces need to be secure and contiguous. As an approximation, about 100 to 150 sq ft/person should be allowed. Security is a serious issue both because of the confidentiality of the information and also because of the cost of the computer equipment, much of which is extremely portable.

The interview should be led by the lead programmer of the consultant's team; it is recommended that the leader of the client's team be present. The agenda should be tiered according to the priority of the information; it should be preceded by a presentation by the leader concerning the updated global material that may particularly affect the group being interviewed (e.g., revised space standards or the organization of adjacent departments). Any limitations placed on the net area or

---

[6]If the plan includes concurrent interviews, obviously two rooms or more would be required. If the graphical display is part of the strategy, multiple sets of display material must therefore be produced to furnish these rooms so that the global parameters are universally communicated. It is extremely difficult, however, to keep these displays updated and uniform as the global parameters change in response to discovered common and compelling details. In addition, one of the principal reasons for this approach, the ability to grasp the project in a single glance, is easily forfeited.

personnel allocation for the group need to be addressed in the preliminary presentation. Prior to the interview, an agenda should have been sent along with the questionnaire (this is covered in more detail in Chap. 5). The information gathering during the group interview should be addressed in this order:

1. Space list and other quantitative data along with projections
2. Group or function organization chart
3. Intradepartment functional affinities and work flow
4. Interdepartment affinities and work flow
5. Requirements for special building services
6. Identification of major equipment and discussion of the equipment data sheets
7. Discussion related to specific spaces (this should be done with the room data sheets in hand if they are part of the program questionnaire and final document)
8. Addressing of qualitative issues, goals, concepts, and other criteria
9. Detailed AEC

Throughout the discussion, the leader, as facilitator, should direct the discussion with evocative ideas to describe abstract concepts and thus help the people being interviewed express their needs and aspirations. These ideas include common design issues, criteria, and program objectives and concepts; lists of those most frequently encountered are given in Appendix A. In addition, the interviewing team must bring to the table experience on similar projects so that these ideas can be addressed in the light of current practice and standards of other organizations.

Leading the interviews is a difficult task, requiring high-level abilities in the art of communication, creative thinking, leadership, team building, organization, and diplomacy. Many of the issues occur frequently, however, and many of the techniques that are suggested in this text will be improved by experience and training. As previously mentioned, a careful reading of Chap. 5 will acquaint you with some of the subtleties.

Workshop Wrap-Up

It is possible to conclude the workshop by the creation and presentation of a balanced draft program at the end of the session, but more often than not there is insufficient time to come to a verified and supportable document on all but the simplest projects. For simple projects for which this is the goal, the strategy should be to schedule an all-day (or afternoon and evening) team work session on the day prior to the final day of the workshop. During this work session, the team will collate and tabulate all the quantitative data, create or refresh all of the graphic data (organization charts, flowcharts, design concepts, etc.), create an overall schedule, and compile a cost evaluation of the project. Toward the end of the day or, at the very latest, the following morning, a meeting should be convened with the global decision makers and the program presented. Should there be any conflicts concerning the scope of work, quality, and cost, compromises will be made and the program balanced on the spot. The results will then be presented to the entire group on the last day of the workshop.

For the larger or more complex program, however, often the final session is held merely to share, in a general way, the information that has been gathered, to inform the participants of the next events on the schedule, and to thank them for their effort. The work of creating the draft program and its subsequent review with the client team then becomes the vehicle for any final decisions and balancing that need to be done.

Draft Program

The preparation of the draft program, in which no significant imbalance in cost, quality, or scope is revealed, takes about one week for projects of average complexity. If meeting notes are required, this may add another week or two for the preparation and confirmation process. Should corrections and clarifications be required, this can usually be done by telephone, fax, or overnight courier. Meetings may be required with key representatives of the owner's team for resolution of significant issues. In addition, for complex buildings with many programmed requirements, it is usually advisable to have confirmation interviews with many of the departments to review the material again to correct any errors and add missing details. This added sequence of events will, of course, add time to the schedule.

Owner Review of the Draft Program

For projects of average size and complexity, a week is usually sufficient to review the project. Many times, however, the complexity of the owner's decision making and approval process may require longer time, even for the simplest projects. A month or more is not uncommon. This should be anticipated in the initial strategy meeting and the schedule adjusted accordingly. The people involved in the review need to be informed in advance so a timely review of the program can be completed. Once again, to ensure a prompt return, the material is best distributed over the signature of the most senior person available in the organization.

Final Program Document Preparation

For projects of average size and complexity for which the presentation format does not require fine printing, color reproduction, or special binding, a week is usually sufficient to make the final corrections and produce the document. The suggested contents and format for a program document are treated in some detail in Chap. 4.

Master Plan Program Strategy

The master plan strategy is similar to the strategy above, but, except for the larger projects, it is more simplified. An initial strategy meeting and a brief data gathering period are needed, both of which rarely take more than a week. Often the preparation of graphical material and data analysis can be included in this time period, although many times a second week is necessary. Usually the availability of key personnel on the owner's team determines the schedule. A questionnaire is almost never utilized.

The program workshop and interviews rarely take more than three or four days including initiation and wrap-up, and many times are better described as work sessions with senior executives. The preparation of the rough draft and final document are the same as that for the schematic design facilities program. The sequence of events and strategy are different for each master plan, as is the information to be gathered.

Master Plan Program Case Study No. 1: Strategy for a Corporate Research Complex. A master plan program for AT&T on a site to be utilized for a large complex of offices and research laboratories had a sequence of events as follows:

- The *strategy meeting* lasted about one and a half hours. Present at this meeting were the director of the consultant's team, the leader of the owner's team, and an assistant. The agenda for this meeting was similar to that for the schematic design agenda but abbreviated in terms of the schedule blocking for interviews.

- *Data gathering,* including a site visit and analysis, was completed in two week's time.

- *Workshop interviews* were done in three consecutive daily sessions, convening each day at 9:00 A.M. and concluding at noon. The afternoons were used by the consultant's team to record, collate, and analyze data. On the following morning, at the beginning of each session, the results of each afternoon's labor were reviewed. The initiation meeting was encapsulated at the beginning of the first meeting, and the results of the data gathering and the program premises were outlined. It was not possible to have the global decision makers' meeting until the afternoon of the second day of the workshop as not all participants were available. The global decision makers' meeting was a 30-minute interview with the primary decision maker. There was no desire to complete the draft at the end of the final session because some critical information was lacking and further analysis was required.

- A *draft program* was prepared for review in ten calendar days.

- A *confirmation interview* was held and the draft was reviewed on a line-by-line basis by the assembled team. Copies of the draft where given to the participants 24 hours before the meeting. The meeting lasted four hours with one break of 20 minutes.

- The *final program,* including appendices, was 232 pages long in a standard $8\frac{1}{2} \times 11$ inch format and was finished in about one week's time.

Master Plan Program Case Study No. 2: Strategy for a New Community College Master Plan.   This project was a new branch campus for a community college to replace a collection of leased and scattered storefronts in an urban environment. The college had just acquired a virgin site of about 114 acres. The master plan program, master plan, and first phase of the implementation (which included the immediate construction of an interim facility) were part of a single consultant contract. The client had little more than a timetable, an eventual projected full-time equivalent (FTE) enrollment of 6000, and a rough assessment of gross area based on state guidelines. The sequence of events included the following highlights:

- The *strategy meeting* was divided into two sessions, each lasting one and a half hours. In addition to the standard topics, the agenda included the development of a rough strategy and timetable for community relations events and a strategy for the environmental assessment of the site.

- The *global decision makers' meeting* was convened with the president and three vice presidents of the college; it lasted one and a half hours. From the consultant's team, the planner who was to direct the preparation of the master plan and one assistant accompanied the chief programmer to this meeting.

- *Master plan committee meetings* were held beginning the following week. There were two days of meetings, each meeting being approximately one and a half hours long. The agenda included not only a discussion of student and faculty population projections but also qualitative issues and refinement of what the contents of the master plan documents were to be. While these meetings were being held, a separate team was completing the initial investigation of the site and existing buildings; on the second day of the workshop this group gave a preliminary presentation of its findings to the master plan committee.

- A *draft program* was prepared in one week and sent to the committee for review. It was returned in two weeks, during which time many details were reviewed over the telephone with the chief programmer. Because of the tight schedule, the master plan design team started the planning process as soon as the draft program was issued.

■ The *final program* was completed in a standard $8\frac{1}{2} \times 11$ inch bound format in one week's time.

Detailed Fitout Program

The detailed fitout program document, the strategy to achieve it, and the fitout team have some of the ingredients of the schematic design program but the differences are more pronounced than those of the master plan program. Most frequently, the work is done by the architect, engineer, interior designer, or a specialty consultant engaged by the design consultant; the work is done after the completion of the schematic design as part of a complete design services contract.

Examples of this convention in which a specialty consultant is used are most frequent in laboratory design [for which a laboratory consultant may be engaged by the owner (especially common when a condominium laboratory with separate tenants is the building occupancy strategy)], the selection of furnishings and accessories for corporate offices, and the FFE for a hotel or motel. There may be others of which I am not aware. The exceptions are a result of convention in these niches for which the knowledge of a specialist is needed and is offered competitively by narrowly focused consultants. These specialists exist to bring the state-of-the-art to the client for maximum selection, the latest equipment and practices, and minimum cost.

Most often this kind of program is not in the strict sense a program at all since, without exception, the written program is always accompanied by layouts and design drawings, and the "design" is often the ordering and placement of furniture or equipment. Since the practice varies so significantly between specialties, the best way of looking at the strategy is to explore two of the most common specialties and their strategies for detailed programming:

Laboratory fitout

This process usually starts with a meeting with the department head and/or the laboratory user for each individual laboratory and support space. Usually a team of two is utilized by the programmer for each interview. Armed with a rough plan of the laboratory space, the laboratory module, and a typical laboratory layout (which have all been determined previously in the schematic design program and the schematic design), the unique differences are determined for each particular laboratory. In addition, room environmental requirements, equipment data, and utility requirements are determined precisely at this time. The location of all these spaces are sketched roughly on the spot on a large scale plan. The plans and documents are then refined (but the drawings are usually still rough sketches or overlays) and a package is assembled for confirmation. For an average size laboratory facility, this can usually be accomplished in a week or two. The package will usually contain a refined (but still rough) large scale drawing of the laboratory, a room data sheet for environmental control and utilities, and equipment data sheets [including "cuts" (manufacturer's data) for the proposed new equipment]. The material is reviewed in a confirmation meeting, comments are noted, and the drawing signed by the user group to establish approval. This package is then used as the basis for the final construction documents by the architect, engineer, or laboratory consultant. Experience has shown that this procedure minimizes changes and gives the user groups a high level of comfort. A sample of an appropriate equipment data sheet is to be found in Appendix C.

Office interior fitout program

There needs to be a clear differentiation between the program we are addressing here and the programming of an entire interior space for a building tenant. If the program is for the organization of the space and its general design and layout, including partitions, the programmer should use the previously described process for the schematic design program (the site and its analysis are substituted with the building, the environment into which the program is to be inserted, and its analysis). Most frequently, when there is a separate interior design contract, the fitout program is a part of the scope of work.

Program requirements for a fitout program for an office are usually brief and focus on the budget and schedule. If no program has been done for the interior layout or building, it might be necessary to review some of the issues described in the section on the schematic design program. Some topics that are commonly addressed for this type of program include open office workstation programming; programs for file and storage allocation by personnel and work function; and hierarchical furnishing systems and budget by rank or grade. Often forgotten are equipment data sheets for copiers, computers, and other major (and heat-generating) equipment that is often housed in cramped spaces. In addition, since the environmental requirements are so often similar throughout the entire facility, one needs to be on the alert for a room with special requirements; an AEC form should be filled out for these spaces. It is also good discipline to complete an AEC form for the facility as a whole when doing the complete program, and it is best to divide it into at least two categories: occupied and unoccupied spaces.

Appendix D has both a blank and partially completed example of an AEC form.

At the conclusion of the design phase for the furnishings, equipment, and accessories, the program is developed into a specification and purchase order, but details of these are beyond the scope of this book.

Programming Strategy: Some Notes

Although the processes described above seem rather straightforward and, for the most part, consistent with common sense—no program ever created has been exactly the same as another in content, strategy, sequence of events, or focus. Determination of the unique formulation required for each project is one of the most creative aspects of programming.

This chapter treats the strategy for programming pragmatically, as a sequence of events that are needed for its creation. In a sense, it is a cookbook or management approach and it is not the entire picture. For a theoretical perspective on the programming methodology and the program documentation advocated in this text refer to Chap. 6. It explains the thinking behind the technique and should be helpful in honing your skills. In addition, Chap. 5, which has frequently been referred to in this chapter, is another layer of refinement focused on the operational aspects of the workshop. Chapter 5 also points you toward the bibliography so that you can reach relevant material beyond the scope of this text.

4

Program Document

The final documentation of the program can be organized in a variety of ways, can be more or less inclusive, and can contain a great amount of detail or none at all. Although there is some basic and minimal information required for each program type, the total content and emphasis of each program will be different and will depend on the client's needs, the problem at hand, the resources available, and the perceptions and strategy of the programming team. There are some questions, which when answered, will help you determine the appropriate content and format.

1. *What are the purposes of the program? Who is the audience?* There can be various purposes to which a program is addressed: justification, creation of an estimate for budgeting purposes, supporting material for a financial pro forma, a feasibility study, or instructions to the architect (the master plan or schematic design program). The audience for the document may not only include architects and other design professionals, but also boards of directors, foundations, bankers, occupants, alumni and donors, citizen or political groups, and the general public.

If there will be an extremely wide audience for the program and/or if the information contained within is sensitive and/or confidential, consideration should be given to issuing the document in various forms— one complete and the other(s) edited and organized to control the information or achieve some secondary purpose. For example, one of the objectives in a master plan program for a small private college was to utilize the resulting master plan to solicit donations. The final program and master plan were combined so that each identified project became a removable two page foldout that included a narrative, a graphic representation, and a cost estimate. For a large public community college, the master plan was summarized on the back of a colorful poster and mailed as part of a public relations program. It is also quite common in large projects for which reproduction costs are not comparatively significant to issue a program in a hardbound presentation edition for limited distribution and a general working edition. Often the limited edition is abbreviated.

2. *How much control of the final design is required? What and who are to be controlled? What is the information required to achieve this control?* Programming defines the boundaries within which the physical solution can be evaluated: first thought suggests that instructions to the design team are the only purpose. However, often the control of information and the way it is presented to other audiences may be equally critical.

As regards the control of the design professional who will execute the project, consideration should be given to his or her likely qualifications in the context of the objectives of the final program. If the project is to have a high design profile, the program constraints may need to be carefully loosened to encourage an extremely creative solution. If the opposite is true, and the desired facility is to have an extremely pragmatic and/or conventional solution accompanied by a description for a specific design, a tighter (and perhaps more lengthy) approach is indicated.

A mid-rise speculative office building on an adequate suburban site is a good example of the sort of building in which the program is likely to have few requirements, excepting those regarding cost, rentable area, and efficiency. The strict replication of a simple existing facility on a similar site with the same functional requirements and client may require no program at all. For some public projects, there may be little control over the selection of the design professional as location, political interests, size of firm, equitable distribution of work, or other factors, rather than professional skills, become the dominating influence. The latter situation may need a tough program if design quality is to be achieved.

As regards other audiences, the issue of information control is usually related to hierarchical approval or review within the larger client or owner organization. This is especially true if final authorization is made by people who will not monitor the final design solution for compliance with the program. The questions are: How much information will need to be presented? What facts will be the bases of judgment for this audience?

3. *Over what time period will the program be valid? How much capacity for change and evolution of the program will be needed?* The schematic design program for a specific facility may have a life as short

as the design process that produces the building, say, 3 to 12 months for all but the largest projects. After the project is complete, this program becomes useless paper except for its value as a model for other programs or utilization as part of a later post-occupancy evaluation. The master plan program for a corporation or university, on the other hand, may have a life that stretches over many years: these programs need a built-in mechanism for periodic review and change as the physical plant grows and the mission of the organization evolves. The most typical master plan horizon is five years; this seems appropriate as it keys in with current practice related to long range capital planning timetables and gives the client sufficient time to get through the process of defining, funding, designing, and building the individual facility.

4. *What is the content of the program in relation to the overall planning or mission of the client and the process of designing and building, or more simply stated, where does the program need to begin and end?* There is an entire spectrum of hierarchical documents between the statement of the basic mission of the organization and the occupation of a physical facility. Many of these documents could be called *programs;* the issue is to determine where you are in regard to this spectrum when the task of programming is identified. As an example, for a school, possible questions are: Has the curriculum been adequately defined? What are the utilization efficiencies? For a corporate office building, how does this facility relate to the strategic plan of the company? For all buildings, has the budget been defined so as to differentiate between project cost and construction cost? Are there sufficient funds for the owner to pay for all of the things that normally fall outside the construction cost? One of the programming team's primary tasks should be to identify clearly the limits of existing knowledge at both ends of the spectrum so that the gap may be bridged by the program. The need to build this connection is one of the principal reasons for the wide variation in program content, and a lack of understanding of this context is one of the primary causes of facility program irrelevance and failure.

Elements of the Facility Program

The most useful and frequently recurring elements of a typical program are presented in this chapter as a checklist with recommendations for the content of each topic. This checklist can be used as a reference of elements to determine if anything has been missed in your documentation. The material in this list of elements focuses on the facility program at the master plan and schematic design level—the two most common programming needs. The checklist assumes that programming is only a part of a string of the activities that culminate in the building of a facility: a programming-then-design methodology that assumes that the design team is not necessarily the programming team. The material does not include components related to an expanded definition of programming, including strategic and operational analysis at the beginning of a project or post-occupancy evaluation after the project has been completed.

Also outside the scope of this chapter is the presentation of the results of research studies, sampling, or statistical analysis. These elements are omitted not only because they occur infrequently in conventional practice, but also because they are complex issues in themselves and an adequate treatment here would occupy space out of proportion to their relevance. In addition, since I have seldom used them, I would not feel qualified to offer advice in their application or methodology. There are, however, many specialists in this field and, for those of you who wish to utilize these techniques in your programming, there are references in the Bibliography: see especially Barker (1968), Campbell and Stanley (1963), Michaelson (1975), Sanoff (1991), and Selltiz et al. (1981).

The organization of elements proposed in this chapter and the recommendations on their content and presentation within the document represent a proven, effective, and orderly methodology. In many ways it is an amalgam of contemporary programming practice and utilizes, as much as possible, commonly understood terms and concepts. In doing so, however, it is bland and lacks the impact and stimulating imagery of the idiosyncratic approaches of some practitioners of the programming art. There is much to be said for some of these approaches, as much of the insight and discovery during the programming process is generated by the stimulation of the participants. In these systems, the way that the contents are organized, the content's relative emphasis and names, and the process of creation and presentation depend on a unique theory of programming. The reader can learn much from these systems, and some of the most useful contemporary approaches are briefly reviewed in Chap. 6. In addition, some of the narrative and graphic communication methods of these systems are reviewed in Chap. 5. Whatever system of organization or theoretical approach you intend to use, all of them have common elements of information, and each of these elements has its own effective method of presentation that has evolved as the practice of programming has developed.

The elements of the program document are listed here in more or less the same order that they would appear in a complete program, although it is not likely that all the elements would appear in one document or that the program emphasis would suggest that they be arranged in the same exact order. The many readers that are experienced programmers will find much of what is prescribed below common sense. Some of it, in its effort to be inclusive, is elementary, addressed to the novice programmer, and therefore risks talking down to the vast majority of the text's audience. Among the many suggestions, however, should be at least one or two fresh and useful ideas for the experienced practitioner. Many senior executives will also find it a useful checklist of good practice that can be utilized as an aid to review when the program has been prepared by others. A note on terminology: throughout this checklist the word *client* is frequently used; the meaning of the word to the reader who is an outside consultant is obvious. To the individual within an organization who is cast in the programming role, the word *client* is used to designate the audience of clients within your organization.

Checklist of Program Elements

Introduction

The introduction should focus on the purpose of the document and its relation to the mission of the organization. The introduction should contain the mission statement for this project. The introduction may take the form of a standard chapter or section heading or not; the preferred form is on the client's letterhead as a personal message. It should be written and signed by the most senior individual available in the client organization, the president or CEO, and preferably no more than one page in length. The purpose of the recommended format is to get the attention of the reader, communicate the intent of the document, and define its context.

Preface

The preface should be written by the senior member of the programming team. The contents should be similar to a book preface and may include a historical description of the programming process with calendar dates; a justification of the need for the programming process and document; a brief discussion of the purpose of the program and its organization, scope, and content; the naming of the principal participants in the process; references to supplementary publications or companion documents; and the addition of any points that may have been omitted in the introduction. In addition, for each project, there will always be at least one or more prefatory remarks that are unique. As with a book preface, this is the place for acknowledgments and thank-yous (be sure to remember the names of secretaries or staff members if they helped during the process; they will never forget that their name was on a document read by the chairman of the board, and it is the least you can do). If there is no separate introduction, the contents of the preface should be expanded to include the contents of that section. The preface should be followed by the printed names of the programming team; signatures give a personal touch and are sometimes appropriate.

Table of contents

The contents listing is self-explanatory with the exception of a single issue: It is mandatory that all elements of the document, including graphics, be paginated. With the advent of word processing systems this is now more easily done. I suggest that paginating be done by section, i.e., 1-2, 1-3, 2-1, 2-2, etc., so as to avoid changing all the page numbers when corrections are made. If tabs are possible, use them, along with any other organizing devices such as paper color or dividers to coordinate and clarify the organization system. For some, the program document is a workbook, and most references to the document will be specific in nature, needing constant and convenient access to the information. However, an index of word and topic references, similar to that in a reference book, is a level of detail that is almost never required.

Executive summary

This should be the last section to be written. It should contain a summary of all of the information in the document so that the reader will get an immediate grasp of the contents. The minimum content of this element should be the basic statistics that drive the program, including personnel count, net and gross square feet, cost, and schedule, along with any significant limitations or opportunities related to the site or existing conditions and the mission statement or justification. Often omitted in the summary is cost information, which is buried in the back of the document because of its sensitive nature and the fear that the bottom-line-only reader may look at the cost and go no further. While this initial "sticker shock" is sometimes a real danger, it is usually best, on balance, to include the bottom line here with perhaps a second-order breakdown (i.e., project cost *and* construction cost) to soften the perceived blow, as this reader will, in any event, immediately flip to the back of the document and may confuse the numbers you want to communicate. It is good form to have the first paragraph give highlights of the summary so that the reader with only a minute or so of attention can still grasp the whole. The entire summary should only be one page long.

Priority statement

The priority statement is a ranked list of the most important project objectives (see below and Chap. 6 for the definition and formulation of project objectives); as such, the priority statement is a summary description of the primary means by which the mission statement will be accomplished. A program without establishing priorities does only a part of the job. The reason for this is that, without a clear statement about the relative importance of the principal program objectives, the program is subject to wide interpretation, especially when it is initially translated into the design of the facility. Since the evolution of any component part of the design synthesis will almost always relate to more than one program objective or program concept, without priorities for these ideas, the client has no ruler with which to measure successful achievement and little control over the final result. On the other hand, when a list of ranked program objectives is part of the program, it then becomes relatively easy to make choices and judge whether the resulting design is responsive.

There are a number of approaches that can be used to generate this priority statement. Peña et al. (1987) approach the problem tangentially in step 5 of their system, in which the lead programmer and the lead designer "formulate a series of very succinct statements" that together constitute the *statement of the problem*. These statements are the most important issues related to the specific program and are related to "form, function, economy, and time." They are to be qualitative statements only, deal only with the unique attributes of the problem, and are a "...link between problem definition and problem solving, between programming and design: their primary purpose is to be...an important physical form giver." They recommend no less than four (one for each of the categories above) and no more than ten of these statements. The statements in this system are not ranked as to importance or priority. In practice, the client approves these statements along with the review of the entire document.

Another contemporary and more interactive approach is utilized by Verger and Kaderland (1993) in their system of *connective planning*. They propose a series of rating sheets that are completed in interviews with the client after all the program data, both "subjective" (soft and qualitative) and "objective" (hard and quantitative), is collected and grouped. There are many other approaches to generating priorities, although many schemes of organization bury priorities within other problems and leave them only marginally identified. Both Peña et al. and Verger and Kaderland come closest to the mark, and I believe the approach that is recommended in this text captures the best features of both and simplifies both processes and documentation.

The priority statement as defined here is a ranked list of simple, single issue, and global program objectives. These objectives should be identified initially at the global decision makers' meeting, although many will be discovered as a result of the program workshops; if any synthesis is done to simplify the language, it should be confirmed at the end of the programming interviews and during the review of the draft document. These statements should be succinct and number no less than four or more than ten (the latter limit is related to information overload). These statements may address both qualitative and quantitative issues. They should be written with the client during the programming process as proposed by Verger and Kaderland, but rather than formulate them at the end, they should be formulated at the beginning, refined and clarified during the workshops, and then finalized after all the information is collected and organized. This collection of project objectives may or may not be "form givers" (Peña et al., 1987), but together they should answer the questions: What are the four (or five or ten) most important objectives that the final design solution must accomplish?, and what is their relative importance?[1]

To illustrate the point, here are two completely different examples of statements that get the job done. The first example is a priority statement for a small laboratory renovation at Atlantic Community College in Mays Landing, N.J. In this project, there were more improvements needed than there were funds to do them, and the ranked program objectives became a categorical checklist to evaluate the need for each improvement. The scope of the project was determined in large part by this list. Since this particular project was an interior retrofit of an existing building, there were no design-related objectives that were ranked high enough to appear on the list. The final priority statement listed five program objectives; the numbers indicate their priority ranking:

Priority Statement—Building A Renovations, Atlantic Community College

1. *Budget compliance.*   The funds available are not sufficient to accomplish all of the expressed needs for the complete retrofit of the building. Therefore it is mandatory that the needs be considered in order of priority and that the final project be built within the funds available.

2. *Code and regulatory compliance.*   The building is to be brought into compliance with all current codes. Especially critical is air quality and the elim-

---

[1]Part of the reasoning for this number of objectives may have been the limits of the human mind to manipulate variables; the book, (Peña et al., 1987) however, does not give the reasoning behind this limitation and it might be serendipitous. In any event, about five to nine variables seem to be the range for all but the exceptionally dull or gifted. This limitation was explored in detail by both Miller (1956) and Yntema and Meuser (1960).

ination of exhaust fume reingestion. Although the building generally meets current state and federal codes for the handicapped, there remain some areas of noncompliance that should be remedied.

3. *Laboratory safety.*   Although the laboratories in the building have safety systems required by code, these systems need to be maintained, upgraded when possible, or replaced with better systems as a part of whatever renovation work is done. Many of the problems in the laboratories are due to inadequate ventilation and exhaust hoods that are not up to contemporary standards.

4. *Functional modifications.*   To fulfill the mission of the college, various program elements must be brought up to date. The building is 26 years old and many components, such as the heating, ventilation, and air conditioning (HVAC) system, have reached the end of their expected life. Some components, such as the chemistry laboratories, biology laboratories, and preparation rooms, are just worn out and need renovation and new equipment to continue a useful life. Other elements, such as the lecture room, need technological updating and new equipment to fulfill their functional role.

5. *Operational improvements.*   These improvements include those that will improve the efficiency of the building related to educational mission, day-to-day operational efficiency and maintenance, and energy conservation. Included in this category would also be convenience and cosmetic improvements.

The second example is the priority statement of a new laboratory facility for a Fortune 500 company. These schematic program objectives were developed for this first phase implementation of a larger master planned facility. Many of the program objectives were explored and developed during the earlier master plan programming. The mission statement of the project was "to provide a facility for the development of specialized communication systems on the leading edge of technology for the next 50 years"; the program objectives with the highest priority for this project were as follows:

Priority Statement—Corporate Research Laboratory

1. To create a progressive, creative, high-technology facility that is responsive to the people's needs
2. To establish one of the world's major computing centers and most modern communications operation
3. To promote intensive interaction while providing the appropriate level of privacy for each type of activity
4. To facilitate the efficient reconfiguration of project teams
5. To provide ease of convertibility through the use of universal space
6. To respond to the context of the rural and suburban location

In this second example, the objectives were not ranked. Priorities 1 and 2 later proved to be too abstract and were not especially useful in developing the design. Items 3 through 6 proved to be significant form givers for the final design solution.

Issues, program objectives, and program concepts

This section of the document relates to the more universal ideas that drive the program and make it more than just a collection of data and a space list. It is in this part of the program that the client's hopes, aspirations, and other "soft" qualitative issues are addressed along with basic parameters related to the quantitative issues that are expanded in detail in other sections of the document. For this section of the document, I recommend combining all three terms in a combined format that reflects a structural framework built around design issues, which are then addressed in terms of program objectives and program concepts.

The universal and qualitative information should be expressed in the format of issue, objective(s), and concept(s) as illustrated in the following example:

Issue: Image

Objective: The building design should reflect the high-technology activities in which the company is engaged.

Concept: Consider the use of high-technology architectural materials and expression.

Concept: Consider the expression of technological features such as microwave towers and antennae.

This example demonstrates the preferred pattern and format. Each design issue (abbreviated as "issue") is paired with a program objective (abbreviated as "objective"), and there can be one or more program concepts (abbreviated as "concept") for each of the objectives (it is also common to have no program concepts and the simple paired issue–objective is the complete statement). There can be more than one objective for each issue, and the preferred format is to list each objective as a separate grouping. Note also some of the key vocabulary and syntax for each category: the use of "should be" for objectives and the word "consider" for concepts.

This example and description are excerpted from Chap. 6, where a full treatment of the subject is to be found. In addition, Appendix A is a paired list of the most commonly recurring issues and objectives and concepts. These can be utilized to reveal unaddressed and implicit information at the programming workshops.

An effective format for this part of the program is the use of analysis cards (see Chap. 5): each issue, objective, and concept can be reduced to a single idea on a single card. These cards can then be reduced and printed two or three to a page and printed as part of the final program.

They can be placed either in the body of the document, as an appendix, or not included in the document at all. If the cards are not included in the main body of the document, it is necessary to extract the information, rewrite it in the narrative format suggested above, and place it in this section of the document. Since many of the cards may have diagrams that are hand-drawn, it is time consuming to reconstitute them in a finished format, and this is usually not done.

Space standards

Space standards are the basic irreducible building blocks for most programs. These are standards that are common for the facility overall and usually relate to a repetitive room, workstation, or functional activity. Space standards as defined here not only refer to the size of the space but also to the accommodation of the contents of the space as regards people, furniture, and equipment. Operationally, this definition makes sense as space standards are often determined by what goes in them (e.g., "conference room for eight at a single table"), and they are best illustrated as plan or isometric diagrams in the program. Architectural and Engineering Criteria (AEC) of the spaces are standards of a different level of detail and should be treated separately.

For many corporations and institutions, existing space standards are a fact of life and these become the basis of the raw functional program space requirement data. Many governmental and public agencies publish standards, and many of these become mandatory maximum and minimum requirements, often connected to funding formulas and with little flexibility. This often becomes a problem as function and technology evolve, more space is needed to perform a specific task, and the standards are not updated. A common fault with many standards, which were created when hierarchical systems were the prevalent system of organization, is that they are status related rather than function related.

If space standards exist for a project of any size with repetitive elements, they must be reviewed to confirm that they are suitable and applicable to the project at hand. If they do not exist, they should be created. The creation and testing of these standards can be a significant task, often requiring many trial layouts and, for the larger project, mockup modules or rooms. If the schedule allows, this can be done as a separate work task that precedes the programming itself. More often, a suitable module, office, or workstation size can be arrived at by examining the existing facilities or utilizing standards or examples from other installations with like functions. Often by "benchmarking" the practices and standards of a number of like companies and institutions for similar functions, a suitable preliminary standard may be reached that is adequate for the master plan or schematic design program. The standard can then be developed in detail during the evolution of the design of the facility.

Space standards should be generated by the priorities, philosophy, and mission of the organization. In general the amount of space should be generated by the work flow and function; the quality of the space and fittings and its location may be a result of either functional need or status recognition. Space standards are almost never developed or applied to unique spaces such as auditoria, performing art spaces, or the senior executive suite. It is also unusual to develop space standards for groupings of spaces or workstations, except for large scale master plan programs, as this synthesis is usually left to the design process.

For a retrofit of an existing building or the occupancy of a tenant space in a rental building, space standards will be driven by the fabric of the structure, its column spacing, fenestration and partition modules, and overall plan. For this application, preexisting client area standards should be utilized only with a contingency factor or range of values, or a unique space standard should be developed suitable to the building. Often the incompatibility of space standards and the physical attributes of the existing building into which the program must fit results in insufficient space if the structure was leased without adjusting the normal and expected efficiency to compensate for the variables.

Graphical space standards for a corporate office building and a laboratory are illustrated in Figs. 4.1 and 4.2. Space standards can also be portrayed in a tabular form related to occupancy utilization formulas, such as (net area)/[(student station) $\times$ (efficiency) $\times$ (number of students)] = classroom size, or capacity, such as (number of volumes) $\times$ [(area)/(volume)] = net square feet required for library stacks. If the element is a key building block, the possibility exists that only a slight variation could cause major consequences in the size and resulting cost of a building. It is advisable, in this instance, to verify the standard with a graphical layout as part of the program document. Caution is also indicated when relating the standards to the measuring system and terminology to be adopted for the entire project (see Chap. 8, as there is room for considerable error if strict consistency is not observed).

Organization diagrams

These diagrams are often included in the document to communicate the nature of the organization that will occupy the facility; if the program is

Conference
12 x 20/240 sq ft

Reception
18 x 18/324 sq ft

Office Type A
16 x 20/320 sq ft

Office Type B
14 x 16/224 sq ft

Office Type C
10 x 14/140 sq ft

Workstation Type E
5 x 5/25 sq ft

Workstation Type D
5 x 7.5/37.5 sq ft

Figure 4.1 Graphic space standards for an office building.

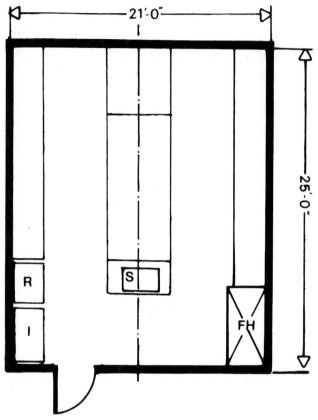

Figure 4.2 Graphic space standard for a laboratory.

for a small piece of a large company or institution it is often useful to illustrate the context of the facility organization in relation to the overall organization of the company. In many instances, the organization chart will reflect the proposed operation of the organization (e.g., interdisciplinary project groups versus departments) and serves as a bridge to create adjacency diagrams and the resulting organization of space in the final plan. The common box and connecting line diagram is the usual format; usually an extensive narrative is not required unless the organization is a key issue. These sorts of charts should only be included in the program if some useful purpose is accomplished; they can often be omitted especially if they do not reflect the way the organization actually operates.

Space lists

The space lists are the core elements of the program: they are the basic foundation upon which the quantitative elements of the program are built. The organization of these elements, their most effective presentation, and their breakdown are different for each project. Normally, they are presented in the form of lists or tables that reflect intended functional or organizational groupings, which are then totaled as a summary. Often, they are accompanied by the aforementioned organization or relationship diagrams.

The space list is always related in time to the requirements of the organization that is to occupy the facility, and these requirements must be keyed to the date of scheduled occupancy. It is good practice to provide separate columns for current requirements, requirements at building occupancy, and similar calculations for five and perhaps ten year projections. Projections of more than ten years are usually not predictable or useful. A consideration of the dynamic nature of space requirements will often generate a decision to build for "requirements + $x\%$ at first occupancy" to allow the organization some time to occupy the facility without the need for new construction. The important point is to relate the facility space program to the expected growth (or shrinkage or need for responsive flexibility) of the organization. For facilities that are planned around a single purpose or function, or if change will happen outside the sphere of influence of the project, a single space list for capacity at occupancy will suffice.

Often, the need to express the change of requirements over time is recognized in a phasing plan. This strategy is especially common in master plan programming in which the growth of a facility is related to specific phases and their implementation, usually over a longer period of time. For this type of project the space requirements are usually expressed in separate columns identified by phase. Often the space requirements for each phase will need to be linked to the specific strategy developed as the project is designed (e.g., central plant versus distributed systems) should this be the case. The program must then be retroactively modified to describe the attributes of the various phases.

Most commonly, the program is first expressed in *net area* or *net assignable area* for spaces or functions related to the mission of the organization—offices, laboratories, classrooms, conference rooms, storerooms, etc. Added to these primary functional areas must be operational support areas such as lobbies, loading docks, kitchens, etc., to make the facility function. These spaces are also net or net assignable areas and they should be determined or, at the very least, verified against intended function by the programmer; they are often understated or omitted entirely in preliminary functional programs. Table 4.1 is a checklist of some of the most common operational areas along with recommended net and gross area determinations. In Chap. 8, there is a complete discussion of categories for all types of spaces, rules for their application,

TABLE 4.1 Common Operational Areas

The designations of Net Area and not-Net (Gross Area) for the spaces follow convention; for many of the special areas such as loading docks and lobbies, which seem to have no convention, this table suggests one.

Area	Usually net area	Usually not net area
Entry vestibules		x*
Lobbies	x†	
Enclosed loading docks (dock space)	x	
Enclosed truck bay loading (truck space)		x
Maintenance storage rooms and workshops	x	
Janitor's closets		x*
Private toilets	x*	
Public toilets and attached lounges		x*
Mechanical, electrical, and communication equipment rooms		x‡
Circulation—vertical and horizontal between net areas		x*
Circulation within a room or dedicated function	x	
Circulation between workstations in open office		x*
Kitchens, food service, dining, and vending	x*	
Mail rooms	x*	
Office equipment rooms	x*	
Garbage and trash holding, recycling, and storage rooms	x	
Security office and console and security locker rooms	x*	
Maintenance and physical plant offices and locker rooms	x	
Storage rooms for occupants	x*	
File rooms, vaults, and records storage	x*	
Automobile parking		x§

*These definitions cross-reference other systems of measurement and seem to have wide consensus on their designation.

†Only to the extent that the size of the lobby exceeds the space required for passage through the lobby. This phantom corridor should not be considered net area and should be deducted from the space of the lobby in the program area tabulations.

‡If selected mechanical, electrical, or communications rooms are dedicated to a single tenant in a multitenant building, these are considered part of the *rentable area* (RA)—see Chap. 8. But for programming purposes when generating total net and gross areas and ratios, they should not be considered part of the net area. In addition, when a single piece of equipment is dedicated to the primary mission of the program, say an emergency generator that serves a single computer, the area housing this equipment should be considered as net area. If, however, the equipment serves multiple pieces of equipment, the space that houses it should be called a mechanical room and *not* be part of the net area.

§If the program includes enclosed space for a few cars this can conveniently be put in the gross area calculation. If the parking is not enclosed, it should not be tabulated for program purposes in the space lists. If there are many parking spaces in the program, enclosed or not, they need to be accounted for in the cost evaluation. This is best done by including a line 1a in the 17 line format and separately tabulating a unit cost for on-grade parking or a parking structure.

and an appropriate vocabulary. The programmer should explicitly define the mensuration system that will be used as the standard to build the program document; it is also good practice to insert the entire standard as an appendix since most of the published standards and the standard system proposed in this text are not too voluminous.

After tabulation of the required net area, it is the usual practice to extrapolate a gross or total area as a percentage of the net area. This percentage is based on the building type, qualitative judgments, and parameters established during the programming phase, and programmatic decisions related to plan organization, utilities configuration, and other factors. The formula [(net area)/(gross area)] $\times$ 100 generates the building efficiency. In accord with the rules described in Chap. 8, the efficiencies for some common building types are shown in Table 4.2. If you change the rules and the categories, as rental agents often do under the umbrella of local standard real estate practices to maximize the rentable area, you get, of course, completely different results. It is not unusual, for example, to have office floors 95 percent efficient when using these sorts of rules, and such numbers often create a communication problem for the programmer utilizing a more universal system.

The efficiency determination for the program is one of the most significant decisions the programming team must make; it drives the design quality, allows or proscribes building organization strategies and subsystem possibilities, and of course determines, in large part, the ultimate size and consequent cost of the facility. It should be one of the last decisions to be made during the programming process, but it is absolutely essential that the efficiency determination be included in the program as it is the basis for the project cost.

A common temptation and consequent mistake is to adjust the efficiency in response to a budget overrun. If the final adjusted efficiency falls within the normal parameters of the building type, this may be acceptable. If the proposed ratio is at the bottom end of the range of normal values, you should consider reducing the net area before pursuing alternative strategies. If the efficiency falls below the normal range, and there are no mitigating factors, a reduction of net area is surely indicated. Another approach to resolving a budget or scope overrun may be to attack some of the project's unit costs based on expectations related to finishes, ceiling heights, etc., but changes in these areas usually generate savings only in the 5 to 15 percent range.

It should also be realized that, as the efficiency is driven higher in response to budget constraints, the cost per square foot is likely to increase in response to a higher intensity of use and higher personnel density. In addition, engineering subsystems design will be driven in

TABLE 4.2   Efficiencies of Buildings

These are normal ranges for buildings of average quality for the use. If the building efficiency needs to be increased beyond this, the client is willing to accept lower quality, and you use the methods suggested in Table 4.3, you may be able to add 5 to 7 percent to the high numbers. If, on the other hand, the building needs to be of a higher quality, then you should use a factor 7 to 10 percent less than the lower end of the range.

Building	Efficiency, %
Offices	
Corporate headquarters	50–60*
Standard	60–70
Legal or medical	50–65
College	
Classroom buildings	60–75
Undergraduate teaching laboratories	55–70
Student center	55–65
Dormitory	60–65
Library	60–70
Physical education	65–75
Performing arts	55–65
Research	
Electronics laboratories	60–70
Biology laboratories	55–65
Chemistry laboratories	45–60
Animal facilities	30–50
Schools—High, Middle, and Elementary	60–75
Museum	60–70
Warehouse and storage	70–85

*All of these office area calculations assume a freestanding wholly owned building. Most often this kind of space is tenant space in a rental building and the efficiency shown here is irrelevant because the mechanical rooms and some of the service facilities (loading docks, storage, lobbies, etc.) are remote. The amount of this kind of space will vary from a low of about 15% for the relatively austere building to a high of about 27% of the gross area for a corporate headquarters. This percentage should be added to the numbers shown and will be roughly comparable to rental area (see Chap. 8) for an individual floor.

response to these constraints towards solutions such as rooftop self-contained mechanical units and exterior pad-mounted transformers, switch gear, and emergency generators that may only achieve this efficiency goal and no other. These single-goal-driven solutions often move the costs from initial expenditure to maintenance costs, potentially increase

TABLE 4.3   Factors that Increase or Decrease Efficiency

Factors that Increase Efficiency
  Rooftop mechanical equipment
  Pad-mounted outside transformers
  Pad-mounted outside emergency generators
  Minimum width corridors
  Large rooms
  Few rooms needing windows
  Low code population density
  Large, deep, and compact building platforms
  Buildings with central cores
  Low reliability requirements or no standby equipment
  Large virgin or suburban sites with gentle grades
  Single story buildings
  All electric buildings
  Mild climate
  New building designed for the program function

Factors that Decrease Efficiency
  Central mechanical plants
  Mechanical plants with redundant equipment for high reliability
  Mechanical plants with space for future equipment
  Inside transformers and emergency generators
  Generous corridors and entry spaces
  Vestibules and atria
  Many small rooms
  Many rooms needing windows
  Very high code population
  Small, narrow, irregular, and extended floor plates
  Multiple cores or scattered fixed facilities
  High reliability and standby equipment requirements
  Restricted urban sites or sites with steep grades
  Buildings more than six to eight stories high
  Severe climate
  Retrofit or remodeling of an existing building

the lifetime cost and decrease the life of the system, and may not be compatible with other goals. It is also a good idea to look at the program goals and the site for factors that may affect efficiency. Some of the factors that can increase or decrease efficiency are listed in Table 4.3.

It is inevitable that the owner will compare the proposed efficiencies for the new facility with personal experience, and usually the most available experience is the facility that is currently occupied. Once again, the system of measurement, definition of terms, and the need to include all areas are critical to a fair comparison. As an example, in Houston in 1985, I led a programming team for a new 285,000 sq ft office and computer facility for Chevron Geosciences that was to replace an outgrown, two story, leased facility. The original structure was designed as a speculative office building and had gradually been improved by Chevron to accommodate a major computer center. The efficiency proposed for the new structure by the programming team was 65 percent. The owner's calculations revealed that the existing structure was 85 percent efficient...why were we being so extravagant? An analysis revealed three principal reasons for the difference.

The first reason was that the owner had requested wider corridors because the existing code-minimum width corridors were dark and confining.

The second reason was one of program language—the owner had utilized *departmental gross* (the sum of net plus intradepartmental circulation) instead of *net area* (see Chap. 8 for definitions) in his calculations of the existing building's efficiency.

The third reason related to the housing of the mechanical equipment. It was decided that, for reliability, ease of maintenance, and longevity, a large central mechanical plant was to be included within the new building. Our inspection of the existing building revealed that all the chillers, air handlers, and the existing emergency generator were sitting on pads in the parking lot! The program efficiency requirement for the new building was finally negotiated to 68 percent: the final building was 66 percent efficient.

Affinities and grouping

The relationship of spaces to each other is best expressed by means of simple diagrams. There is a wide variety of styles that may be utilized for these diagrams, ranging from freehand sketches to hard-line drawings. There is also a range of terminology—*relationship diagrams* and *origination/destination overlays* are two of the more common names. Figure 5.5 has diagrams that show two popular styles. Experience has shown that loose and freehand sketches convey the information best and that the nonrectilinear shape is less likely to be mistaken for a proposed room layout. If the chosen programming technique includes the use of single idea analysis cards (see Chap. 5), the sketching techniques for the adjacency diagrams should be compatible.

Another common technique to describe adjacencies is the adjacency matrix, an example of which is shown in Fig. 5.4. This type of chart is easy to prepare, and it is often used when time and resources do not allow the preparation of affinity diagrams. Its strength lies in the ability to display a great deal of information about the adjacency priorities of a large number of functions compactly, its weakness lies in its lack of image—the design team must put great effort into determining patterns and grasping the whole from this type of chart (most often they will create their own affinity diagrams from the matrix to grasp the program relationships).

For the simplest project, adjacencies can be described narratively: when the attributes of each space are described in a standard format on a room data sheet, often a brief adjacency statement is entered, e.g., "adjacent to the theater box office," as a part of the data. However, even for the smallest project it is recommended that at least one diagram be created to illustrate the overall relationships of the spaces. For ease of reference and image recognition, the adjacency diagram should be located next to the space list for that grouping. For the larger project there is usually a hierarchy of diagrams, one of them illustrating the entire program.

Flow diagrams

Not required for every project, but for the factory or industrial plant in which the process and movement of people and goods determine the building, the flow diagram is essential. Other examples for which the flow diagram might be required would include transportation terminals for trains, trucks, and buses. Sometimes it is useful to calculate flow volume and holding capacity requirements roughly to determine the size of roads, walks, corridors, and waiting or holding spaces such as lobbies and event prefunction spaces.

Room data sheets

For the simpler project or those projects comprised of mostly unique spaces with low repetition, often the most effective strategy of organization and presentation is the utilization of the room data sheet. In practice, it is most often seen in the academic or corporate program prepared by an in-house committee. This approach utilizes a prepared format on a single sheet for each room or workspace to describe all of the program details. This may be seen as a vertical rather than horizontal information slicing method and, in its pure form, it obviates the need for separate AEC tables, adjacency diagrams, space standards, and equipment data sheets (EDS), albeit with loss of some detail. If the room data sheet approach is chosen as the program format, it will often be the bulk of the simple document.

There is a great deal of merit to this vertical slicing approach, as it often picks up special requirements in a simple narrative fashion for the special room or function. Many alternative means of organization ignore these room by room details that can be very helpful to the design team and very comforting to the user when the requested specifics are explicit. One of the disadvantages of this method of organization is that it becomes extremely bulky for the larger program because it does not take advantage of the economy of expression possible for repetitive spaces with tables and lists—there are always many sheets of paper because the information density tends to be low. In addition, the organization of information does not lend itself to ease of manipulation and pattern recognition for successive design phases. As an example of the latter problem, during schematic design, the engineer cannot, without going through every room data sheet in the program, grasp the number of laboratories that have the need for piped vacuum to decide whether a central or distributed system makes the most sense.

The following room data sheet is extracted from a recent program for a university music building; it was prepared by a faculty committee and is typical of the type.

Room data sheet

Room name: Orchestral music office

Number of rooms required: 2

A. *Space purpose and type of activity:* Office for the directors of orchestral music

B. *Number of occupants:* 1, faculty

C. *Space relationship:* Near instrumental ensemble room; near orchestral library

D. *Visual relationship:* None

E. *Furniture and equipment:* Upright piano, desk and chair with computer workstation, two side chairs, audio playback system, files, music stand, and book shelves

F. *Electric lighting:* No special requirements

G. *Electric power:* Accommodate the equipment

H. *Special systems:* Telephone and/or data connection

I. *HVAC:* Control of temperature and humidity is important

J. *Plumbing:* None

K. *Special finishes:* Floor finishes must be smooth so that equipment may be moved easily

L. *Special needs:* Isolate acoustically from adjacent spaces

Since this example was prepared and completed by a faculty committee, what it gains in direct communication, it loses in technical precision. The design team then must develop specific quantitative criteria (or design with subjective interpretations of the needs without the development of criteria) for all physical systems. Yet, the narrative descriptions related to room function and purpose, adjacency, furniture and equipment (which often defines the room shape and size), special finishes, and special needs, are important data that is directly expressed and easily captured in this format.

For the larger and more complex program that does not vertically slice the requirements into room data sheets there are, however, some alternative approaches to capturing the information related to specific rooms in the program:

■ *Provide a narrative alongside the space list.* This is usually done at the lowest level of the breakdown. If space standards are used for repetitive spaces, an accompanying narrative will usually be sufficient to pick up the occasional and exceptional detail for these spaces also. As an alternative, the room requirements can be treated as footnotes to the space list. This is a good approach if there are only a few special rooms and the data is not too voluminous or detailed.

■ *Provide limited room data information for each room in a standard format.* Perhaps list just a few categories not included in the AEC or EDS formats, i.e., space purpose and activity, space relationships (you can omit diagrams), visual relationships, furniture and equipment, special finishes, and special needs. Alternatively, *a narrative without organization* is often effective if the special information is only bits and pieces and a standard format would leave many blank spaces. With this format each page of the program may contain two to four rooms. This room data can preferably follow the space lists or, alternatively, the AEC tables in the document. This is a viable approach if there are many rooms with special and unique needs and if a greater level of precision is required for the architectural and engineering systems, which may, for example, be listed in the AEC tabular format.

■ *Develop a separate section of the document that would include only each room that has special requirements.* This could be an appendix referred to by tabular footnote. This approach makes sense if the special requirements are voluminous and would overwhelm the general information flow, of the program with a high level of detail. Special laboratories with heavily documented unique equipment, operational flow, and access requirements would be typical examples of indications for the use of this mode of information organization.

The utilization of room data sheets or one of the alternatives described above depends on whether the communication of the program information will be helped or hindered. The question to ask is: What is the form that captures the information completely, weeds out the most repetitive, blank, and noninformative chaff, and presents the data in the most succinct and accessible way? The answer will be different for each program.

Architectural and Engineering Criteria

The quantitative parameters of a program, especially one at the schematic design level for a specific project, are not complete without the inclusion of the environmental requirements for the various spaces. This is especially true when the building is a laboratory, hospital, or other complex structure with specific parameters and great variation. Some engineering/architectural firms prefer to establish these criteria later during the initial design phase, but most find it more effective and convenient to prepare it as part of the program document. Since the requirements will often reveal a significant design and cost impact, I believe it is best to make these discoveries as early as possible and therefore recommend that it be done as part of the program document rather than as a separate and later statement.

Even though the principal application of the AEC table is for the more complex project, it is a good exercise to include these criteria even for the simple office building for which a first impression suggests that there are no special criteria. There are. Even the simple office building has occupied and unoccupied spaces, hours of operation, acoustical and privacy requirements, and rooms with special heat-generating sources such as copier rooms. If each office is to have a laser printer or the conference rooms need to be darkened and have provisions for special equipment it is important to know this at the program level, and the inclusion of AEC is the most effective way of prescribing these accommodations.

It is easiest to put these requirements in a tabular form, and an example of both a blank and completed AEC table is given in Appendix D. The suggested form provides a column for each room *type*; therefore if the building program is simple with many repetitive elements, the AEC table will likewise be simple and have only a few columns. The example illustrates a table that should be sufficient for most uses. Should the building in question be a laboratory or hospital, the table should be expanded to account for a multiple of piped gases and utilities.

Codes, ordinances, and regulations

Most simply, this is a listing of the various legal requirements that relate to the utilization of the site and the construction of the building. Include the names of the written documents and the enforcement agencies; if possible include a contact name and telephone number. Should there be a significant site constraint, such as building setback requirements for an urban site or covenants related to the restrictions of use, this section may be expanded to include some details. This is the section in which significant regulatory form givers or constraints to the building should be flagged. It is usually not necessary or constructive, however, to do a detailed code analysis as part of the program: this should be done by the design team as an initial task of the later design process. It is often convenient, for the smaller program, to insert the names and contacts for utilities in this section. For the larger program or the master plan program there is usually a separate section devoted to utilities.

General criteria and standards

These criteria and standards relate to the project as a whole. They differ from codes and regulations in that, although there are legally imposed thresholds for many of the criteria, they are driven mostly by requirements established within the organization. They include system performance criteria, financial criteria for system selection, and life expectancy criteria for building systems.

System performance criteria that are universal to the structure may be presented separately from the AEC tables devoted to specific spaces or may be included in the table itself. Often missed are structural criteria related to floor loading and vibration, the latter frequently a problem when the structural engineer, without benefit of criteria and seeking greater economy, designs a floor that is perceptibly bouncy, is vibrated by mechanical units, or proscribes the use of sensitive equipment.

Financial criteria for system selection are utilized by the design team to evaluate alternative systems or by the construction manager/contractor to develop value engineering initiatives and alternatives. There are many ways to do this analysis and some of them are quite complex. For most purposes, a simple payback analysis is sufficient and a five year payback is the most common threshold for system or component selection. Normally I recommend to an owner that has adopted the five year simple payback threshold that the design professional be required to perform a present worth life cycle cost analysis on alternatives that, after initial consideration, fall in the three to seven year range.

Normally, the owner/client will provide the assumptions upon which the analysis will be based, including inflation rate, cost of money, present fuel and utility costs, fuel, utility escalation rates, and starting year. Normally salvage value is not calculated as this adds complications to the calculation (you would have to estimate the relative salvage value at the end of the five year period). Many of these assumptions may be included in the program; most often they are furnished separately by the owner/client as the need arises. Evaluations of operating costs, maintenance costs, and construction costs will be made by the design consultant or construction manager/contractor. To ensure uniformity and the expected level of analysis, it is necessary to specify both the criteria and the method of calculation in the program document.[2]

Life expectancy criteria for building systems is required to perform financial analyses related to component selection. It should be included as part of the criteria for the program. The recommended life spans for most systems are given along with a range in Table 4.5. The programmer should review his or her preliminary recommendations with the client or owner and compare them with their historical maintenance experience to determine the appropriate system life expectancy. Most readers familiar with similar lists will notice that the recommended life expectancy for electrical and communication systems and nonstructural partitions is considerably shorter than most. This more accurately reflects current experience and trends in all but the most static institutions.

---

[2]For all calculations I recommend the net present value method. It is not much more difficult than the other systems and requires only that you use Table 4.4, discount factors (many business calculators have these numbers already built in). It is the most commonly understood system, and it considers all relevant cash flows and the time value of money. For example:

	Primary A	Alternate B
Cost	$20,000	$24,000
Savings each year	$0 (base)	$1,500
Number of years with savings	5	5
(the discount rate is 8%)		

Alternate B: $1500 × 3.9926 (sum of .9259 + .8573 + .7938 + .7350 + .6806 from table) = $5,989

Therefore the preferred component is Alternate B, as it saves $1989 ($24,000 − $5,989 = $18,011; $20,000 − $18,011 = $1989. Note that each year would have to be calculated separately if it were to be assumed that cost of operating would escalate differently than the inflation rate upon which the discount rate was based.

TABLE 4.4   Discount Factors

	Present value of $1 at compound interest									
Periods hence	4½%	5%	6%	7%	8%	9%	10%	12%	14%	16%
1	0.9569	0.9524	0.9434	0.9346	0.9259	0.9174	0.9091	0.8929	0.8772	0.8621
2	0.9157	0.9070	0.8900	0.8734	0.8573	0.8417	0.8265	0.7972	0.7695	0.7432
3	0.8763	0.8638	0.8396	0.8163	0.7938	0.7722	0.7513	0.7118	0.6750	0.6407
4	0.8386	0.8227	0.7921	0.7629	0.7350	0.7084	0.6830	0.6355	0.5921	0.5523
5	0.8025	0.7835	0.7473	0.7130	0.6806	0.6499	0.6209	0.5675	0.5194	0.4761
6	0.7679	0.7462	0.7050	0.6663	0.6302	0.5963	0.5645	0.5066	0.4556	0.4104
7	0.7348	0.7107	0.6651	0.6228	0.5835	0.5470	0.5132	0.4524	0.3996	0.3538
8	0.7032	0.6768	0.6274	0.5820	0.5403	0.5019	0.4665	0.4039	0.3506	0.3050
9	0.6729	0.6446	0.5919	0.5439	0.5003	0.4604	0.4241	0.3606	0.3075	0.2630
10	0.6439	0.6139	0.5584	0.5084	0.4632	0.4224	0.3855	0.3220	0.2697	0.2267
11	0.6162	0.5847	0.5268	0.4751	0.4289	0.3875	0.3505	0.2875	0.2366	0.1954
12	0.5897	0.5568	0.4970	0.4440	0.3971	0.3555	0.3186	0.2567	0.2076	0.1685
13	0.5643	0.5303	0.4688	0.4150	0.3677	0.3262	0.2897	0.2292	0.1821	0.1452
14	0.5100	0.5051	0.4423	0.3878	0.3405	0.2993	0.2633	0.2046	0.1597	0.1252
15	0.5167	0.4810	0.4173	0.3625	0.3152	0.2745	0.2394	0.1827	0.1401	0.1079
16	0.4945	0.4581	0.3937	0.3387	0.2919	0.2519	0.2176	0.1631	0.1229	0.0930
17	0.4732	0.4363	0.3714	0.3166	0.2703	0.2311	0.1978	0.1456	0.1078	0.0802
18	0.4528	0.4155	0.3503	0.2959	0.2503	0.2120	0.1799	0.1300	0.0946	0.0691
19	0.4333	0.3957	0.3305	0.2765	0.2317	0.1945	0.1635	0.1161	0.0830	0.0596
20	0.4146	0.3769	0.3118	0.2584	0.2146	0.1784	0.1486	0.1037	0.0728	0.0514

TABLE 4.5   System Life Expectancy

When designing systems or components of systems, the expected life shown below should be the basis of design selection and life cycle cost analysis (including salvage value) unless otherwise stipulated by the client.

Systems	Life, years
Architectural (shell and core)	40
Elevator (cab upgrades at 10 year intervals)	40
Structural	40+
Mechanical	25
Plumbing	25
Electrical	10
Office fitout, furnishings and finishes	3–10
Public spaces	25
Laboratory casework and fittings	25

Equipment Data Sheets

While the data contained in these sheets is at a higher level of detail than the balance of the schematic design program, and the principal use of these sheets is during the later schematic design and design development phases, there are instances when their use in the initial program document is indicated. They serve a purpose here when the size and dimensions of spaces are predicated on a special piece of equipment or a series of machines connected by a work flow or process. Often, for a major piece of equipment, environmental conditions, overhead clearance, floor loadings, compass orientation, heat generation, vibration sensitivity, magnetic field requirements, and the like combine to drive the design solution and must be included in the program. An example of an equipment data sheet is given in Appendix C.

It is usually not necessary at the level of detail of the schematic design or master plan program to have the form entirely completed. The form should be sent to the user requesting the information that is needed now; the form can then be completed at a later stage of the project development. Usually the forms are inserted as part of the appendix of the program and referenced in the space lists or room data sheets.

Site evaluation

Although programming as a process can relate to nonphysical results, the focus of this text is on programming for the planning and building of physical facilities and, most particularly, facilities for human occupancy. In this kind of facility there are almost always two basic components of the program equation: the program of needs and objectives and the physical environment in which it is to be placed. When the facility program is prepared as the basis for site selection, the program of needs and objectives becomes the criteria for the selection of the site.

For the new facility, the environment is the site. For the program to be housed in an existing structure, the building *and* its site become the environment. Although the processes for the evaluation of both situations are similar, the manifestations and methodology are different and are best treated separately. The focus here is on site evaluation for a new building: the methodology for organization and analysis of the program for an existing facility is more fully described in Chap. 3, and the program documentation for the retrofit building analysis is described following this section.

There is a school of thought that suggests that the site analysis should not be part of the facility schematic design program, and that the facility program should then be more narrowly defined as only the written needs and objectives. The inclusion of the site analysis is, of course, a matter of choice, but I believe that a schematic design program for a new facility is incomplete without a site analysis (unless a site analysis has been completed as part of a previously prepared master plan). The primary reason for this is related to the need for cost information; another is that many program concepts relate to the site or can only be evaluated in terms of the site. In regard to financial issues, the site is often the source of much of the cost impact related to the program. How, for example, would the need for an expensive sewage treatment plant be identified and accounted for in the program? Or, as another example, how do we factor in the existence of a floodplain that restricts the use of the site and thereby mandates higher costs generated by the necessity for a high rise building and structured parking? A program without a site analysis is a program without a cost estimate, and a program without a cost estimate is not much of a program at all.

For the master plan, it is common to organize the planning into three parts: the master plan program, the site analysis, and the master plan itself. In this system of organization, the site analysis is not part of the program (which is defined in the narrower sense described earlier) but because of its larger importance becomes a separate document in its own right. It is best prepared on a parallel time track with the program by a separate team so that information may be shared; both are completed, however, as a prelude to the master planning process.

The site analysis, for the most part, is best portrayed in combined narrative and graphics. For all but the largest projects, or projects for which the audience requires finished artwork, the most cost-effective approach is to prepare a background site diagram in either a finished or freehand sketch format and then draw the various analysis diagrams on reproductions of this background. A drawing generated by a computer-assisted design and drafting (CADD) system and then sketched upon or transported to a PC-based drawing program for the final sketches is an effective higher-technology alternative to the hand-drawn sketch. It is most effective to have the background drawing in the size of the final document say, $8\frac{1}{2} \times 11$ inches; this keeps the ideas large and omits much of the unnecessary detail. It is best to have each drawing focus on a single aspect and then combine the most important features in a composite diagram. For the site analysis related to a master plan, the background diagrams should obviously be used for the preparation of the final master plan documents. A list of information on the site analysis drawings might include the following:

- Legal description and boundaries
- Zoning and legal restrictions (include land use restrictions, rights of way, easements, setbacks, etc.)

- Natural features
- Soil characteristics
- Subsurface characteristics (rock, underground streams, etc.)
- Vegetation plan
- Topography and slope analysis
- Site drainage (including floodplain, if any)
- Climate and microclimate (including a wind rose with prevailing seasonal winds is handy)
- Temperature ranges, rainfall and intensity by season, humidity, snowfall
- Utility plan (this may be divided into the various utilities if they are complex)
- Site access, access opportunities and constraints, and adjacent or internal traffic patterns (vehicular, pedestrian, other)
- Manufactured features
- Composite features
- Constraints and opportunities
- Adjacent land use and surrounding physical environment (existing and potential)
- Shadow patterns from adjacent structures or natural features
- Time and distance factors (often a 5, 10, and 15 minute walking radius will effectively communicate the scale of the site)
- Views from and into the site

In addition, some smaller scale maps might be utilized for a more regional perspective including the following:

- Off-site utilities
- Watershed boundaries
- Traffic and transportation
- Site location map

If possible, aerial photos of the site should be procured. Should existing aerial photography not be available and the funds not allow new photography, satellite photos of all of the continental United States (and for the world at a smaller scale) are available at a nominal cost and can be enlarged to an appropriate size with more than sufficient detail for all but the smallest sites. Sometimes the aerial photography reveals an unexpected pattern or a historical condition that points the way to the most effective site utilization. Figure 4.3 shows two diagrams in an effective freehand format. For many creative ideas on how to display site information graphically, see White (1983).

Existing facility analysis

If the programming is for the occupancy, or retrofit and occupancy, of an existing structure the site analysis described above is replaced in the program by an existing building analysis. Although site analysis may also be included in such a program, e.g., a change of occupancy requires a change in parking requirements, this is usually not the case, and the program is confined to the facility itself. The strategy for the retrofit program is described in Chap. 3; here we will confine ourselves to the documentation that is the subject of this chapter. The documentation for the retrofit must include three parts: (1) the condition analysis—an analysis to determine the existing physical condition of the building, (2) a suitability evaluation—its ability to accommodate the program and its elements, and (3) a cost evaluation to determine the cost to accomplish this.

Condition analysis: If the building is to be purchased, the analysis of the building at the program level should include a field report of an inspection describing each system by each discipline, ascertaining the capacity and condition of each component of the structure. If the building is to be leased and is fairly new, often the information will be available from the lessor. If the structure is an existing one, owned by the client that is to be converted to a new use, often data on its condition will be available and will only need updating. A recent facility audit, if it is available, will usually contain all of the information necessary. Often information on subjects such as handicapped compliance, and the existence of asbestos, polychlorinated biphenyls (PCBs), and other toxic chemicals, will have to be gathered, some of it by specialty consultants. The evaluation of the building does not need to be exhaustive, just enough to identify its shortcomings and opportunities in reference to the intended occupancy.

Suitability evaluation: The building's ability to accommodate the program not only relates to its gross area but also to such factors as its likely efficiency, structural bay spacing and load capacity, floor plate depth, area, and configuration, code compliance for its intended use, vertical transportation, floor to floor height, ease of floor penetration, etc. The questions to be answered here are: How well does the program

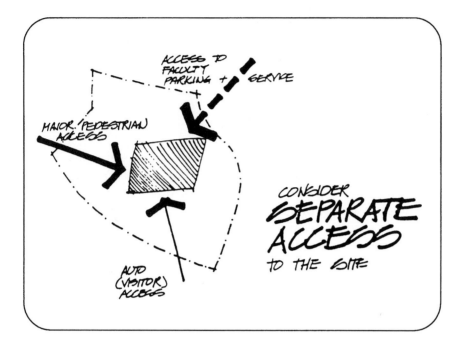

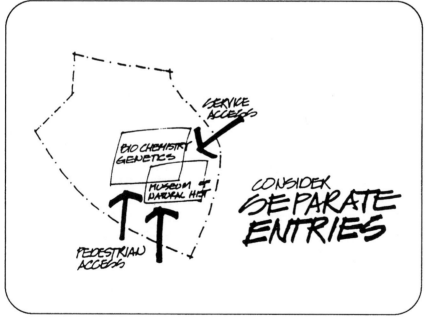

Figure 4.3 Site analysis diagram. There should be a diagram for each factor.

fit the building? Are there compromises that must be made acceptable? Often the penalty to be paid is one of additional gross area due to reduced efficiency and less than desirable layouts and adjacencies.

Cost evaluation: With the information of the condition analysis and suitability evaluation in hand, a list of improvements to bridge the gap from the program needs to the existing facility is made. This list usually cannot be made until a general design strategy regarding both the various systems and the arrangement of spaces is determined. This list is then evaluated as to cost in accord with the strategies outlined below and in Chap. 7. The proposed approach that generated the cost data should be included as backup to the cost evaluation summary or placed in the program appendix.

Cost evaluation and budget development

Few clients have unlimited financial resources and, for most facilities, the evaluation of construction cost at the program level is always one of the crucial issues. For some programs there may be little knowledge of the cost of the needs prior to defining them, but there is always an idea, albeit not always explicit, as to the limits of spending that seems reasonable to fulfill the objectives of the program. Frequently, the cost limits are set in advance and the challenge is to program the facility to accomplish the mission utilizing a fixed cost as one of the parameters. Cost, quality, and quantity of space form a three-legged structure: when these three elements are complementary, the program is balanced: when they are not, at least one of the elements must be modified.

Cost estimating at the program level is completely different than cost estimating for a project in design; at the program level cost demands its own language and approach. The methodology recommended in this text is called *program cost evaluation* and a complete description of the approach and its documentation is to be found in Chap. 7. In regard to documentation, which is the subject of this chapter, it is usually sufficient for most schematic design programs to have *the 17 line cost evaluation* as a stand-alone summary of cost. In many instances, the client will have a mandated format. Whatever format is utilized, it is essential to communicate to both the client and the reader the construction cost, the larger project cost, and the appropriate contingencies for each, so that no confusion arises and common fundamental errors are avoided.

For a master plan program, often a cost evaluation is not required. If it is, the categories described should be similar to the schematic design program except that a breakdown by phase is often required and the cost elements are often treated more broadly. Frequently, major cost issues related to the initiation of the master plan such as the furnishing of utilities (especially off-site utilities) are described in some detail. Should a further breakdown be necessary, it should follow the 17 line format summary. If the cost evaluation workbook in Appendix D in this text is used as an interviewing and analysis tool, it may be included in the program appendix.

Schedule

The schedule relates the program to both timing of process and time of completion for the programmed facility. For clarity the schedule is best portrayed as a simple Gantt chart accompanied by a narrative. The schematic design schedule should show not only the programming process, but also the schedule for the design, construction, and occupancy of the structure. For the master plan, the schedule may illustrate phasing on a longer timetable.

For many schedules, the crucial issues may be the timetables for various agency approvals: this is especially prevalent in master plan programs for sensitive sites that may include wetlands, the presence of toxic waste, or the habitat of threatened or endangered species. Almost every design professional can relate a horror story about these kinds of delays, and the regulatory environment only continues to tighten. Other common issues include sanitary sewer applications and storm water retention. The discovery and incorporation of these issues into the schedule should be part of the programming process, and often a civil engineer with experience in local regulations and their enforcement or a specialty consultant may be required to join the programming team to furnish this data.

The schedule is tied directly to cost by its relation to inflation and escalation (see Chap. 7 on how to incorporate the financial factors in the cost evaluation). In addition, the schedule is the vehicle that relates the program's quantitative data to the changing requirements as the organization evolves over time, i.e., what will the population be at initial occupancy, five years later, and ten years later?

Unresolved issues

During the programming process there will be issues discovered that cannot be resolved, and these must remain as questions to be addressed during later phases of the project. Many of these issues can only be resolved by design synthesis. For example, the statement for a retrofit program that suggests "it would be desirable if all of the sales and marketing department could be fitted onto the third floor of the building" is a concept that needs testing by actual layout. Other issues cannot be addressed because of timing. An example of this would be the forthcoming approval or disapproval of an initiative, say, the issue of a sewer permit or setback variance by an outside authority. Another would be an ongoing investigation of some marginal aspect that will not be complete by the time of issue of the program but is not important enough to warrant delaying it. Occasionally, an issue will surface during the programming process that will either delay the issue of the program or cause it to be corrected and reissued: in practice, however, this is extremely rare.

All of these unresolved issues should be collected in one section of the program to alert the client and design professional and to prevent them from falling through a crack. The most effective format is a simple list of these issues with a brief description and (if possible) a proposed timetable for their resolution.

Other kinds of information

It is impossible to be exhaustive in a checklist and there will, on occasion, be a call for other topics that are to be treated as part of the typical master plan or facility schematic design program. There will always be a need for these special topics in the program with a special focus. Two of these topics that are occasionally included in programs with a special focus are design guidelines and site selection criteria.

Design guidelines: These are often called *design parameters, design fulfillment criteria,* or a host of other terms. The reader, who by now is familiar with programming terminology, will immediately recognize these as design concepts and, as such, an extension outside the recommended programming boundary. As discussed in the section devoted to program concepts above and in Chap. 6, these design concepts should remain as part of the master planning or schematic design process, as including mandatory design concepts will stifle design creativity, the very commodity for which most clients hire design professionals. The proscription of design guidelines in the program should not, on the other hand, be confused with the requirements for them in master and urban planning, where they should be included and are often a vital result of the process. The creation of these documents, however, is outside the scope of programming.

The inclusion of design concepts in the program, however, may be useful when control needs to be extended over the design because of concerns related to the abilities or potential solution of the design team or likely design team. An example of an occasion when this approach proved advisable was the programming of the headquarters of a major pharmaceutical company in France. They had already selected an architect for the project, and the architect produced a design that was not responsive to the sensitivities of the neighbors or the objectives of a new corporate leadership. It was thought inadvisable to terminate the architect, so a program was written to express the new requirements and, because the architect's ouvre seemed not particularly sensitive to the stated program objectives, design guidelines in the form of concepts related to the site, site access, specific materials and imagery, etc., were added to the program document.

Site selection criteria

Often a program of needs is created as the basis for the selection of an appropriate site. In this type of program, the site analysis is replaced with quantitative and qualitative criteria to aid others in the selection of a site for the project. In addition to physical parameters such as size to accommodate the building footprint, parking and roads, or appearance to accommodate the need for image and a pleasant working environment, etc., are added other factors related more to the organization itself and its mission. Some of these factors may include demographics such as population profile related to worker, user, or customer, average traveling distance, site access, present and future utilization of adjacent land, utility availability and cost to provide, land cost, cost premiums if any to develop the land, site visibility, access to airports, and public transportation. For the larger project, the issues may get quite complex and may be outside the skills of the programming team. Should this be the case, specialty consultants for site acquisition, demographic analysis, etc., should be added to the team. In addition, because of the current level of regulation related to land use, it is advisable to add civil engineers and environmental consultants to the site selection team.

Appendixes

As in all documents, appendixes are used to add detail and supporting documentation that would interrupt the flow of information if contained within the body of the text. The programming process and emphasis will determine the contents. If the appendixes become too voluminous, consideration should be given to having them separately bound. Appendixes for a typical schematic design program may include the following:

- Meeting notes from the interviews
- Reproductions of analysis cards (if not included in the body of the program)
- Regulatory agency or utility letters of approval, intent, or commitment
- Reprints of critical regulatory data
- Reports of specialty consultants that support the program analysis; the most common include geotechnical and environmental (including the existence of asbestos, PCBs, and other toxic chemicals) traffic, roof condition analysis (retrofit), and reports related to acoustical conditions, vibration, etc.
- Surveys and analysis of existing building conditions and systems (retrofit projects)
- Detailed analysis and reports related to specific issues, e.g., utility routing options
- Equipment data sheets for equipment that will have significant impact on the program

For the master plan program, the appendix may add material on a more regional basis, including demographics, analysis of adjacent properties and neighborhoods, and impact studies in a hierarchy of scales for a variety of issues and interests.

As discussed in Chap. 3, meeting notes from the programming workshops may or may not be taken. If they are taken, they should be part of the program appendix. Often they are voluminous enough to be bound separately. If meeting notes are not taken, it is essential that a list of the meetings and the attendees be in the appendix: many will judge the validity and strength of the program contents based upon who participated in the process.

5

Tools and Techniques of Information Gathering

Introduction

This chapter focuses on refinements in the mechanics of programming. Since most of the information is gathered in the programming workshop, many of the techniques in this chapter focus on this activity—how to initiate the workshop, how to run it, and how to bridge an impasse creatively if it occurs. Many of the essential workshop techniques have already been treated broadly in Chap. 3 (if, for some reason, you skipped this chapter or need to refresh your memory, please go back and read the part related to the workshop strategy). In addition to the operational mechanics, some of the graphical tools that will help you in your efforts are described in this chapter.

Preparing for the Workshop: Agenda

Preparation for the workshop means not only organizing the data that you have collected and putting it in a format to communicate it, but also preparing the strategy that you will use to work with the people from whom you will get the information. Many of the logistical items, such as the space for the workshop and the requirements of the program team, have already been covered in Chap. 3 and will have been decided at the initial strategy meeting with the client's team. Here we will look at some additional details that may prove helpful.

After you have prepared the questionnaire (if any), you should prepare a detailed agenda for each workshop interview and send it to the individual who will be leading the client's group for that specific session. For the most part the agenda can be the same for all interviews (including, with some modifications, the initiation meeting) and can be in a standard format. An effective format suggested here follows standard good business practice. The timing indicated is related to a one and one-half hour meeting; your published agenda should only include the italicized titles, not the descriptive material below the title.

1. *Introduction* (three to five minutes). This is your orientation speech, which should include (1) the purpose of the programming process and the objectives of this meeting in the context of the overall planning and construction process (all of this information will have already been given in the orientation meeting, but it is good to repeat the highlights here for those who might have missed the meeting or were there and either could not hear or fell asleep), (2) the history and present status of the information basis for the discussion, especially any changes that have been made since the first orientation meeting, (3) the high points of the global decision makers' meeting, including the mission statement and any boundaries or constraints that will affect the participants' needs, (4) a review of this agenda for any changes, (5) a statement about how attendees are expected to participate, and (6) the type of information you expect to have by the end of the meeting.
2. *Review of existing data* (five to ten minutes). This is an overview presentation of all the knowledge gathered and assumptions made by the programming team related to the group, interest, or department that is the subject of the interview.
3. *Review of department or group program* (72 to 80 minutes). The topics should be addressed in order of priority so that if the meeting runs over and cannot be continued in a later block of time you will have discussed the most important information; the balance can be picked up either later in the design process or as work assignments to be completed and sent to the programming team. The recommended order to be included in the agenda is as follows.
   a. *Space list and other quantitative data along with projections*
   b. *Group or function organization chart*
   c. *Intradepartment functional relationships and work flow*
   d. *Interdepartment relationships and desired adjacencies*
   e. *Addressing of issues, objectives, concepts, and criteria related specifically to the department*
   f. *Requirements for special building services*
   g. *Discussion related to specific spaces (this should be done with the*

*room data sheets in hand if they are part of the program question-
naire and final document)*

h. *Detailed AEC*

i. *Identification of major equipment and review of the equipment
data sheets*

Much of this information can be gathered in a standard format if a
questionnaire has been previously issued to the participants. If the
questionnaire has been issued (see Chap. 3), the questionnaire can be
used as the agenda for this part of the meeting. As an alternative,
standard forms to be filled out can be attached to the agenda or, for
the simpler program, requested in the cover letter that accompanies
the agenda. If the latter is the strategy, however, sufficient time must
be given between the issue of the agenda and the meeting to allow the
work to be completed. Not all the information listed above need be
requested for this meeting, but you will need to tell the participants
what you expect. The ideal situation, if time allows, is to have the
questionnaire returned one week prior to the workshop interview so
that the responses can be analyzed and perhaps even put in a rough
draft of the final format so inconsistencies can be discovered. Most
frequently, however, this is impossible.

4. *Wrap up* (two to three minutes). This includes identification of unresolved issues, work to be completed, and required follow-up meetings. If confirmation meetings are needed, the timing for these
   should be agreed upon.

A cover letter should accompany the agenda; this letter should cover
the high points of the introduction and explain what is to be accomplished at the meeting and how the addressee can prepare for it. If the
client comes to the meeting without preparation, it is often impossible
to cover all the needed issues in the one and one-half hour time slot allocated for an individual department workshop. The time for the workshop should not be extended, however, because of attention span limitations and productivity decline. Therefore, every effort must be made
by the programming team to have the client prepare as much information as possible prior to the meeting.

Preparing for the Workshop: Standard Forms

One of the ingredients of an effective and efficient programming process
is the standard form, which eliminates much of the repetitive work. As
forms are used, they get refined and the quality of the information is
improved. With any programming form (as with any survey form), however, there is danger of having more and more questions added in the

interest of getting more and more data. This natural tendency must be consistently resisted and the form regularly pruned to simplify and omit rather than add questions; each additional question increases the chance that the form will not be completed or completed at all. In addition to the 17 line cost evaluation form, which, along with its accompanying workbook, is explored in detail in Chap. 7, there are two other forms that I have found useful and universal enough to include on the computer disc that accompanies this text. The use of both these forms is discussed in Chap. 4. Prune them as you think necessary:

Equipment data form: Design data for both fixed and portable equipment (Appendix C)

AEC form: Room by room criteria including utility requirements in a convenient matrix (Appendix D)

Preparing for the Workshop: Questionnaire

Chapter 3 suggests the contents for a typical and generic questionnaire, but in practice each building type specialty will require its own questionnaire, focused on its special needs and that must, in addition, be edited for each project so that the questionnaire remains as succinct and focused as possible. As part of their programming methodology each organization should develop a generic questionnaire that can be easily modified to suit each project. In addition to the questionnaire there is other information for specialty building types that might be more easily gathered by the use of a standard form (tenant options and paint colors for a residential rental improvement schedule would be a good example), but these are beyond the scope of this text.

Preparing for the Workshop: Analysis Cards

If analysis cards (more on these later in this chapter) are used at the workshop interviews, it is typical to prepare cards that show the information that has been accumulated to that point including the mission statement and the visions and constraints produced at the global decision makers' meeting. In addition to these project-related cards, it is also useful to have generic analysis cards that are preprinted with the issues, objectives, and recurring concepts listed in Appendix A. In addition to the evocative prompts, diagrams that illustrate the ideas may be added to the cards to increase the impact of the text. These kinds of graphic materials are very useful as a catalyst both to begin the programming process and jump-start it again when it stalls.

Preparing for the Workshop: Graphic Net Area Display

Many programming projects begin with a functional program describing net area generated by a formula. This program creates a list of net areas by functional requirement that are required to achieve the mission of the project. Many times this tabulation with a multiplier is used to generate gross area and a budget. Rarely is the list comprehensive, but like any other information it is a starting point. If there is enough of a breakdown, this space list can be prepared prior to the workshops as a graphic to illustrate the major components of the program. Later in the chapter there are suggestions for various ways of preparing and manipulating this sort of graphic information.

Running a Workshop: Leadership Role

Programming workshops are a unique meeting format for most of the participants. Since the programmer's objective is to listen to people, gather information about their desires, and determine how to fulfill them, the meetings are usually positive and upbeat. Assuming you are talking to the right people, the principal problems are usually those of creative input, information overload, time constraints, and focus. This is where the workshop leader needs to be effective. Some thoughts follow.

On creativity. Many new and creative ideas are caused by dissent, dissatisfaction, or negative information. Often, when this kind of information surfaces in the workshop it represents opinions and feelings that may have been suppressed by an unresponsive and often authoritarian culture and are now being released in what is perceived to be a non-threatening environment. This negative or contrary information should be recorded and revealed anonymously; if the analysis card system is used it should be posted without attribution as an idea to be considered (this is similar to brainstorming and the two-step process of idea first and then judgment). Later, reactions to the idea can be solicited from higher levels of the client hierarchy. Because of time demands, no contentious point should be debated at any length in the workshop.

On boundaries. Inform all the participants what decisions they can make and what the boundaries are in which they are working. The quickest way to discourage participation and destroy enthusiasm is to give the impression that you are able to accomplish more than you can. For example, if the budget only allows $20,000 worth of improvements to a department, if a department is only allocated 3,000 sq ft of space, or if the final budget or area is subject to approval by the president and this is only the first iteration, be certain that these constraints are made explicit. In addition, although dissent is encouraged, venturing outside the boundaries of the problem by revisiting the mission statement, exploring alternative options that have already been rejected at the functional program level ("we should have gone back to the site on Broadway instead of purchasing this site on Fullerton Avenue"), and like excursions should be discouraged.

Summarize.   As you proceed from item to item on the agenda you should give or get clarification of vague statements, promote evaluation of generalizations, and, as a deliberate procedure, give or solicit summaries and conclusions before moving on to the next topic.

On focus.   Having an agenda and tracking the meeting by summarizing as you go along will avoid most sidetracking and irrelevant discussions. Changing topics and drawing conclusions prematurely also need to be controlled so that sufficient time is given to each topic on the agenda. Jumping back and forth from one topic to another is a natural part of any meeting; however, it needs to be held within reasonable bounds. Coming to a conclusion before there has been sufficient analysis or problem definition is a frequent problem, particularly among a group of aggressive managers who may often tend to resist protracted discussion and often propose an answer for a problem immediately after hearing it stated. This expeditious approach is appealing, and a quick answer will often get a bandwagon of supporters who will join in the unwarranted validation of what is often a bad idea. It is the leader's job to ask "Why is that a good solution?" and thereby slow down the process so that the idea can be subject to an appropriate amount of thoughtful reflection and discussion. The converse of premature conclusions—the protracted discussion—also needs to be controlled; when the conversation turns pointless and ideas stop flowing, it is best for the leader to choose an appropriate moment to jump in and ask for a conclusion or summary. If a conclusion cannot be reached, perhaps a separate issue meeting is indicated (more on this later in the chapter), or alternatively, the topic can simply be recorded as an unresolved issue to be included in the program and addressed during the later design phases (see "Issues" section, Chap. 4).

On time.   Start on time and end on time. Wait to start five minutes at most and then only for the key participant. Do not lock the door or use any strict methods to control promptness; programming is often a task that has been added to the participant's burden. Often people will drift in and out of the workshop sessions to address other urgent business;

this hardly ever gets out of hand. Utilize the agenda for pacing the flow of information. In the end, if you have incorrectly estimated the amount of time required, intervene toward the end of the meeting and discuss alternative tactics for retrieving the balance of the information. One alternative would be to continue the meeting in another available time slot. It is better to get half the information well documented than have all of it useless. Pace yourself and the team so that you maintain the necessary intervals between meetings.

Running a Workshop: Group Dynamics

How groups assemble and interact has been studied by many disciplines; all have approached the subject with divergent interests. By far, sociologists have done the most controlled research in this area, but business people have not been far behind. Business interests are concerned with making the group an effective tool for decision making or getting things done; sociologists focus principally on the interaction of the group as it relates to the individual. There is a vast literature on the subject and this text can only cover the basics for the reader. For those with a continuing interest in this fascinating subject and a desire to improve their skills, there are references in the bibliography that will give you a starting point.

Group size

- The number of persons in a group affects both the distribution and the quality of the interaction (Mills, 1967).

- As groups increase in size, participation becomes less dynamic—adjacent ranks become more alike both in output and receipts (Stephan and Mishler, 1952).

Commentary: Small groups invite intimacy, candor, creativity, and achieve real results. If groups number over 10, then the dynamics of theatrics and group acceptance come into play. People try to impress their colleagues or their boss. Suggested action: since small is better, only invite those that need to be there.

Patterns of communication

- As members become better acquainted, inhibition drops more for larger groups than smaller groups (Slater, 1958).

  Suggested action: This can be both a positive and negative phenomena—positive because you may get more creative ideas, and negative if the participants get so comfortable as to forget the purpose of the session. To minimize the latter, continue to drive the meetings forward with the agenda for all the workshops; if anything, the structure should tighten as you get toward the end of the session.

- Even when interaction is free and open, a systematic pattern (of communication) tends to appear (Mills, 1967).
  Suggested action: Be aware of the developing patterns of communication as the workshop progresses. Be certain to get information from the appropriate individual, not just the loudest, most verbal, most prepared, or most senior. Personality, status, assertiveness, and previously established patterns of deference and communication may establish the basic pattern of communication for the workshop. This is especially true if members of the group have all worked together before. This pattern may be rigid and immediately obvious, subtle and loose, or a unique combination of both. Deliberate caution is suggested so as not to equate contribution with stereotypes of physical attributes (good looking, big, corpulent, etc.), culture, profession, race, age, gender, or status. In addition, be alert for the occasional destructive character types such as the authoritarian, negative personality, and the "high mach" (Barron, 1985) manipulator who will try to twist the programming process to achieve personal goals.

Group effectiveness

- In regard to group effectiveness, it has been found that cooperative groups perform better than competitive groups. They exchange ideas more freely, are concerned with completing the problem, experience less difficulty in communication, coordinate their activity through dividing functions and pooling results, show clearer insight and better judgment in deciding their next steps, and solve puzzles faster (Deutsch, 1949).
  Suggested action: Do not pit one group's needs against another's and do not assume fixed allotments. If there are limited resources that must be shared, call a joint meeting or a separate issue meeting for the involved parties to sort it out. Often the opinion of the programmer as an outside authority, unbiased except for the desire to satisfy the mission statement, can act as a catalyst for an effective compromise. Focus on the problem and attack it as a group; create the reality of all the contributors working as a team to achieve a common goal.

- Success in accomplishing the goal becomes an "interactive spiral"—superior performance and productivity become in themselves causal factors, inspiring enthusiasm, easing communications, and allowing closer coordination. "[N]ew energies and new social and technical skills increase the likelihood of success. This spiral relationship may prove to be one of the most important principles of group dynamics." (Mills, 1967).

Suggested action: As you move through the workshop process, focus on the successes, not the problems. In a protracted and complex process identify benchmarks so achievement can be recorded. If things go smoothly and progress is made, take the opportunity to make sure everyone knows it. If the group seems to be discouraged, call a progress meeting and focus on what has been accomplished.

■ Groupthink is that warm, agreeable, and paralyzing process of decision by hierarchical deference and fellowship that always results in mediocrity. Critical thinking is suspended unconsciously because of the positive feelings between the group members and their leader. Groupthink gave us the Bay of Pigs invasion and The House Un-American Activities Committee. Some of its symptoms include the understatement or rationalizing away of all problems, the suppression of all conflict to the prevailing view, a rosy and simplified view of the world as it affects the decision, the illusion of group invulnerability, and the negative stereotyping of critics.

Suggested action: If you suspect that this phenomena is happening, suggest ways to remove the cause—have the power structure change by having the most senior member skip some meetings, collect contributions from participants anonymously, play the devil's advocate, or encourage alternative ideas by the use of nonjudgmental techniques (see alternative strategies below).

■ Effectiveness and participation fall off after two hours.
Suggested action: If the agenda suggests more time is required, breaks should be scheduled and the meeting divided into two or more segments; the duration of the breaks should be at least 20 minutes, preferably longer.

The individual in the group

■ A person who has skills or knowledge about a specific aspect of a problem feels comfortable with and has pride in the contribution made to a group effort—this is called operating in an instrumental role. "[A] person enters the instrumental role in a group when he (1) conceives of the group goal, (2) accepts it, (3) commits his personal resources, intelligence, skill, and energy toward accomplishing it, and (4) gives its accomplishment higher priority than his own goals, the group's norms, and the existing pattern of emotional relationships among members." (Mills, 1967).

Suggested action: Be sure you have communicated the goals of the process and how it will affect each individual positively; get people involved and motivated; get them to contribute what they are capable of contributing to the programming process and thereby play this instrumental role; everyone has something to contribute.

- The presence of those who are committed to ends other than the group goal or who display disinterest or distaste for the task at hand tends to undermine the effectiveness of the group as a whole (Rosenthal and Cofer, 1948).

  Suggested Action: As soon as you detect such a person, take immediate steps to remove them from the process; in a workshop meeting, try to ignore them or diminish their role. Note that this is not to be confused with constructive dissent, which should be encouraged.

- The individual's first impulse in a group will tend to be negative toward a new idea. This seems to be a result of what Tversky and Kahneman (1988) call the *loss aversion theory* wherein the individual or a group of individuals adopts a conservative framing of the issue because of the greater concern for possible loss than the potential advantages of the decision.

  Suggested action: Try to have people focus on evaluating the negatives of a new idea realistically rather than rationalizing additional reasons to accept the conservative solution.

Running a Workshop: Separate Issue Meetings

During the course of the workshop issues will arise that are outside the authority and power of the programming team to resolve. There are two types of issues: (1) those that cannot be resolved at the present time and need either study by the design team or elapsed time to come to a conclusion (the latter would include rulings by outside commissions, analysis of soil borings, etc.) and (2) those that relate to policy, sharing of resources, organization, or other functional program issues. The first type of issue should be addressed by simply posting it as an unresolved issue in the program document and accounting for it with an appropriate contingency in the cost evaluation if it has a cost impact. The second type of issue often requires a decision by top management or study by a special committee. This should be done simultaneously with the programming process by having the senior client representative determine who should resolve the difficulty and then assign the task. If a wall display is used, the results of their work should be posted. Usually the programming team only defines the issue and does not participate in its resolution.

Running a Workshop: Alternative Formats

Most programming workshops will consist entirely of meetings with small groups around the conference table. It is not uncommon, however, that critical segments of the programming process need to adopt other formats because of the unavailability of key decision makers or remotely located specialist consultants. The principal alternative formats are video conferencing, the conference call, the computer conference, and electronic mail.

The video conference

Even though it is becoming more common that the larger client will have facilities on the premises, most often the conference will be held at a special rented facility off the premises. Because of this and because the communication difficulties with this method require more preparation time than the face to face meeting, it is imperative that the leader be even more methodical about the agenda and process. Because of the medium, the conference will be more formal and not as effective as face to face meetings; the participants will have difficulty in gauging signals when to talk, interruption protocols, nonverbal responses, and reactions. Experienced participants will be redundant and repetitive to ensure their message gets across, and remarks are often inappropriately extended because the control of the leader and subtle nonverbal signals of the participants are not apparent. All of this slows down the pace and the conference usually becomes a series of speeches rather than a free-wheeling creative session, and since the mind can process thoughts at four to ten times the speed of speech, the problem of sufficient attention is exacerbated.

If it is within your power to do so, some of these problems can be minimized by the correct setup of the conference room. Rather than sitting on one side of a table, have more cameras and monitors and sit on all sides of the table (the groups at both ends need to talk to each other also). All these cameras should be fixed to the wide angle position and pick up every participant at all times so that nonverbal signals and reactions can be perceived. An alternative configuration is to have a fixed camera for each individual. It is best to have both, but this is usually beyond the capabilities of most installations. An attendant-operated or voice-actuated camera focusing on the speaker is the minimum equipment required for the video conference, but this format is not as useful.

If you and your participants are new to this medium you will be intimidated at first, but here are some helpful hints:

1. Assume you are always on camera. Avoid wiping your nose or adjusting your clothing. Do not forget to gently cover your microphone if you are having a side conversation.

2. The camera magnifies facial expressions. Use it to your advantage and smile; be animated and use gestures to add vitality; use a variety of facial expressions; be as natural and comfortable in tone of voice and posture as you can—relax.

3. Be certain you speak to the camera and do not watch yourself on the monitor. If you have notes, lay them flat on the table and do not look at them while you are speaking.

4. Do not wear white because the camera will adjust the contrast so your face looks dark; men should wear medium-toned shirts and clothing; women should wear medium-toned blouses and omit sparkling jewelry and heavy makeup.

5. Be deliberate in your contributions—your statements should be concise; you should spell out unusual names or terms; identify yourself the first time you speak; if you have questions, address the question to a specific person by name as if they were sitting across from you.

If you are the convener of the conference you should do everything you can to prepare the participants for a successful show. If you are doing the conference at a studio, often you can get expert advice for your participants just prior to the conference. Makeup services are often available and your participants will appreciate the gesture. Confirm that each of them is fully prepared by distributing the agenda, giving each of them a package of instructions and assignments for specific issues if appropriate.

As the electronic revolution continues toward virtual reality this kind of conference will become more useful. The programmer should keep aware of the latest developments in this medium and be able to work with technical people to set up the equipment and operational format to make the conference most effective.

The conference call

Leadership and control are extremely difficult in this medium, so it is best to be extremely deliberate and structured. Since all visual cues such as identification, eye contact, body language, physical signals, appearance, personality, and charisma are completely lost and verbal cues such as voice intonation and interruption protocols are severely constrained, this is not the medium to use for a creative session. As with the video conference, the meeting is usually a series of disconnected speeches. For programming, however, in which only the simple collection of data or opinion is required, this is often a very useful medium. It is most often used when the opinion of a single individual such as a specialty consultant or senior individual is critical. It is very important that for this kind of meeting an agenda be distributed and specific time agreed upon well before the call. The orientation speech should be precise and should include the protocols for speaking and participation. For meetings of more than four to six people, a technical staff person should be available to set up the conference room, make the connections, and address any technical hitches that occur during the call.

Regarding the operation of this meeting the leader should require specific protocols including: the identification of the chairperson and all the participants at the beginning of the meeting, identification by each speaker before making their contribution ("Bob here..." or the like is usually sufficient), and, if relevant, the addressing of each question to a participant by name even when the person is sitting at the table with you and the person on the other end of the conference call is merely listening. At the end of a comment a consistent phrase such as "over" or "back to you" will diminish the hesitations and simultaneous speaking and, because it is not natural to most people, this or some similar phrase should be specifically required by the leader for the larger conference. But the best way to make this medium more effective is by reducing the number to less than six participants. If many participants are merely there to listen, an alternative strategy may be to have only a few participants and consider the balance as audience that needs to be informed. In the latter instance, you will still need to identify both the speakers and the audience to the participants on the other end of the line so that no embarrassing faux pas occur. In addition, it is appropriate for the leader to acknowledge comments from audience members and to let them speak if they have an important point to make.

The computer conference and electronic mail

Computers, computer networks, and electronic mail (E-mail) are rarely used for programming yet, but the possibilities of these media cannot be ignored. The format for this kind of meeting is usually one on one, although it is possible with projection devices to use groups at both ends. Alternatively, there can be serial group participation by everyone acting individually with their own computer. If the latter procedure is used, this is certainly not a conference in the usual sense. Since the medium is one of instantly communicated written messages, the meetings will be even more structured than either video or telephone conferences. Communication is more precise and there is no disagreement about what is written, although what is written may be subject to various interpretations. Advocates of this process of communication suggest it generates better and more completely thought-out reactions, allows messages to be sent as information to all or completely anonymous or confidential information to an individual, and suspends time and space in that you can take a little or a lot of time to react. Disadvantages include all of those of the video and phone conferences in addition to the requirement for additional time. This format may be useful at the present time as a communication device for the lead programmer to communicate with one remotely located key individual.

Graphical Tools: Introduction

Most people are verbal thinkers, but designers, architects, and engineers are visual thinkers. Programming is the bridge between these thinking languages, and therefore the program should incorporate as many graphics as the budget and time allow. The very best messages are those that contain both pictures and words such as illustrated analysis cards or diagrams with accompanying text. The documentation of existing conditions can be illustrated through photographs, site analysis diagrams, graphs, and charts. Likewise, in the body of the program itself there will be affinity diagrams, site diagrams, graphs, and charts. If you wish to extend the program toward design, Alexander diagrams (see Figs. 6.7 and 6.8) and design guidelines (see Chap. 4) may also be added.

This section of the text reviews the most useful and typical graphics utilized in both the programming process and final program document and suggests how to go about creating and using them. Where graphics are well known to the reader, such as pie charts, bar graphs, organization charts, and flowcharts, I have not bothered to add illustrations. They are all available in popular business computer software, and the software you choose will determine the possible format.

Graphical Tools: Graphic Net Area Display

This is a tool that will communicate the net area of the project as a graphic so it can be communicated to the client and manipulated during the workshop to balance the programmed area with the available resources. This type of display was originated by Peña of CRSS on what came to be known as *brown sheets* (the apocryphal story is that the original CRS office was over a butcher shop and the CRS staff borrowed the brown paper off the butcher's roll; later CRS had this paper made pre-cut with printed graph lines, but still kept the brown color). The graphic displays all of the net areas by listing each of them in some categorical grouping, i.e., "purchasing department" at a consistent level of detail, then listing all the groups (subtotaling as necessary), and finally presenting a grand total at the end along with a gross area conversion number so that the total can be related directly to the cost evaluation. Areas are shown both graphically to the same scale and numerically in the graphic and totals. An example of a single-page display is shown in Figure 5.1. For a complex project it is typical to have many pages; usually each page will illustrate two to four departments or similar sized groups of people and activities.

Operationally, the sheets should be large enough to be seen by the workshop participants when pinned on the wall. I find that 30 × 42 inch is a standard sheet size for both drawings and printers, is roughly proportional to 8½ × 11 inch (for later reduction and inclusion in the final document), is about the largest size easily handled by a single person, and is large enough to display a good deal of information. The basic data on the sheet can be created by hand or by computer. The graphic depiction of the areas should be in a contrasting color to the background for ease of comprehension.

A hand-created combination that works is white paper, various colors of self-stick removable post notes or contact paper cut to size, and colored chalk or chalk pencils for the tabulations. There are many others, including the original brown paper, white labels, and white chalk combination used by CRSS. The difficulty with all these approaches is that there is a practical limit to the number of times you can change chalk marks on paper. Although a bit less portable, white porcelain enamel steel sheets, colorful sheet magnets in desired shapes, and colored markers are a good combination that can be changed endlessly. Often, if programming an educational or corporate facility, a dedicated whiteboard or steel chalkboard can be made available for this purpose, obviating the need for portable sheets. If you suspect that the area tabulation will be contentious, you might consider this approach. The objective is to make whatever system you choose workable and responsive.

For the large project, the technologically inclined and equipped consultant or facility director can create the area diagrams and tabulation in the computer in full color, bring it to the workshop on a laptop PC,

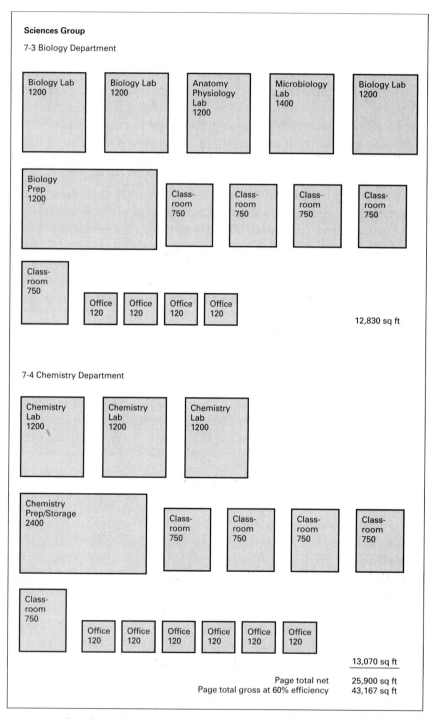

Figure 5.1 Graphic net area display. There is no particular convention as to the dimensions by which the areas are created except that they be compact; if there is a known dimension for a particular space, however, it could be roughly expressed in the representation.

and project it on the wall. Using popular word processing software, the diagrams and numbers can be manipulated and totaled simultaneously. At the completion of the session a printout can be made immediately. The only disadvantage of the computer system is that only one page at a time can be viewed and it is difficult to get a holistic grasp of the tabulation.

Graphical Tools: Analysis Cards

The analysis card is a 5 × 7 inch filing card upon which, with words, pictures, or both, a single idea is expressed. Analysis cards for programming were originally an innovation by Willy Peña of CRSS. Prior to their use for programming, they were used by Walt Disney to make storyboards for animated films. Now they are used routinely in many disciplines for problem solving. General Pagonis, the logistical supply commander for Desert Storm, utilized a wall display of analysis cards to coordinate the largest secret military supply movement in history, the now famous shift to the north to support the end run around the Iraqi defenses of Kuwait (Pagonis and Cruikshank, 1992). The utility of the analysis card system lies at once in its flexibility (cards can be added, removed, or relocated) and its ability when utilized in aggregate form as a wall display to allow comprehension of the program at a glance and immediate access to any part. There are some disadvantages to the system if the programming project is large and complex and time is short: (1) The scale of the graphics limits the working group size to about 20 or 30. This is not a problem in a workshop meeting, as the groups will usually be smaller than this, but it is a difficulty in group orientation or confirmation meetings when the group could be considerably larger. (2) The wall display is unique and fixed and difficult to replicate or move. This obviates the use of multiple teams simultaneously programming large projects and requires all participants to meet serially in a single room.

These difficulties will occur infrequently, however, and for the most part analysis cards are an effective visual aid for the programming process. Here are some operational hints on how to utilize these cards:

- Each card should represent a single issue, objective, or concept.
- Preprinted cards should be prepared before the workshop for the most commonly occurring generic issues, objectives, and concepts for the project type you are programming. These cards should be based on the listing in Appendix A, and contain both words and evocative diagrams. They will be used to stimulate client response. Use only as

many of these topics as are necessary, and add others that you know are particular to the project type.

- Preprinted cards should be prepared before the workshop with all (or a summary of all) the unique project-related information that you have gathered. These cards should primarily address global issues such as overall project size and total budget, but should also include the primary divisions of the program by naming departments, divisions, etc., so as to provide the armature of the program organization. These cards are used as the basis of confirmation for the assumptions you have made (the entry point) regarding the program requirements. These cards may be brought to the global decision makers' meeting; they should be combined with any new information gathered at this meeting to form the beginning of the wall display that will be filled in as the workshop progresses.

- Group the cards on the wall by issue, interest, or department in rows of seven to ten cards taped together on the back so they can be conveniently folded like maps for relocation or retrieval in groups .

- Have an assistant programmer in the meeting whose sole job is to prepare, clean up, and add or delete the cards in the wall display as the meeting progresses. Another assistant can become the official notetaker if meeting notes will be required (see Chap. 3 for a discussion of this strategy and Chap. 4 for the need for meeting notes).

- As cards are deleted, cross them out with a big X and leave them up for a while so future participants can see ideas that have been considered and rejected. Often if the program reaches an impasse or takes off in a new direction, these ideas may become useful (see "The Technique for the Intermediate Impossible," for the theory behind this approach).

- After the workshop is finished, the cards can be utilized as part of the final program document or used only as the basis for the document (see Chap. 4 for an evaluation of both of these approaches).

- The analysis cards may be easily prepared on the computer and printed with a laser printer using any popular word processing software. Diagrams can also be prepared on the computer. Figure 5.2 illustrates a preprinted analysis card prepared on the computer (the original was prepared in WordPerfect, utilizing Times New Roman TT Italic in 36 and 24 point type). During the workshop, cards can be prepared with felt tip markers and cleaned up or clarified later in the same medium; alternatively they can be reconstituted on the computer. Figure 5.3 illustrates an example of this kind of card.

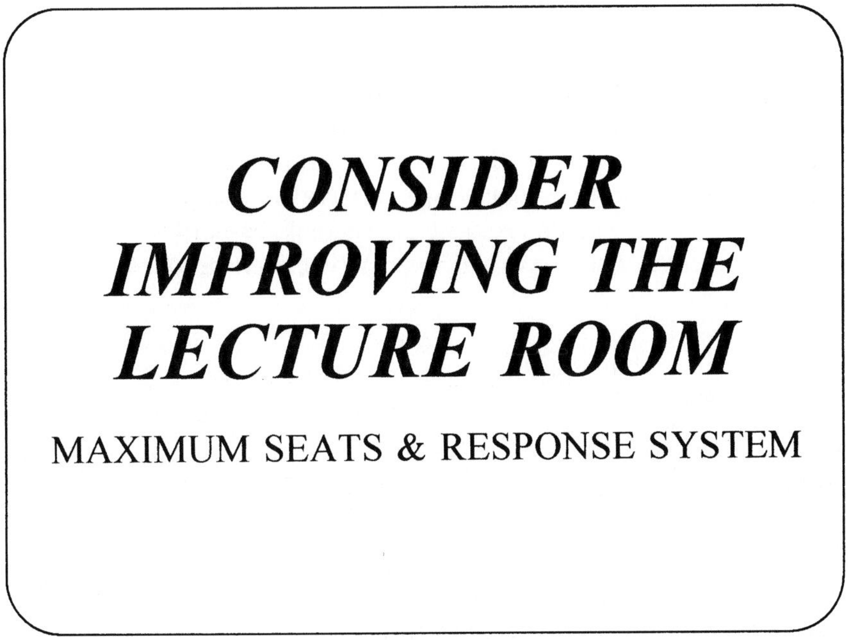

> # *CONSIDER IMPROVING THE LECTURE ROOM*
>
> ## MAXIMUM SEATS & RESPONSE SYSTEM

Figure 5.2 Analysis card—finished. This card was prepared from a rough original on a computer.

CONSIDER A SOLID BARRIER TO SCREEN THE GARDEN.

Figure 5.3 Analysis Rough—An example of a card prepared in the workshop interview.

■ For the workshop, you will need a big blank wall for the wall display; 20 to 40 ft long is fairly typical. A surface that can be pinned is best; one that can be taped will do. This wall should be one of the criteria for selecting the workshop space. Alternatively, I have had portable corkboards and chalkboards brought in to use if the walls of the workshop were precious wood, were filled with objects and artwork, or were all glass.

Graphical Tools: Flowcharts

Many programs, especially those that include industrial processing of some kind or another, are best explained by a flowchart. Other applications of flowcharts may include traffic volume and circulation diagrams related to the site analysis. For the average program, these diagrams should be done freehand. Should they need to be spruced up, they can be recreated by computer utilizing graphics software.

Graphical Tools: Affinity Matrix

The *affinity matrix* or activities relationship matrix is the first tool used to record the relationships of functions or groups within the program. In its simplest form (see Fig. 5.4) it lists each space in the program and

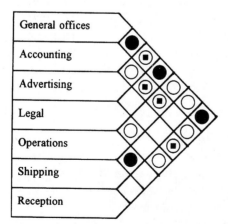

Figure 5.4 Affinity matrix. In this form it is a half matrix. Although you can use numbers to designate the need for adjacency, it is better to use graphic symbols that vary in density—dark is strong affinity and absence is no affinity, so that patterns are immediately obvious at a glance. The example uses three marks to represent four levels of affinity; you will rarely need more.

uses a hierarchical notation (usually at three or four levels) to record the need for interaction. Except for the simplest of programs, there will need to be a hierarchy of at least two levels of matrix diagrams: (1) department matrices for each of the departments showing the intradepartmental relationships and (2) an interdepartment matrix illustrating the entire facility. Implicit in these diagrams is that proximity will increase interaction and that the relationship need is physical. There is no proximity implication for a telephone connection, nor does it now need to be accounted for.

As a tool to be used by the design team the affinity matrix is useless as it exhibits only the subtlest of patterns. It is only the first step and must be translated into an affinity diagram (see below) to be useful. This translation is most often done as part of the programming process as it involves interviewing future occupants and making corrections as the relationships are clarified by the process of translation.

Graphical Tools: Affinity Diagrams

Affinity diagrams (also sometimes referred to as *correlation diagrams, relationship diagrams,* or *interaction nets* by some programmers) show the relationship between program elements. They are the graphic of choice for this purpose and most readers will be familiar with the diagram. It is best done by illustrating functional areas as nonrectilinear freeform shapes and then connecting them by lines. Figure 5.5 shows two styles of these affinity diagrams.The weight or number of lines illustrates the strength of the affinity between the functions. For programming, these diagrams are best done in hierarchically arranged and richly interactive groups (by department or function, for example). These groups can then be aggregated into a picture of the entire program (see Chap. 6 for some in-depth discussion of the theory).

Graphical Tools: Statistical and Numerical Display

Often past history, present analyses, and future projections of population, traffic, or material quantity will be clarified by the use of graphs. In addition, cost analysis and distribution of elements are often displayed better graphically than as a series of numbers. As the reader knows, the utility of graphs is their ability to show patterns and anomalies so they can easily be grasped. With the advent of business graphics software, it is now easy to display numbers in a variety of popular graphic formats including bar charts, pie charts, and linear graphs. Applications to programming would include population projections, pro-

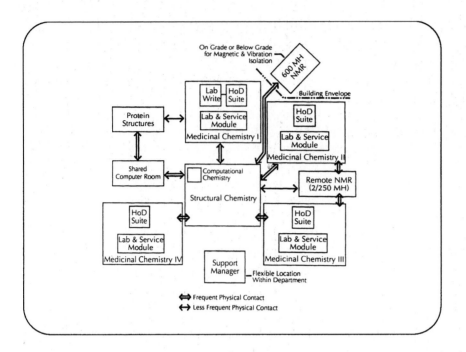

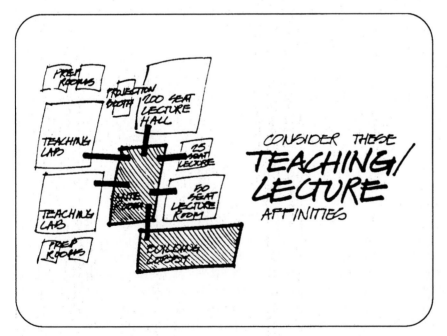

Figure 5.5   Affinity diagrams. Two examples of effective diagrams.

jections related to facility availability, land use distribution, net to gross ratios and area by category, and cost distribution by element or category.

Graphical Tools: Alexander Diagrams

There are two types of what I call *Alexander diagrams* [so-called because they were invented by Christopher Alexander to explain his system of design in *Notes on the Synthesis of Form* (1964)]: the highly abstract point-and-line relationship diagram that summarizes the essence of the functional attributes of a related group of program elements and the succinct graphic image. These diagrams are similar to the more familiar relationship diagram but extend the concept graphically and conceptually in both directions—toward greater abstraction and toward design. The theory behind these diagrams and some examples are to be found in Chap. 6.

Graphical Tools: Blocking and Stacking

Blocking and stacking are really a preliminary design device used to determine the ideal method of filling a building envelope with program elements. Blocking is the aggregation of area into a block of space, usually at the department level; stacking is the placement of the block within a building volume. The primary use of blocking and stacking is in exploring alternative arrangements of departments and other spaces to determine fit or achieve an ideal adjacency relationship. Many times it is done three-dimensionally so that vertical adjacencies in multistory buildings can be explored. The primary use of blocking and stacking is related to renovation or tenant lease programming for which a physical facility is already in place. It is often used as a bridging intermediate step between programming and design. It is a crucial part of the program if the program is utilized as a feasibility study to evaluate the usability of a structure under consideration for lease or purchase. In many situations, this technique can be used in a meeting with the future occupants of the facility as an interactive workshop.

Physical tools can vary from the elaborate to the mundane. At the mundane end of the spectrum, pieces of stiff paper, cut to scale and colored to represent functions or departments, are manipulated on prints of the building plans. At the elaborate end, a multilevel clear plastic model with precut wood or plastic elements in various colors can be used. Future developments in this area will include the use of the computer with a graphic program to manipulate areas, including "morphing" programs to squeeze and manipulate department configurations to fit the building envelope. By use of a projection system this could become an interactive session.

Use of the Computer

The reader who has proceeded this far has come upon many aspects of both the process and documentation of the program in which computers are suggested or implied. As you progress further there will be more. Most of the contemporary applications of this tool are really in their infancy regarding this discipline principally because the facility program, like the individual building, is a unique creation not subject to many of the labor-saving aspects of computer applications. Today, principal programming applications are the tabulation of numbers, the creation of graphs and charts, the creation of standard forms, word processing and desktop publishing, and the manipulation and reproduction of graphic elements such as photographs, drawings, charts, net area diagrams, and analysis cards. In the near future, the computer will be used more frequently as an interactive communication device; in addition, as our efficiency in processing information increases, this should eventually enable us to prepare the complete draft document right in the workshop. In the more distant future, virtual reality and the communications revolution may bring us the completely electronic workshop.

For the consultant or facility director who programs facilities frequently (even if the projects are of only moderate complexity), it is essential that the computer become part of your programming toolbox. As you develop your applications and train your personnel, the efficiency of processing and displaying information will be constantly improved. Programming is one area in which utilizing the computer can have a dramatic influence on the time and effort that are required.

Advanced Strategies: Overcoming the Impasse

The tools and methods described in this text, along with some knowledge and experience in the parameters of the facility type, will give you the skills that you need to program in almost any situation and bring the process to a successful conclusion. On occasion, however, you may reach an impasse if either the program cannot be balanced, agreement cannot be reached, or any forward movement seems impossible; it is at this point you will need to apply more advanced techniques. These techniques are not "tricks" but merely ways of stimulating creativity and channeling it for productive purposes. Their application is both for you as an individual, for your team, and for the client programming team in a group setting. All of the methods suggested below have been used for many years and, in the appropriate situation, have been proven effective. As with all tools, it is up to you to choose the best one for your problem.

Advanced Strategies: Introduction

As the leader of the programming team it is up to you to identify the point at which the normal and ordinary programming methodologies are not working and to develop ways in which to resolve the difficulties and maintain the momentum of the process. Creating new ideas or directions as the individual leading the program and then introducing them into the normal process should be attempted first. Some of these techniques are suggested below. Alternatively, if you are an outside consultant or a facilities director, you might consider organizing some of the advanced group techniques for your in-house team. If this does not work, then you will need to approach the client representative and explore alternative strategies to bring the process to a successful conclusion by applying these group techniques in the workshop. The use of these advanced strategies can obviously apply to either one aspect of the program or the entire process.

Advanced Strategies: Group Tactics

Brainstorming techinque

Brainstorming is a creation of Alex Osborn described in *Applied Imagination* (1953). The objective of this system is to generate ideas. Its normal format is to have individuals in a small group setting verbally generate all the ideas they can; these are then recorded on chalkboard or easel pad by the moderator. The rules include the following: (1) the objective is to create as many ideas as possible: quantity, not quality is the goal, (2) spontaneity and free association are encouraged: the wildest ideas are the best, and wilder extrapolation and building on these ideas are even better, and (3) suspend all judgment and evaluation: no approval, compliments, or disapproval are allowed. Only after the session is finished is the evaluation made by the group.

Operational suggestions include restricting the time to about 30 minutes, with 45 minutes being the outside limit if the ideas are still flowing (but always try to stop just before you run out of ideas); having at least six but no more than twelve people, some of whom are part of the problem solving team and a majority are people with completely diverse interests not related to the problem; having a separate notetaker who is adept at condensing the essence of an idea into a succinct statement; and having another notetaker write every idea down, even if it seems only a slight variation of another. As the leader, you must define the boundaries of the problem, keep the process moving if it stalls, slow the exchange down so all the ideas can be heard, and start and stop the session. If possible, it is best to have a day or so after the session before a separate session is convened in which the ideas are culled for repetition and evaluated; in practice this is often not an option because of time constraints. At the very minimum, however, there should be a long break between the brainstorming session and the evaluation session to complete the logical and critical mental shift.

Commentary: This is an approach that is valuable for generating program concepts; it is not good for the evaluation of complex questions. It can be a refreshing change of pace for a group, especially one with quiet, inhibited, or reserved members. It should be looked upon as step one in the two-step process of idea creation and idea evaluation. Be careful everyone plays by the rules and the session does not degenerate into "tossing around a few wild ideas" and simultaneously evaluating them. Slower paced, but perhaps more palatable to the group that is really reserved or part of a rigid authoritarian culture, is a variation in which everyone is encouraged to write three or four of their wildest ideas on a slip of paper and the moderator posts them anonymously. To get people to relate to other's notions, have another round of three or four ideas and post them, and so on. Usually three or four rounds are the maximum; ideas fall off rapidly after that. If you want more ideas, stimulate the group by the use of the random word (see below) and have another round or so.

Single-text technique

The one-text procedure is an effective device for resolving disagreement in two situations: (1) if the positions of two or more parties are so far apart that a face to face agreement is not possible or (2) if there are many parties involved and a consensus cannot be reached. This is the technique of *shuttle diplomacy.* The method involves having the programmer become a third party mediator and utilizing successive drafts of the program or its contentious part as a single text to be modified until every one is satisfied. At the end of the process, all the parties are faced with a simple "yes" or "no." The most famous one-text procedure was the 1978 Camp David Accord in which after 13 days and 24 drafts, with the United States acting as the third party mediator, both Egypt and Israel signed the agreement.[1]

Commentary: If you reach a point of impasse, using the program or pieces of it as a single text and shuttling successive drafts between the parties with conflicting or diverse interests is often the only way to do the job at all. You might also find this procedure a handy tool when the parties are in remote locations. The keys to the success of this method are the creation of options and the patience of the mediator.

Nominal group technique

This is a technique designed by Delbecq et al. (1986) to generate ideas in a more controlled format than the brainstorming session and then evaluate them. It is a highly structured process that is effective in identifying elements of either a problem or a solution and setting priorities: (1) Each participant makes a preliminary list of ideas. (2) Each participant in round robin style orally states a single idea that is written on a flipchart or board by the moderator in the contributor's own words. The rounds continue until all ideas have been recorded (individuals can "pass" if they have no contributions for that round). (3) After all ideas have been recorded, the leader reads them and solicits questions from the group; the questions are to clarify the meaning of the idea, not to evaluate it. A brief discussion ensues on the criteria for ranking. (4) Each participant chooses up to nine ideas and then ranks them. (5) These rankings are then recorded on anonymous ballots. (6) The ballots are passed to the leader for preliminary tabulation and posting. (7) The group then discusses the results, especially focusing on wide variations in ranking for possible misinterpretation of information. (8) A final vote is taken on the ranking.

Commentary: This is a good technique to eliminate hierarchical deference, the smothering of minority opinion, and "groupthink." In programming, it can be a useful tool to identify and rank program issues, especially if they are contentious or vague. The leader should pace the discussion, set the exact rules for ranking and voting, and avoid interpreting or steering the contributions as they are recorded and discussed.

---

[1]The observation has been made that this technique is analogous to the process of architectural design and documentation. It is a most obvious analogy when the architect designing a house for a couple finds that they are in complete disagreement and, as a result, adopts the technique of interviewing them separately, using the design drawings as a single text. After many iterations and when the design is the best compromise possible, it is presented for a "yes" or "no" approval to both. One could stretch the single-text analogy still further by saying that the preparation of the facility program and all instruments of service, the drawings and specifications, are merely a single-text approach with a wider audience.

The technique of analogy

This technique was developed by William J. J. Gordon and is described in *Synectics* (1961). It uses four types of operational mechanisms: (1) *personal analogy,* in which the individual relates the problem to personal experience, (2) *direct analogy,* which uses parallel facts, related technology, general knowledge, etc., (3) *symbolic analogy,* which utilizes impersonal objects or images as metaphor, and (4) *fantasy analogy,* which gives permission to relate to the ridiculous, impossible, or simply weird. The operational mechanism is the small group problem solving meeting that focuses on a single problem or issue. To be effective the rules must include the "idea first, evaluation later" suspension of judgment structure that is used in brainstorming, although here it does not have to be as rigidly applied and the two phases can be merged as part of successive loops during the session.

Commentary: This is a technique that has great appeal to the design professional as it is really a structured group version of the design thinking process. If design professionals are participants, this kind of session will often generate many useful ideas. It is related to the technique of the random word and evocative word described below.

Other group strategies

The strategies presented above are the ones most likely to be useful to the programmer. For most readers they are more than they will ever use. If none of them appeals to you, however, there are many more. Included among them are some that the reader is likely to recognize: the single question format and the ideal solution format (Larson, 1969), the Delphi method (Dalkey, 1967), Maier's posting format (Maier, 1963), Wright's 494 agenda (Wright, 1975), PERT and its variation SAPS (standard agenda performance system) (Phillips, 1966), and one of the first contributions—"buzz groups" (Phillips, 1948). An overview of many of these systems can be found in Mosvik and Nelson (1987); for those readers who want a more detailed treatment, the original sources are listed in the bibliography.

Advanced Strategies: Individual and Group Tactics

Lateral thinking

Lateral thinking is a concept and term originally conceived by Edward Debono and first published as *The Use of Lateral Thinking* (1967). Since then Debono has written more than 25 books on the subject, and these have since been translated into 20 languages. A list of some of these are in the bibliography. The concept identifies two types of thinking: logical and lateral. Lateral thinking creates ideas and logical thinking evaluates them. In many ways, the creation of lateral ideas is similar to brainstorming, but with a slightly different twist. Debono is more analytical and helpful than Osborne regarding the creation of these alternatives. Whereas Osborne uses the "wild ideas" created as free associations as part of his system, Debono goes about helping us create these ideas as part of a process of lateral thinking. Since this process is a key methodology used in the programming theory supporting the system recommended in this text, it is explained in more detail in Chap. 6. However, there are two tactics that he developed as a result of this concept that are useful to include here: *the technique of the random word* and *the technique of the intermediate impossible.*

The technique of the random word

The random word deliberately introduces discontinuity into the process of thinking. The relevance of the word to the problem at hand is established *after* it has been chosen. The random word changes the entry point to the problem and its sole purpose is to generate new ideas. Drawing the spectator into the creative process by giving their works truly random and irrelevant names was a favorite device of the surrealists—the meaning of the work was thereby enhanced and created as unique for each person. At first thought, it seems incredible that any truly random word could have relevance to the subject at hand but the patterning process of the mind actually makes it impossible for any stimulus to be irrelevant to another once it has been brought into juxtaposition and focus. The reader with some knowledge of psychological technique will also recognize the similarity of this concept and the semantic differential of Ozgood.

The operational technique works either in a formal group setting such as a brainstorming session or for the individual as an exercise. In practice, about three minutes is best and five minutes is the longest one should devote to a single word; longer durations run out of ideas or energy. Random nouns are best and, as a rule no selectivity should be used. In a group setting, the facilitator selects the word, and the ideas are recorded without evaluation in accord with the rules of the brainstorming session. The use of the *random word* as a creative tool, however, is not as frequent as the use of the related concept of the *evocative word,* which is an everyday tool in the programmer's toolbox if the programming system in this text is utilized.

In a sense, one of the building blocks of the programming structure outlined in this text, the objectives and concepts in the checklist in Appendix A, operates as random words but these words are chosen to relate to the issues and do not demand the kind of creative stretch that a truly random word requires. To the client, however, many of these words represent concepts or aspects of the program that have not been heretofore considered and, as such, evoke creative thought. They are *evocative words* (I am indebted to Willy Peña of CRSS for the first use of the word in this context) rather than random words. The same creative patterning of the thought process that is stimulated by the random word is stimulated (albeit at a much lower level of abstraction and a higher level of control) by the use of these evocative words. Contrary to the proposed time limit of the basic technique, however, as much time as is necessary should be devoted to each topic in the workshop interviews.

The technique of the intermediate impossible

This is another approach to the introduction of discontinuity in logical and linear problem solving. In its pure form, this is a lateral thinking approach (Debono, 1971, p. 83) that uses an idea that seems ridiculous in itself as a bridge over an insurmountable obstacle blocking the train of logical thinking. The ideas themselves are often created in nonjudgmental creative environments such as brainstorming or free association. A key element of the method is to suspend negative judgment and not proceed up the yes–no decision tree. In practice, the awareness of this methodology will encourage you to put these unworkable or ridiculous ideas aside rather than discard them, in the knowledge that if you reach an impasse in your logical thinking, tracing your path back to this discontinuity may furnish a breakthrough to an alternative path of success.

For the programmer, the insight is to suspend final judgment on an initially rejected idea until the process has proceeded beyond the issue. Often a change of reference or framework in the program will make a once judged foolish idea attractive in the new context.

The morphological forced connection

This is another generator of ideas, but uses the controlled (as opposed to free) association of two or more elements. It is the adult equivalent of the popular children's books composed of three or more adjacent sections that can be flipped at random to get unique combinations: by flipping heads, middles, and ends of familiar beasts, truly strange beasts are created.

Its most popular form is adjacent columns of words; usually three or four columns are the maximum that are usable—any more and the connections are less creative and more confusing (unless they are specifi-cally structured to be compared in this manner, say, an extensive listing of mechanical properties). The most useful format is "attribute–attribute–noun"; another useful combination is three or four attributes or nouns. Another variation is to take the factors in groups of two or three at a time; the total number of combinations is determined by ele-mentary probability equations. An example of the technique utilizing groups of three attributes in three columns related to the phrasing of a program concept is shown in Fig. 5.6. The most useful application of this strategy is the creation of alternative attributes.

Change in thinking language

When first confronted with a problem, people will unconsciously choose a strategy and then perhaps unconsciously switch from one strategy to another. It is more productive, however, to be aware of the strategy you are using and then consciously change it if it does not work. There are three basic thinking languages that we use. The most prevalent in west-ern culture is *verbal thinking,* followed at some distance by both *visual*

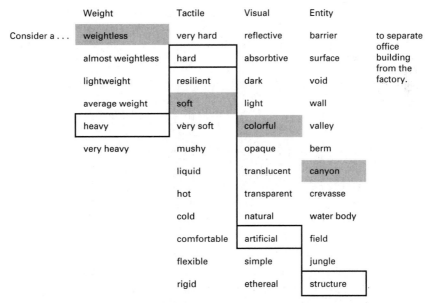

Figure 5.6 Morphological forced connection chart. A generator of alternative attributes that is especially useful for program concepts and design concepts. The combination connected with solid lines is rather conventional; the shaded attributes begin to show the creative possibilities. This method is a controlled version of the use of *the random word,* another creative technique that is also discussed in this chapter.

thinking and *mathematical thinking*. Most people tend to think predominantly in verbal terms, which are more metaphorical, condensed, and abstract than visual thinking. Speech, writing, inner speech, and their common use of language mirror the verbal thinking process. This mode of thought is most effective in solving logical problems, perceiving abstract concepts, and communicating experience. Visual thinking, on the other hand, uses the experience of the apparent physical world and creates models and metaphors to solve problems. It is the primary thinking strategy of the designer, the primary end user of the program. Since the program uses both means of expression, it is useful to think of the program itself as a bridge between the verbal thinking of the client and the visual thinking of the designer. Mathematical thinking relates to physical problems asking for quantitative data and is an essential method for solving these kinds of problems. Its applications in programming are obvious and universal.[2]

In programming, the changing of thinking languages to solve an impasse is most useful at the hazy juncture of the program objective (verbal), the program concept (verbal and/or visual), and the design concept (certainly visual). It is here that the physical manifestation of what is said and drawn can be manipulated until satisfactory communication is achieved, and it is at this juncture that the power of the diagram is most compelling.

Technique of alternative strategies

As opposed to the general strategy of change in thinking language, alternative strategies are conceptual processes that may use any or all three of the languages—it is the same tactic but on a different level of abstraction. This is a useful tool that suggests overcoming the impasse not by creating new ideas as suggested by Osborn and Debono, but rather by reexamining existing ideas using different approaches. Becoming aware of the strategy that you are using to solve a problem is useful so that if the process bogs down or comes to a dead end, other alternatives can be explored.[3] In their *Strategy Notebook,* Interaction Associates (1972) lists

---

[2]A complete review of the concept of thinking languages with many examples from literature and the arts is to be found in *Notebooks of the Mind* by Vera John-Steiner (1985).

[3]James L. Adams (1979) relates that John Arnold, founder of the Design Division at Stanford University, had a checklist of strategies [which was first published by Osborn (1953)] put on a deck of cards that he would flip through for problem solving. The analogy to the analysis card system utilized for graphic program display is obvious.

66 strategies and their powers and limitations along with a simple exercise.[4] The strategies listed in the Notebook include:

Buildup	Display	Simulate
Eliminate	Organize	Test
Work forward	List	Play
Work backward	Check	Manipulate
Associate	Diagram	Copy
Classify	Chart	Interpret
Generalize	Verbalize	Transform
Exemplify	Visualize	Translate
Compare	Memorize	Expand
Relate	Recall	Reduce
Commit	Record	Exaggerate
Defer	Retrieve	Understate
Leap in	Search	Adapt
Hold back	Select	Substitute
Focus	Plan	Combine
Release	Predict	Separate
Force	Assume	Change
Relax	Question	Vary
Dream	Hypothesize	Cycle
Imagine	Guess	Repeat
Purge	Define	Systemize
Incubate	Symbolize	Randomize

Many of these thinking strategies are used in the normal train of events when the program is conceived and assembled. This is especially true for program objectives and program concepts. The point is to change the procedure by which ideas are formulated to effect change and eventual resolution.

---

[4]This book regrettably just went out of print. A similar list of strategies, although not nearly as complete or handy in its treatment, is to be found in Sanoff (1977).

Other data gathering techniques

In addition to the workshop interview as the primary source of information about the program as the future desired state, other information
will need to be secured to complete the program. A full listing of the con-
stituent parts of a program, with priorities indicated, is included in
Chap. 4. For the existing facility, physical inspection and documentation are required; for the new facility, a site visit is required. The level
of documentation and focus of these inspections depend on the purpose
of the programming effort, and this is also treated in detail in Chap. 4.
If the programming effort is for a building type unfamiliar to the programmer, a literature search, including design handbooks and manuals, statistical data, regulatory manuals, and published examples of
similar projects, should be made as part of the programming effort.

In rare instances, data on similar projects or the programming team's
experience might not be sufficient and you will have to resort to behavioral research to determine some aspect of the program. This is most
common when there is some question or characteristic unique to the
specific problem that must be addressed at the program level. Examples
might include questions such as "If the doctor's parking lot were moved
to the corner of Broadway and Lincoln and a shuttle provided, would
you still drive to the hospital or would you take public transportation?"
or "How would you arrange your classroom seating to teach most effectively?" The answers to these kind of questions can usually be gathered
by simple questionnaires (as we have seen, however, structuring a good
and simple questionnaire is not simple), but the acquisition of some
kinds of data may need more extensive behavioral research. Since most
programmers are not experienced enough in these methods to plan and
execute this kind of project, it is suggested that a specialty consultant
be retained. This is especially critical if the results of the research will
have a profound effect on the program content or cost. If, on the other
hand, the effect on the program will be minimal, the time and financial
resources are available, and you or your staff have a personal interest
in such endeavors, you may want to do it yourself. For those that are
interested, I have included a short bibliography on the subject that
should give a starting point.

The use of research

To my knowledge, there exists no comprehensive, recent summary of
environmental design research done at a level of abstraction that is of
interest and immediate use to the facility programmer. Most of the literature is available only in papers on behavioral science that are diffi-

cult to access. Subjects such as the effect of distance on communication, perception of space, how people move through spaces, how to create natural conversational groupings, and a host of other topics have been the subject of research. The contributed papers for the national conventions of The Environmental Research Design Association (ERDA), are a rich source for both hard and soft data. Much of the data and prescient observation exists as individual nuggets, buried deeply within texts on perception, art, design, and sociological theory. The programmer should be aware of the current literature and gradually build up a library of data that can be used as behavioral and perceptual facts to help the client make decisions during the programming process. The bibliography at the end of this book has many references that contain this sort of information.

6

Programming Theory

How you program may include a theoretical framework or not. For the simplest of programs there is no need for structure and even for the moderately complex program you may decide that a simple rundown of the various checklists, tables of content, and the contents of Chap. 4, the program document, are sufficient for your purposes; indeed, a program, that is better than the average document produced in contemporary practice can be achieved in this way. However, to produce a document that is a significant improvement in the communication of the client's intent, a methodology of organizing your thinking and portraying your information is needed. This chapter is devoted to the development of a conceptual framework and the improvement of your data gathering and analysis techniques to achieve that end.

Some Conceptual Frameworks

Most of the texts on the subject of programming devote a substantial proportion of their pages to the development of a conceptual framework for identifying and categorizing information. Three of the most comprehensive systems like this are Palmer (1981), Peña et al. (1987), and Duerk (1993).

The matrix as a framework for information is used by all three of these systems. Palmer's diagram, Fig. 6.1, has *human factors, physical factors,* and *external factors* as one dimension and *ascertainments, predictions,* and *recommendations* as the other dimension. Peña et al.'s diagram, Fig. 6.2, has *goals, facts, concepts, needs,* and *problem,* which are then each explored and defined in terms of *form, function, economy,* and *time.* Duerk's diagram, Fig. 6.3, has the same *goals, facts,* and *concepts,*

	Human factors	Physical factors	External factors
Ascertainments			
Predictions			
Recommendations			

Figure 6.1 Palmer's matrix. Three "categories of information" and three "conclusion types." (*Reproduced with the permission of The American Institute of Architects under license #94096. This license expires November 30, 1995.* Further reproduction is prohibited.)

	Function	Form	Economy	Time
Goals				
Facts				
Concepts				
Needs				
Problem				

Figure 6.2 Peña et al.'s matrix. Five procedural steps and four design considerations. (*Reproduced by permission of CRSS*)

Issues	Privacy	Security	Image	Etc.
Facts				
Values				
Goals				
Performance requirements				
Concepts				

Figure 6.3 Duerk's matrix. Five information categories and an infinite number of design issues. (*Reproduced by permission of Van Nostrand Reinhold.*)

but adds *values* and *performance requirements* and explores and defines all of these factors in terms of design issues.

Another, simpler approach to categorizing information is a checklist of topics; indeed, many of the matrix systems have standard topics and checklists within each of the boxes. Peña et al. (1987), for example, has a rather extensive listing in the aforementioned matrix called an *information matrix*. Palmer (1981) fills the squares with subcategories. White (1972) takes a completely different approach, and his system of programming is simply a checklist. It is probably the most complete list of topics related to programming available anywhere; he calls them *traditional facts*. I would call many of them goals and concepts (as he, in fact, does). One of the problems with this list and the reason it is not reproduced here is the lack of any hierarchical structure and the wide variation in detail; many of the topics listed by White do not need to be part of most schematic design or master plan level programs.

In some systems, there is, overlaying the categorized information, another process and/or logical construction that helps to define the terminology and organize the information in accord with priority and hierarchy—helping define what is important and what is not. The two most structured are Peña et al.'s [illustrated in *Problem Seeking* (1987)] and Duerk's [described in *Architectural Programming* (1993)].

Peña et al.'s model relates each of their categories of information, goals, facts, concepts, needs, and problem, to a five-step chronologically linear process. Each step is defined in terms of form, function, economy, and time:

Step 1   Establish goals

Step 2   Collect, organize, and analyze facts

Step 3   Uncover and test concepts

Step 4   Determine needs

Step 5   State the problem

Step 4 is the balancing of the program in which the quality and quantity of space are aligned with the budget and schedule; step 5 is a synthesis by the programmer and designer of short and succinct qualitative statements "no less than four...dealing with form, function, economy and time." Step 5 is described as "the link between problem definition and problem solving, between programming and design." It is a written communication between the designer and the client to confirm the designer's understanding of the program.

Duerk (1993) creates a model that is more hierarchical; she illustrates it as a branching diagram (Fig. 6.4). The mission statement gen-

Mission Goal Performance Concept
Requirement

Figure 6.4 Duerk's branching diagram. From *Architectural Programming: Information Management for Design* (1993) by Donna P. Duerk. (*Reproduced by permission of Van Nostrand Reinhold.*)

erates goals, which generate performance requirements, which generate concepts. The process is described as "an algorithm for a rigorous programming process" (Duerk, 1993, p. 9).

There is a great deal of similarity in the approaches of Duerk and Peña, much of it disguised by differences in terminology. Both of them use a second way of organizing thought in conjunction with the initial structure, which, although necessary to make the system comprehensive, makes them difficult to comprehend as a whole. Verger and Kaderland (1993) and Duerk (1993) all contribute the notion of categorizing information by *design issue*. This approach is also the one suggested in this text. Verger and Kaderland (1993) use the term *dynamic clustering,* which achieves the same organization of information by design issue, but in a workshop environment with the client. The approach of clustering by issue is the key to eliminating the matrix and making the organization of information more obvious and accessible.

A Proposed Conceptual Framework: Background

The first question to be asked of the systems described above or, for that matter, any structure that categorizes thought is—is it necessary? If it is not, it is just an unnecessary layer of thought management that filters direct communication and needs to be excised. If one looks at a simple facility program, mission statement, space list, budget, and schedule, and asks "What's missing?" the answer is not very much. However, the whatever is missing is the essence of the gap between a good comprehensive program and a mediocre program, and a conceptual framework is the only way to bridge this gap—only with a method can the programmer organize, cull, and prioritize the vast amount of information typical for the larger project in a way that can easily be grasped and manipulated by the design team. The problem with most conceptual frameworks is that they strive to be universal and elegant (in a mathematical sense) and in doing so become a procrustean bed of facts, many of them trimmed or stretched ridiculously to fit the framework.

When we look at the entire spectrum of programming activities and interests, we find only two areas in which it helps to have information structured in a conceptual framework: (1) the larger, more universal considerations and notions related to quality—objectives, aspirations, concepts, and needs, and (2) the process to gather, evoke, synthesize, and express them. Everything else can be relegated to standard formats, checklists, criteria, surveys, statements, and tables. For example, the cost evaluation system described in Chap. 7 is, by itself, an effective algorithm for determining cost and needs no further structure; if there are larger considerations related to cost such as phasing and capital cost versus operating cost, these can be treated separately as universal considerations in the recommended theoretical format. Striving for a completely consistent logical structure and format for the entire programming process and documentation is not useful. Programming to be effective and simple should be "messy" thinking—thinking in structures which although having internal, logical consistency are not holistically consistent.

The first building block in a structure to address these two areas of concern is a simple checklist of design issues (see Appendix A), which are expressed in a specific format. The essential attribute of the objectives and concepts generated by this checklist lies in their source—*it is only information gathered from the client.* Although it is one of the programmer's primary functions to gather information, discover patterns, and act as a catalyst to evoke the client's thoughts and contributions, *information is not created by the programmer.* There are some essential exceptions to this rule, however, but these are related to generic facts that the programmer, because of his or her experience and research, brings to the table. Among them may be historical building costs, design and construction schedules, building type efficiencies, code and regulatory data, results of research and analysis, surveys, and standards and practices of similar institutions or companies, which, when revealed to clients, will help them crystallize their thoughts.

By focusing on identified design issues only, one of the essential problems relating to the matrix structure—the compulsion to fill every box in order that the information is complete and comprehensive—is eliminated. When the client does not have an opinion or thought about an issue, it can be left up to the design team to resolve that issue in the design of the facility—*the design is the completion of the prescription, not the program*—and to create information to fill the categorical box is either useless or an unnecessary restraint on the design team. This issue-based approach not only eliminates useless paper and distraction but also reflects what actually happens in practice: treating every issue exhaustively in a matrix format will exhaust the team and the resources and is, in the end, unnecessary.

A Proposed Conceptual Framework: The System

Universal and qualitative information should be expressed in the format of issue, objective(s), and concept(s) as illustrated in the following example:

Issue: Image

Objective: The building design should reflect the high-technology activities in which the company is engaged

Concept: Consider the use of high-technology architectural materials and expression

Concept: Consider the expression of technological features such as microwave towers and antennae

Objective: The building should be an advertisement for the company and the products it makes

Concept: Consider the use of lighting to give the building a presence from the highway at night

Concept: Consider the exposure of some high-technology elements on the interior that can be seen from the exterior at night

Concept: Consider a sign, pylon, tower, or marker to identify the company

These two examples, related to what is obviously a high-profile, high-technology corporation, demonstrate the preferred pattern and format. Each design issue (*Issue*) is paired with one or more program objectives (*Objective*) and there can be one or more program concepts (*Concept*) for each objective (it is also common to have no program concepts and the simple issue–objective pair is the complete statement). As shown above, there can be more than one objective for each issue, and the preferred format is to list each objective as a separate grouping. Note also some of the key vocabulary and syntax for each category: the use of "should be" for objectives and the word "consider" for concepts. Further on in this chapter there is a more detailed treatment of the definition, formulation, and use of these kinds of statements. Here is another example.

Issue: Image

Objective: The building should reflect human values and the process of creativity rather than be a reference to the high technology that is the company's product

Concept: Consider the extensive integration of building and landscape

This example addresses the same issue of image treated above, but for a high-technology company with a different philosophy. This statement should generate a completely different design response by the architect and illustrates why it is crucial to communicate these issues, concepts, and objectives as part of the program document. Another way of addressing the image issue is to go and "hire an architect who does work like that" and often this is done when an individual decision maker projects his or her vision by singlehandedly selecting the architect. When the decision is made by a selection committee, however, often the preferences of the users are thwarted. However, one of the advantages that can be secured by having a comprehensive program prepared prior to the selection of the design professional is that it can be used as a lever to select the architect. You could, for example, use image preference (or functional approach, or any other desirable trait) as the means to make a short list or final selection.

For many projects, in addition to the more universal issues, there are specialized areas of interest that, because of their importance, need to be treated at a higher level of detail so that the program can be fully defined. For simplification of terminology I prefer to also call these *issues* but they are issues in the sense of "the issue of." This approach is analogous to the dynamic clustering of topics suggested by Verger and Kaderland (1993) for "multiple channel communication." It is another example of the pragmatic, but messy, thinking approach that I advocate. An example illustrates this kind of grouping:

Issue: Biology laboratories

Objective: Furnishing of convenient and flexible electrical power and communication

Concept: Consider the use of overhead exposed cable trays

Concept: Consider the use of reel-down electrical power similar to commercial automobile garages

This a convenient format to list all of the ideas of the client so they are easily available to the design team. The format is most useful when there is a lot of information at the same level of detail. If there are only a few fragments, often the easiest way is to use a simple narrative alongside the space tables or as a footnote to the space tables. These and other approaches to capture this kind of information are discussed in Chap. 4 in the section devoted to room data sheets.

Because of their importance in communicating vital program information, it is worth exploring the meanings of the terms *issue, objective,* and *concept,* their relationships to each other, and how to go about creating statements for each of them. The definitions of each of these terms as used in this text are as follows; a more detailed examination follows the definitions.

Issue.   An abbreviation of *design issue.* A topic, most of which recur, related to some aspect of design fulfillment. It is a statement, the answer to which will contribute to the achievement of *the mission statement* (see Chap. 4 and the Glossary for the definition of the mission statement).

Objective.   An abbreviation of *program objective.* Objectives define either quantitatively or qualitatively the result to be achieved by the final design and construction of what you are programming. An objective addresses a single issue and defines the final result or state of being to be achieved. There can be more than one objective for each issue. A collection of the highest priority objectives becomes *the priority statement* (see Chap. 4 and the Glossary for a description of the priority statement).

Concept.   An abbreviation of *program concept.* Concepts are means to achieve the program objectives. They are less abstract than program objectives and more abstract than design concepts, which are specific and specify *how* the program concepts are to be realized. There can be many program concepts for each program objective, and there may be many design concepts for each program concept. Design concepts are not part of the program document except when design guidelines are included; see Chap. 4 for a discussion of when this might be appropriate.

Design issues

Although, at the beginning, every project will have a list of explicit design issues to address, most of the issues that will affect the final outcome of the design will remain either not addressed or simply implicit until revealed by the programming team. Most of these issues, at least the most important ones, recur and are expressed in this text as a list from which you can select the applicable terms and then expose them to your client for review and later development. There are many such lists published, but most of them are not really useful because they are either too general and abbreviated, at various levels of detail, or mix what I would call concepts, issues, criteria, and facts into a single undifferentiated tabulation. This kind of list makes the program impossible to grasp as a whole. As a result, this text contains a list of design issues (issues) that recur often and, since the issues are first addressed as program objectives, the issues are paired with the most common recurring objectives and concepts in Appendix A.

Program objectives

Program objectives are statements that define both qualitatively and quantitatively the result to be achieved by the design and construction of what you are programming. When they relate to quantitative issues such as schedule and cost, they can be very specific. When they relate to qualitative issues and are expressed as an ideal state of being to be achieved, they should be at a relatively higher level of abstraction. As a rule, program objectives are more abstract than program concepts and less abstract than the mission statement. A selection of the most important program objectives becomes the priority statement. Recognized in this way, these objectives express and clarify the most important ideas related to the fulfillment of the mission statement.

In related literature and many of the referenced texts, e.g., Duerk (1993) and Peña et al. (1987), the reader will find the word *goal* utilized in place of, or interchangeably with, the word *objective*. The terms are interchangeable and for consistency throughout this text we have chosen to use the latter.

In the formulation of these program objectives, the same cautions related to formulation and level of abstraction as described for the preparation of analysis cards (see Chap. 5) or project concepts (see below) need to be observed. The final result should be measurable in some way, albeit subjectively. For example, the statement that "the final design must reflect that we are a good company" is probably too abstract to be useful as a program objective, whereas the statement "the design must have a solidity reflecting the substantial nature of the company" is more useful, and the statement "the final design must take advantage of the spectacular view of the mountains to the west" is more useful still. The statement "the construction cost must be no more than $20 million, including furniture and equipment" is an appropriately stated quantitative program objective without need of further abstraction.

Program concepts

Program concepts are perceived means to achieve program objectives. They are, for the most part, qualitative in nature, and, although the program team should strive for a consistent level of detail appropriate to the task at hand, they can occur in the program at almost every level of detail. Program concepts are often useful as concrete examples that clarify the meaning of a program objective, which is at a higher level of abstraction and often more difficult to communicate. Program concepts in themselves, however, are at a higher level of abstraction than design concepts. Often program concepts are the client's preconceived notions of how the design or components of the design should be executed. In practice, however, most of them are created during the programming process as a logical result of the flow of information and contributions during the workshops. Some of them will be good ideas and some, obviously, will not. Some can be evaluated during the programming process and some must wait until the design of the project to prove their worth (the latter may be treated as issues, which are included below as part of the programming contents). Program concepts are the primary vehicle for the fulfillment of the qualitative requirements of program objectives. Since program concepts are the bridge between program objectives and design, it is worth some consideration of what they are, how they are formulated, and what their relationship is to the program objectives and the process of design.

Program concepts are part of the information gathered by the program team. They are either brought to the program by the owner as a preconceived notion or they are developed in concert with the owner during the interactive workshop interviews. Program concepts may be suggested by the programming team to stimulate the owner's thinking, but they should never be wholly created by the programmer; this would be design.

Program concepts must always be at a level of appropriate abstraction. Design concepts are to be avoided if possible. If the program concept is at a low level of abstraction, then the concept should be prefaced with the word *consider* to signal the design team that this is an idea to be explored but that it is not a fiat. The programming team cannot be too careful in walking the tightrope between appropriate control and the stifling of creative design; narrow and prescriptive concepts at a low level of abstraction are to be avoided. The programming team must seek the highest level of abstraction possible for each concept, both to distill the essence of the idea, and give the design team the widest latitude for creativity. The limit of abstraction should be a test of the statement's utility. The goal should be to create a performance envelope as large as possible without sacrificing meaning. For example, here is an idea expressed in an ascending order of abstraction and consequent design latitude:

1. Build a 6 ft high red brick wall along the east property line (a design concept).

2. Consider a solid wall east of the building for acoustical and visual isolation (a design concept with a higher level of abstraction; except for the word *consider* it would be too prescriptive).

3. A visual and acoustical barrier should be created to shield the building from the busy street to the east (a program concept with an average level of abstraction).

4. The project design should protect the occupants of the building from the noise and visual distractions surrounding the site (a program concept with a high level of abstraction).

5. The project design should protect the occupants of the building from the noise and visual distractions surrounding the site by reducing the existing ambient noise level of 75 to 50 dB on the site and 35 dB within the building: screening views at the ground level to a height of 6 ft is required (a program concept with a high level of abstraction but combined with the addition of specific criteria).

6. Create an island of quiet tranquillity in a noisy urban environment (a concept with a very high level of abstraction: it may not be very useful).

7. The development is to be an island of tranquillity in a noisy urban environment (a qualitative objective, written as a state of being).

It is obvious from the example that design concepts, program concepts, and objectives can form a seamless continuum from the abstract to the concrete for a single idea; this is why these terms have, in the past, been so difficult to describe and differentiate. Notice, for example, the change from objective to concept in 6 and 7 above—it is achieved simply by rewording the same statement from a state of being to a specific idea. There are, however, some guidelines for developing, differentiating, and evaluating the terms:

Program concepts are different from program objectives or design concepts. They relate to a specific function of doing rather than an ideal state of being (an objective). Program concepts are less abstract than program objectives and more abstract than design concepts. A program concept relates *what* needs to be done to achieve the objective: a design concept describes *how* it will be (or could be) done.

A program objective can be realized by a number of program concepts, and each program concept should be able to generate many design concepts. This quality is a good test of how effective these statements are:

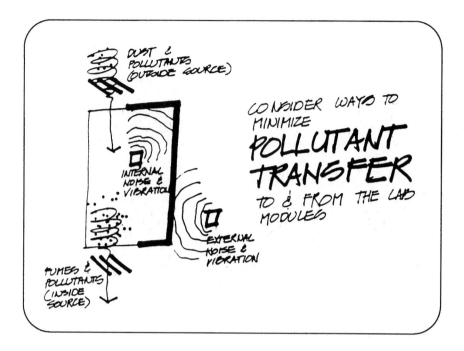

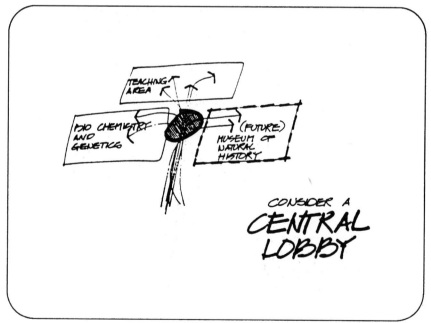

Figure 6.5 Program concepts with diagrams.

if a program concept generates only one or two design concepts it is probably too narrowly stated and should be revised.

A good program concept is specific and measurable, although the evaluation may be based on subjective judgment rather than strictly measurable quantities. Note the difference between program concepts 4 and 5 in the preceding example. Concept 5 in addition to the abstract statement includes specific criteria. Stating a requirement in this way, although making it more measurable, suffers from a mixture of levels of detail. Often specific criteria will need greater thought than the time and resources devoted to the program will allow and, unless crucial to the program intent, are likely to be at a higher level of detail than is required. The flow of information within the program seems to work best hierarchically, and the detailed requirements are therefore best left to the general criteria and the AEC tables, which are, in the proposed system of organization, to follow later in the program document. This sort of expanded program concept format should only be utilized when the sections devoted to criteria are omitted from the program.

Program concepts should be single ideas stated as succinctly as possible. Although it is common to portray program concepts as simple statements, for maximum communication they are best accompanied by a simple diagram. Figure 6.5 shows two samples of effectively portrayed program concepts. The diagrams are best done freehand and should be as abstract as possible to distill and focus the message. *Problem Seeking* (Peña et al., 1987) contains many abstract concept diagrams (Fig. 6.6 is an example) that are excellent to use for the evocations of the client. In practice, however, the final concept diagrams for a specific program will tend to be more specific and less abstract than those illustrated in Peña et al.'s text. The ideal diagram is simple and has a strong visual impact: it clarifies the meaning of the concept. As for the statements themselves, they are best written in the form of an imperative command or action followed by the statement of the idea. The use of the word *should* as in item 3 of the preceding example is also a useful structure. If the program concept is at a low level of abstraction or a suspected design concept, the statement should be preceded by the word *consider* as in item 2 above, once again to increase the latitude for creativity of the design team. As a program concept, item 4 above would probably be most appropriate and useful for a schematic design or master plan level program.

Theoretical Background

As with all ideas, the conceptual framework of the programming system prescribed in this text is built upon the foundations of others. The CRSS

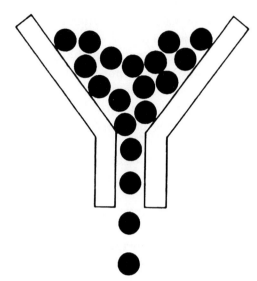

Figure 6.6 Peña et al.'s concept diagram: data clog. From *Problem Seeking* (1987) by William M. Peña et al. Reproduced by permission of the AIA Press. There are many of these kinds of abstract diagrams in this book.

system outlined by Peña et al. (1987) was the basis for the principal mechanics of the system. The limited theoretical system, design issues–program objectives–program concepts, is based on the earlier theoretical work of Christopher Alexander in *Notes on the Synthesis of Form* (1964), and Paul Watzlawick, John Weakland, and Richard Fisch in *Change: Principles of Problem Formation and Problem Resolution* (1974). The hierarchical multiplication of elements is based on the insights of Duerk (1993). In addition, the various works of Edward Debono including most especially *Lateral Thinking for Management* (1971) are key to the understanding of how to creatively navigate this system.

Christopher Alexander is probably most familiar to the reader as one of the authors of a series of three books published in the 1970s related to what was conceived as a new approach to architecture. The three books, *The Timeless Way of Building, The Oregon Experiment,* and *A Pattern Language* (1977) were popular with students in the 1970s and are related to earlier work in that they describe patterns and elements that can be used as the basic building blocks of design. Since they were written in the 1970s by professors at The University of California at Berkeley, they reflect the era that witnessed the eruption of *Mother Earth News,* the Beatles, the "hippies," and the back to nature movement. As a result, the books advocate a populist approach to design so that the "self-conscious professional" can be eliminated.

This arbitrary and self-conscious professional as the principal reason for the uncomfortable fit of modern architecture was also the focus of the earlier work by Alexander (1964)—it was an unnatural way of building. Since Alexander did not like the modern architecture of the 1950s and 1960s (in retrospect most would agree that there was not much to like), the three later books eliminate this problem by throwing the design professional out with the bathwater. For example, by combining, in various ways, the 253 patterns described in *The Timeless Way of Building* (1977), people can design and build a better home for themselves and their families. Stripped of its populist rhetoric, this book contains the results of a good deal of research and prescient observation and is a rich lode of common sense ideas for the professional. Many of these ideas are sufficiently abstract to form the basis of program concepts. But it is the earlier work that bears more directly on programming theory.

Notes on the Synthesis of Form (1964) is, like Debono's work, based on the way that the human brain works. It is proposed as a rational system of design that replaces the irrational design process. It begins with a rigorous hierarchical concept based on the mathematics of set theory, and in the end, because the number of variables, even for the simplest problems, are staggering, it suggests that the designer use convention and intuition to reduce the number of variables put into the equations. Although this mathematical approach to design has not had great appeal for architects, the bases of many programming theories and techniques grew out of this work, and a better understanding of it will help you structure and express your programming efforts more effectively.

Information overload is the primary problem confronting the designer during the process of design and one might think that increasing the data in a facilities program only contributes to this problem. On the other hand, not giving the designer sufficient information and constraints will allow the designer to solve the problem with a limited amount of information from which they may select data that has little relevance to the client's priorities. This is, in fact, the case for most projects with inadequate programs that are, in the end, judged as unresponsive. Alexander proposes that to resolve the dilemma of information overload versus information sufficiency, the process of programming must reflect inversely the process of design, and therefore the structure of the problem should be portrayed in the same way the design is formulated (construction and deconstruction if you will) in a hierarchical tree.

Even the simplest of design problems, say, the design of a simple device such as a pencil, if completely described, will have too many variables to be grasped as a whole. We know, for example, that there are limits to a person's ability to manipulate variables or do mathematical problems in their head, and although this varies for each individual, at a certain point it becomes necessary to pick up a pencil and paper to do the job effectively or at all. A complete description of the variables of the architectural or planning problem will overwhelm the human brain unless a structure is devised. How does the designer proceed? What is the structure of the program that will mirror this process and therefore facilitate a solution that more or less correctly balances all of the program elements?

Alexander proposes that the effective designer proceeds both by a hierarchy of ideas and by the isolation of variables into subsets, which, although rich with interconnections themselves, have little effect on other sets of variables. In this way, each part of the design problem can be divided into a set of variables that are within the capacity of the human brain to manipulate holistically. The concept of isolation by hierarchy is expressed more clearly by Whitehead and Russell (1927) and in a later work by Watzlawick et al. (1974): the latter is discussed below in more detail. Alexander, however, gives us a key insight for the treatment of variables that are at the same level of detail and a practical overview of how the hierarchy of ideas can work in the programming and design process.

Alexander's approach identifies what he terms *misfit variables* and he graphically depicts them as vertices of a diagram connected by causal linkages (Fig. 6.7). He further defines these misfit variables as needs or requirements (equivalent to program objectives in the proposed system in this text) that must be satisfied positively [p. 136 of Alexander (1964)]. The causal linkages between these vertices are denoted by a plus sign if they are positive and supportive factors or by a minus sign if they are negative or conflicting factors. He proposes that the linkages can be more than one line to designate the strength of the relationship (but I would not recommend more than three so as to keep the hierarchical relationships clearly perceptible).

Readers who are familiar with the philosophy of Hegel will recognize the similarity of Alexander's diagram of vertices and links with Hegel's diagrammatic grouping of concepts into the well known triad of thesis, antithesis, and synthesis or Jung's later tetrad of the fourfold aspect of the universe. Programmers will recognize the basic pattern of the relationship diagram, of which this is the seminal basis, and readers familiar with statics will immediately see a graphic and conceptual analogy to the isolation of structural elements for analysis by the use of a free body diagram.

The process of describing the problem holistically begins by deconstructing the problem into a hierarchy of classes by proceeding from the general to the specific. The reader will immediately recognize in this structure an analogy to the verbal expression of the hierarchy of thought—design issue, program objective, and program concept—of the proposed program structure of this text. An example would be access (highest level), site and building (next level), and employees, visitors, vendors, etc. (at the lowest level). The terminology in this example is taken from the list in Appendix A.

The utility of understanding Alexander's diagram lies in the requirement that the programmer discover the variables that have an effect on each other and group them so that, to the maximum extent possible, their variations within the subset will fully describe the problem at the lowest level of division and simultaneously have a minimal effect on the variables in a different subset (Fig. 6.7). This arrangement will give the design team the information in a format that can be easily manipulated but not easily misunderstood.

The second step is what Alexander calls "the realization of the program." This realization of the program is accomplished by working backwards up the hierarchy by first optimizing each subset and expressing it as a diagram. Then, each subset is combined with other

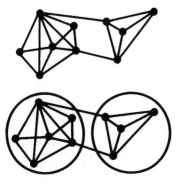

Figure 6.7 The isolation of interdependent requirements. The upper diagram illustrates requirements (the vertices) connected by lines (interdependent requirements). The lower diagram illustrates their isolation by dividing the requirements into two groups at their weakest links. By doing this, the richly connected variables are able to be manipulated with minimal effect on the other group. These are what is referred to in this text as *Alexander diagrams*. They were conceived by Christopher Alexander. (*Reprinted by permission of the publishers from* Notes on the Synthesis of Form *by Christopher Alexander, Cambridge, Mass.: Harvard University Press, Copyright © 1964 by the President and Fellows of Harvard College.*)

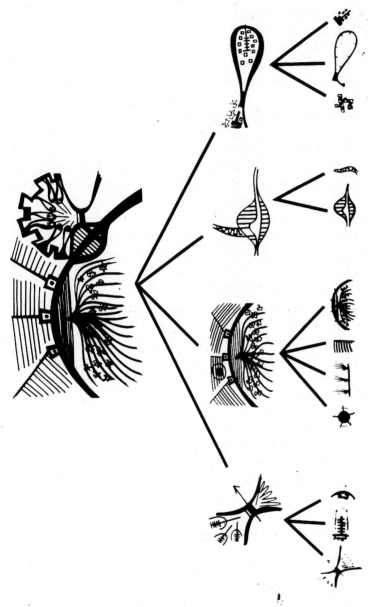

Figure 6.8 Alexander's diagram—the realization of the program. The intermediate step between the program and design. Each icon in the branching diagram is the resolution of a set of isolated interdependent variables. The aggregate of these icons is *the realization of the program*. Figure 6.10 relates this intermediate step to the programming system in this text. (*Reprinted by permission of the publishers from Notes on the Synthesis of Form by Christopher Alexander, Cambridge, Mass.: Harvard University Press, Copyright © 1964 by the President and Fellows of Harvard College.*)

subsets at the same hierarchical level (which are now themselves variables) to the next hierarchical level and so on, until the hierarchical tree of design problems as a whole is optimized and constructed (Fig. 6.8). This second step crosses into a gray area between program concept and design concept and marks the end of the program-then-design process advocated in this text.

Although Alexander's system of organization suggests a way in which a program could be assembled and provides the basis for the creation of images that were later developed by Peña as a crucial part of his analysis card graphic display system (see Chap. 5), it has been criticized as a synthesis-then-design approach that "does not provide a general image of the issues a design must address...and provide a structure to organize their use."[1] I believe, however, that as regards the *general image* Alexander goes just far enough when he stops at the aggregate of abstract images that describe the program. The missing ingredient, the parti, the overall vision, the grand synthesis, or the "aha," is the domain of the designer, not the programmer. A well-crafted facility program should be equally valuable and stimulating to a Tschumi, a Graves, or the average architect down the street. The final design solution should be as varied as the architect's approach, and the program document should stimulate this variation; to do otherwise would rob the client of the benefit of the architect's creative synthesis of the problem—the very commodity for which the owner hired the architect.

There is, in fact, a case to be made for the programmer to consider the program complete at the end of the collection and grouping of the variables and a description of their connections, leaving the "realization of the program," the creation of the abstract and succinct diagrams, to the design team. Using this approach, the program would be complete without the addition of these diagrams or design guidelines. This latter approach is the most common in general practice and is the approach the programmer should use except in those circumstances when the program (or component of the program) is sufficiently unique to require this intermediate step to clarify the issues in the owner's mind and thereby communicate it as an immediately comprehensible image to the designer.

The power of the graphic image is such that it deserves a short diversion to explore the way it communicates to the designer and the client. The old cliche "a picture is worth a thousand words" reflects the reality of the way we think. Joseph Chilton Pearce, in *The Crack in the Cosmic*

---

[1]Korobkin (1975), p. 30.

Egg: Changing Constructs of Mind and Reality (1971), among others, would go even further and suggest that reality is modified by the way we think about reality—"the mind mirrors the universe which mirrors the mind."

We think mostly in patterns and images. Every text on improving your memory suggests that you form images to remember verbal concepts, names, sequences of numbers, or anything. Designers, most of all, think in images when they design. But these images are not those with the superficial connotation of appearance alone, they relate to the individual designer's knowledge and mirror of the universe. In the mind of the designer, these images center around analogies, homologies, and metaphors. Korobkin (1975, p. 10) suggests that these images are generated at three levels of abstraction: *cultural images,* generated in "evolutionary time," which form the background or general environment; *general images,* which exist as archetypes or models; and *response images,* which relate the problem in hand to similar problems of the past and their subjective solutions.

Image (in the simplistic sense of appearance to communicate meaning) is a key program issue to be communicated to the designer. The difficulty in communicating any image requirements, however, is the problem of being excessively prescriptive. Therefore, in communicating a specific image, the programmer should strive to achieve the highest level of abstraction possible, i.e., with cultural imagery or, at most, general images. Response images that are communicated as specific design solutions are dangers to be avoided. Maintaining the appropriate level of abstraction is a key determinant in deciding whether a diagram should be included or not. If too prescriptive, omit the diagram and utilize a description at the appropriate level of abstraction to stimulate the designer's own subjective diagram and image.

Change: Principles of Problem Formation and Problem Resolution (1974) by Paul Watzlawick, John Weakland, and Richard Fisch affords us some insights on the concept of interaction within a group of variables and within a hierarchy as a means to grasp mentally a problem as a whole. To do this they introduce (1) the theory of groups and (2) the theory of logical types.[2]

---

[2]From *CHANGE: Principles of Problem Formation and Problem Resolution* by Paul Watzlawick, John H. Weakland, and Richard Fisch, by permission of the authors and W. W. Norton & Company, Inc. Copyright © 1974 by W. W. Norton & Company, Inc.; the descriptions given here are condensed versions of the original text.

The *theory of groups* offers us some insights as to the possibilities and limitations within the richly interactive group of elements that is considered at one level (or class) and is isolated as Alexander describes it (see above) (the original work by Évariste Galois was a paper written in 1832 that created group theory, a field of mathematics that has had a profound effect on quantum and relativity theory). According to the theory, a group has the following properties:

1. It is composed of members that have one similar characteristic. For purposes of relating this to programming theory, these members can be groups of issues, concepts, or objectives. They can be anything, however, as long as they have that single common characteristic and the combination of two or more members is itself a member of the group. The addition of positive whole numbers is a good example of this characteristic.

2. The members of the group can be combined in various sequences, but the outcome remains the same. Positive numbers added together is again a good example for this characteristic.

3. The group contains an identity number, which when combined with any member maintains that member's identity. For example, this number is 1 for multiplication, i.e., $7 \times 1 = 7$, etc.

4. Every member of the group has a reciprocal such that in combination with this number, the identity number is created. In multiplication, the reciprocal is the number itself, i.e., $7 \div 7 = 1$.

The theory of groups related to programming gives us the basis for understanding the manipulation of variables at the most elementary level; Watzlawick et al. (1974, p. 10) calls this change within a group a first-order change. This kind of manipulation will only solve a limited range of problems, and is analogous, for example, to trying more of the same procedures when the process does not work. If the enemy is not intimidated by small threats, use bigger threats. This methodology is, by far, the most common way of solving problems, and persisting in its application in the face of mounting contrary evidence has been the source of many great historical mistakes including, for example, Vietnam for the United States and Afghanistan for the former Soviet Union. If we want to solve more intractable problems we must use a different approach and look outside the theory of groups.

The *theory of logical types* designates each of the components of a totality as members as does the theory of groups, but the totality of the members is called a class rather than a group. The essential axiom of the theory is that *...whatever involves all of the collection must not be* *one of the collection....*[3] A population of 20 million is both quantitatively and qualitatively different from the individual who is one of the 20 million and the behavior of the 20 million cannot be deduced by multiplying the behavior of one individual by 20 million. The notion of class also suggests a hierarchy of conceptual thought that is useful if a change of reference system, or framework is indicated to clarify an issue or solve a problem. The notion requires that when you talk about the members of a group as a class, you must talk in terms that are not a member of the class itself. To do otherwise leads to paradox and confusion. If we want to talk about a language we must do so in terms of a metalanguage. To talk about the metalanguage we must use a metametalanguage, and so on. Transcending the group and using this metalanguage to solve problems is the insight provided by this theory. Watzlawick et al. (1974, p. 10) calls this change of change a *second-order change.*

A good illustration of this concept is the concept of spatial dimension. You can conceive in a tangential and mathematical sense but not comprehend visually a universe with dimensions higher than that in which you exist. Following the mathematical postulation of universes of higher orders of dimension late in the nineteenth century, many unsuccessful attempts were made to describe the fourth dimension. By describing a two-dimensional universe, Edwin Abbott in *Flatland: A Romance of Many Dimensions* (1884) came closest to the mark of describing not only the difficulties of comprehension but also, in my mind, the clearest illustration of the difficulties involved in perceiving second-order change.[4]

In Abbott's two-dimensional universe of triangles, circles, lines, and squares the effects of a three-dimensional universe could be postulated but not visualized. For example, the passing of a sphere through the universe could be postulated as a result of the appearance of first a point and then an ever increasing and then decreasing circle ending in a point

---

[3]Whitehead and Russell (1927), p. 6.

[4]For those who have already read *Flatland* and enjoyed it, *Sphereland* by Dionys Burger (1965) is an interesting sequel that also contains a synopsis of the earlier work. For those among you who have not already read *Flatland,* the original work is still in print by, at last count, five different publishers.

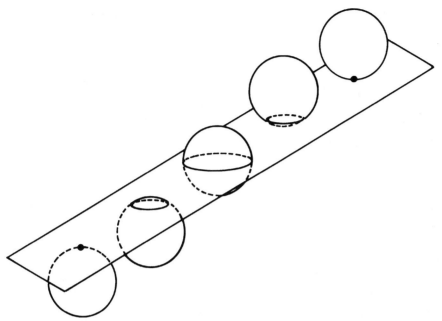

Figure 6.9   A sphere passes through Abbott's flatland. An analog of second-order change.

and then disappearing (Fig. 6.9).[5] From these observations, the existence of the higher-dimensional universe could be postulated by the mathematicians of the two-dimensional universe and the properties of a sphere calculated. From our higher-order universe the phenomena were, of course, easily comprehensible and obvious.

There are some important programming tactics that can be deduced from the consideration of these theories together: (1) the initial approach is to aggregate each richly connected idea as a member of a group and work consciously within this context, optimizing the members of the group as a whole (logical levels must be consciously realized and kept strictly apart), and (2) if the problem is intractable, utilize the strategy of going from one level or class to the next to create a discontinuity and create the change required.

The hierarchical structure of the proposed programming system is based on these two concepts. If two or more program concepts are mutu-

---

[5]Marcel DuChamp in the first decade of the twentieth century produced a series of sketches of various forms passing through planes illustrating the phenomena.

ally contradictory and one of them must be chosen over the other, the programmer should move up to the next class, the program objective, to obtain the criteria to make the choice. Should program objectives conflict, the choice is made by the ranking of the priority statement. In actual practice it is rare that you move more than one class upwards to resolve a conflict in a lower class.

As an example in facility programming terms, consider the program objective of acoustical isolation under which is paired the program concepts of noise and barrier. As the noise increases the barrier must get thicker and heavier to maintain the same level of isolation. But if the source of the noise gets louder by a significant degree, say by the introduction of the requirement for a jet engine testing stand as compared with ordinary conversation, more of the same solutions will not work without inordinate expense and/or space; therefore a change of the second order, such as relocating the testing facility to a remote site, is required.

Programming, like design, is an iterative and heuristic process. Both of these activities have an identical identified beginning—*the mission statement.* The program describes in detail *what* needs to be done to fulfill the mission statement; the design describes, in phases of ever more explicit detail, *how* to do it. As such, both processes can be viewed as continuous and successive iterations along an ever branching path of choices. At issue are the questions: How does the orderly and responsive design process proceed? How does the program help the designer realize a creative and inclusive integration of all the program objectives?

Designers are intuitive people who have developed their methodology over an entire career. For the most part, they would not be as analytical and methodical in their method as the structure proposed for the program in this text. However, most designers approach problems in more or less the same way, working from the abstract to the particular, and the basic sequence of events, program to mental (or explicit) diagram to design, is universal. Portraying this programming-to-design path shown in Fig. 6.10 as linking the program to design by way of Alexander's intermediate hierarchical diagrams is probably close to reality.

In this process diagram, the lowest level of abstraction of the programming process, the program concept, connects to the design process by way of the design concept, which is really an abstract idea (a diagram) of how to arrange a small number of variables that can occur at any level (the design concept can relate to the whole project or only a small detail). Visualizing the process in this way suggests a continuum from programming to design, from a hierarchy of detail and thought to

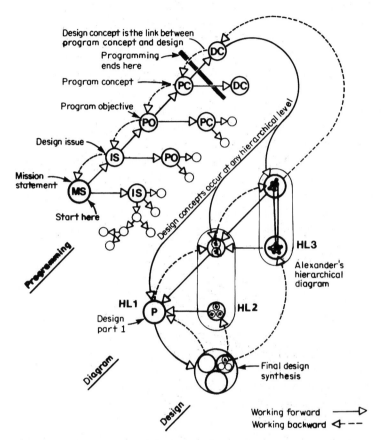

Figure 6.10 Theoretical program diagram. The path from mission statement to design synthesis.

a language of visual expression, and allows for a shift in level and a reexamination of the lower-order tenets as part of a higher-order process (second-order change) back and forth along many orderly paths. This is useful since when you proceed from a verbal description (in the program) to a diagram (which may or may not be part of the program) to the design, often the greater understanding that results will prompt the reexamination of some of the lower level assumptions and requirements (working backwards). By visualizing the process in this way, outright chaos will be prevented when making a conscious switch between levels, but at the same time, the optimization of the design by means of reframing or lateral thinking will be stimulated. An example of the usefulness of this construct is the design synthesis ("aha!") of a single element from two or more seemingly disparate elements of the diagram or program. The creative possibilities of this approach reveals the utility of grouping the variables; the making of creative second-order change in this environment will minimize the effect to the structure at the lower level.

Some designers might find all of the above very interesting, but I believe it is too analytical and structured to be useful for most. One could make the case that it substitutes a self-conscious process for the unnatural self-conscious professional (an example of second-order change). The utility in attempting to understand the structure of the program-then-design process, however, is to determine how best to write an architectural program such that the design process is responsive to the objectives of the client. I believe the system described in this section satisfies this objective and that the continuation of the structure into design offers the designer, who is so inclined, some tools to increase his or her creativity.

But data is meaningless unless we look at it with an idea; each person will see something different depending on the idea which they use. This is the "mirroring of the universe" that Joseph Chilton Pearce (1971) talks about. The scientific method of hypothesis and verification is a common example of this *mythos* preceding *logos*. This choice of factors and area of attention are two of the three basic determinants of what Debono calls *first-stage thinking,* the problem of defining the problem. The third determinant is the point of entry.

Both Alexander and Watzlawick et al. also describe ways that we think, and the conceptual system of programming described in this text is structured in accord with the tenets of group theory and the theory of logical types that they use in their work and the understanding of the need to group and isolate variables according to both class and common characteristics. The understanding of these concepts is the key to the holistic grasping of a complex problem and the manipulation of its elements. Although there are many works on how we think and the different strategies that may be employed, Edward Debono in his many works on lateral thinking provides us with methods of navigating this intellectual structure. Starting with *The Use of Lateral Thinking* (1967), Debono has devoted a lifetime of study to the process of creative thinking and is the richest source of well thought-out ideas in this field. In this chapter I have focused on only those ideas that seem most seminal to my thinking related to the theory of programming in this text. The programmer interested in honing his or her skills would be well advised to put many of Debono's works on his or her reading list. Listed in the bibliography are the best among them.

Logical thinking is single-dimension linear thinking. It proceeds along a "yes"–"no" path and reaches a conclusion in single discrete steps. It can be pictured as a decision tree proceeding from the general to the particular. It is deduction and it abhors gaps in reasoning and data; it looks for answers and meaning. It is how we do most of our thinking, but it is not a creative process. You must create ideas before you subject them to this rigorous process.

Lateral thinking is the term coined by Debono for nonlinear creative thinking. Lateral thinking as described by Debono proceeds along different paths than logical thinking.

- It is generative of change and change for the sake of change and the creation of alternatives.
- It looks for what is different, not what is right or wrong.
- It uses information to generate new ideas not for meaning but for quality.
- It makes deliberate jumps in logic so as to reveal new possibilities.
- It welcomes chance intrusions and explores the seemingly irrelevant.

Altogether, lateral thinking is a methodology of creating alternatives. The reader will recognize in the first three parts of the list the tenets and methods of Alex Osborn's creation, the brainstorming session, and the now familiar theory of logical types and the scientific method in the fourth. In actual practice, lateral thinking is alternated with logical thinking—lateral thinking creates an idea, logical thinking validates it, logical thinking reaches an impasse, and lateral thinking may or may not create a way around it. Roger Fisher and William Ury in their landmark *Getting to Yes: Negotiating Agreement without Giving In* (1981), identify *inventing options for mutual gain* as one of the four key elements of successful negotiation. This tactic is, in a sense, lateral thinking as opposed to the logical and conventional approach of "(1) premature judgement; (2) searching for the single answer; (3) the assumption of a fixed pie; and (4) thinking that 'solving their problem is their problem'" (p. 59). The goal according to Fisher and Ury is to create as many options as possible, especially if you are not aware of the objectives of the other party. It is unwise to negotiate who gets which half of the apple when one party really wants the fruit and the other wants the peel and seeds.

The idea of how to put the facility program together, what information to have, and how it is expressed will have great influence on the perception of the problem by the design team that will execute the project. Since, as we have discussed above, the designer will translate the program into his or her own level of experience and methodology and only pay attention to the patterns that are meaningful to him or her, it is imperative that the client's priorities be as explicit as possible so they will not be ignored.

7

Program Cost Evaluation

During any phase of a project, facilities managers need the most accurate project cost evaluation possible. This is especially crucial at the predesign and programming phases, when budgets must often be set and money appropriated before the design process begins.

The process for doing a cost evaluation at the program stage is unique, requiring its own vocabulary, attitude, and methodology. Historically, this has been done by rule of thumb and ad hoc judgment. This chapter describes a process that codifies and organizes the procedure to provide an accurate early assessment of construction costs and risks and presents a format for communicating the information. As a matter of vocabulary, the term *cost evaluation* is used rather than *estimate* to differentiate this process from the traditional take-off and its variations.

The people with the most knowledge—the architect, planner of labor and materials, or the facilities administrator—are the most qualified to evaluate the cost of a construction project during the early programming and design phases. Construction managers and contractors are useful sources of information for historical costs and geographical market conditions, but their estimating methodology, typically based on a take-off of materials and systems, has little relevance when there is no physical basis for cost.

It should be noted that determining cost at the preconceptual phase is hazardous, even for the simplest repetitive building. The cost evalu-

Note: Much of this chapter was originally published as "Program Cost Evaluation" in *Critical Issues in Facilities Management,* Vol. 7, *Planning, Design and Construction* (1990) by The Association of Physical Plant Administrators of Universities and Colleges and is reprinted here with their kind permission.

ation at the program level must have appropriate contingencies at a level that recognizes that the exact scope of work and quality is still unclear. It is almost certain, however, that whatever number is determined, the focus will be on this bottom line, and it will be difficult (if not impossible) to increase this number after an appropriation has been set and approved.

It is important to know the priorities that have been identified by the organization and the facility's prospective occupants. If the facilities required (rather than the cost, will determine the project scope—often true for specialized research and development, pilot plants, etc.), the estimate can be delayed until early design is complete or a higher contingency or range of cost at the program level is provided. If, however, there is a fixed budget for construction (this is by far the most usual case)—even an implied one—it must be exposed at the beginning and used to determine the validity of the balance of the program.

The only cost evaluation methodology available at the predesign stage is one based on a model comparison method, i.e., similar buildings. The closer the model is to the proposed project in size, location, quality, function, and time, the lower the contingencies that are required. The typical program cost evaluation process can be separated into eight discrete steps:

1. Gather cost-focused information
2. Define project cost and construction cost
3. Select a model
4. Identify applicable premiums and reductions
5. List unknowns and develop appropriate contingencies
6. Present the evaluation in an appropriate format
7. Perform a reality check
8. Describe the basis of evaluation and list assumptions

Each of the steps is treated here in detail. It should be noted that if a fixed limit of either project cost or construction cost is mandated, the process can be worked backwards to generate the appropriate program scope and quality.

Gather Cost-Focused Information

The architect/planner needs to gather all the information that has the potential to affect cost significantly. There are two broad categories: (1)

the client's needs and timing and (2) requirements of the site (or locality, if the site has not been selected). If the project is programmed by the client or a separate consultant, there may be sufficient information on the needs to be satisfied. Typically, however, these programs do not focus on cost issues and must be supplemented by other data. If the project has been programmed by the architect with cost evaluation requirements in mind, there should be both quantitative and qualitative data to make the job easier and the evaluation more accurate.

Define Construction Cost and Project Cost

At the program and preprogram stage, it is essential to determine the future occupant's expectations and assumptions. This is especially important if you are an infrequent builder. A brief drill with the occupants, utilizing a standard form, will not only focus on what you expect the architect to control, but also will expose any hidden costs that you have not considered in determining the total project budget. In addition, the switching of items usually in "other" costs to construction costs will indicate an upward adjustment to that category. The line-by-line description of the 17-line format (described later in this chapter) provides a good beginning for this process. The descriptions provided are not exhaustive, but they cover most of the items normally encountered.

Select a Model

The model can be a single building, a composite of two or three buildings, or a collection of qualitative facts based on prior experience. The best model is a single building, recently built by the client's organization and similar to the proposed project in size, location, quality, and function.

The least complex building, such as an office building or simple classroom building, will often be a candidate for a generic approach. Methods for more complex buildings could include Gantt charts with scatter diagrams of similar projects or lists of historical costs. Often your best source of information will be an architect or contractor with experience in the specific building type. The availability of data and knowledge of details of relevant projects is critical if such an approach is taken; there is no substitute for current experience.

Whatever format is adopted, it should be simple, brief, and most important of all, consistent. It is of no use to perform this task for unique projects for which historical data will have little chance of future application.

Identify Applicable Premiums and Reductions

A premium is a known factor that will add cost compared to the model, and a reduction is a known factor that will reduce cost. Since the model constantly changes, it is most efficient to create a checklist of factors that can be scored as a premium, a reduction, or a neutral (no effect, not applicable, etc.) relative to the model. These can be scored or weighted to generate a numerical total, or a preliminary cost estimate can be determined of what each premium might contribute to the bottom line. Should a high–low dollar amount be generated, the difference between the two numbers may be treated as a contingency amount. This could be factored by up to 50 percent; not all the worst-case scenarios will happen.

The accuracy of the results of this analysis depends upon the number of unknowns; the object is not to come up with a cast-in-stone numerical premium, but rather to get a feel for some of the factors and risks and to communicate them. It is here that experience and judgment make the difference. If some of the unknowns are too large for your requirements, some further investigation and more detailed analyses on specific factors are indicated.

For those who believe that a high degree of accuracy is possible, remember that many of these premiums (owner, time, construction market, construction operations) will still exist at bid time after the building is fully designed and documented and a detailed estimate based on a take-off of materials is complete. The cost evaluation is really an estimate of what the successful low bidder will include in a bid for these factors. It is an estimate of an estimate, closer to a game of poker than a scientific process.

An accurate final estimate is only possible because by the time the construction documents are completed, the premiums and contingencies usually can be reduced, for new work, to 5 to 7 percent of the cost of construction in normal and relatively stable markets. These can then be covered by additive or deductive alternatives if a fixed price must be met. All premiums should be reviewed as each phase of the project develops.

List Unknowns and Develop Appropriate Contingencies

A contingency allowance is an amount of money set aside to pay for the unknown. It is not a premium, which we have defined as a known cost addition to the model, although the unknown cost spread of premiums will together help generate the contingency. The first question to ask is: What is the accuracy that we can expect at the program level of development? There are three variables that generate the answer: complexity and uniqueness of the project; amount and reliability of cost-focused program and site information; and the amount of effort and experience the architect/owner team is able to bring to the project cost evaluation.

As much as 35 percent contingency is appropriate for a new research laboratory on a difficult site with little cost-focused program information; as little as 10 percent is appropriate for a "core and shell" repeat of a speculative office building on a simple, known site. Remodeling and retrofit work could demand as much as a 50 percent contingency or more. Most projects will fall between these extremes. Utilizing a thorough cost evaluation procedure, as illustrated here, combined with a comprehensive program could reduce these requirements significantly. In addition, this procedure generates a unique contingency for each project rather than a rule of thumb guess.

It should be noted that, within limits, a contingency can also be the quality and features of a project. Paradoxically, this is usually not appropriate for complex buildings, in which well over half the cost is related to mechanical and electrical systems and subtle changes in quantity, control, quality, maintenance requirements, and flexibility can easily double the cost. This is because with these kinds of buildings, the function is completely dependent upon achieving very specific performance criteria.

Given a roughly defined building function with flexible criteria and a rigid and fixed limit of construction cost and net program area, however, this approach might be the only viable one available. The approach would include utilizing a minimal contingency and requires that the only remaining characteristic, the quality of the project, is negotiable throughout the remaining design phases. The maximum limit of this method would be on the order of a 10 to 15 percent reduction in cost or increase in efficiency from an average quality model after all premiums are accounted for. In no event should this approach be used if the model utilized is of minimum quality for the building function initially. This approach requires constant attentiveness on the part of the architect/facilities manager team to find reductions in quality for each additional cost discovery, along with extreme flexibility and willingness of the client to accept less than the original vision of the project all the way through design and construction. Therefore, it is an extremely trying and negative process, best avoided or mitigated whenever possible.

The first step in developing the appropriate contingency for a specific project utilizing the cost evaluation system is the completion of the premium checklist. The easiest (and least reliable) method of discovering cost uncertainty is to assign a maximum and minimum percentage of cost to each factor that is judged relevant. A more accurate methodology is the assignment of highest and lowest cost; this is especially appropriate for utility costs or off-site improvements for which an average percentage has no meaning. Since accurate dollar costs are almost impossible to evaluate for the majority of factors, most evaluations will be a combination of both approaches. This task is not as daunting as it might seem at first; most factors will be judged neutral or of minimal effect and will be quickly accounted for.

Once the list is completed, you will have a range of high–low costs (or percentage related to model cost) that needs to be factored. The normal approach would be to utilize the average; a more conservative approach would be to use 60 to 75 percent of the high number. The contingencies on the premiums, added to those for anticipated scope change, should be the only contingencies in the program level cost evaluation. As the project evolves from program to design and there are actual quantities, qualities, and systems to measure, the approach shifts gears. Design contingency, estimator's contingency, owner's contingency, and construction contingency become a new vocabulary for the completely different approach required in early design estimating.

Present the Evaluation in an Appropriate Format

The 17-line format shown in Fig. 7.1 presents the information at the proper level of detail and identifies both construction cost and project cost. The usual contents of each of the line items in the form are numbered and defined as follows.

Line 1: Building

This is a cost per square foot of the model you are utilizing, multiplied by the number of square feet in the proposed project. The model should be brought up to the date the evaluation is prepared by using historical escalation (see the discussion of escalation under line 7 below for some subtleties related to this calculation) and rough comparisons to similar projects currently under construction. In addition, adjustments need to be made for geography and construction practices. A potential source of error is using models that are more than six or seven years old; cumulative index addition can generate wide errors. Line 1 usually includes the following items (convention separates building cost from site cost at a line 5 ft from the exterior of the building):

- Architectural, structural, mechanical, electrical, plumbing, emergency and life safety systems, control systems, elevators and lifts

The 17-Line Format

Construction Cost

Line			
	1	Building (............. SF X $ _ _ _ /SF)	$ _ _ , _ _ _
	2	Site	_ _ , _ _ _
	3	Equipment	_ _ , _ _ _
	4	Premiums/Reductions	_ _ , _ _ _
	5	*Contingency (on Construction, Lines 1 through 4)*	_ _ , _ _ _
	6	Construction Cost Today *(sum of Lines 1 through 5)*	$ _ _ _ , _ _ _
	7	Escalation	
		[..... % per year X ..... years (endpoint of construction) X Line 6]	$ _ _ _ , _ _ _
	8	**Total Construction Cost**	
		[(Completion Date: ....); Sum of Lines 6 and 7]	$ _ _ _ , _ _ _

Other Costs/Project Cost

Line			
	9	Fees	$ _ _ , _ _ _
	10	Off-site Improvements/Land Cost	_ _ , _ _ _
	11	Owner Equipment/Furnishings/Special Systems	_ _ , _ _ _
	12	Miscellaneous	_ _ , _ _ _
	13	*Contingency (on Other Costs, Lines 9 through 12)*	_ _ , _ _ _
	14	Other Costs *(sum of Lines 9 through 13)*	$ _ _ _ , _ _ _
	15	Project Cost *(sum of Lines 8 and 14)*	$ _ _ _ , _ _ _
	16	*Owner's Contingency (for Line 8 during the construction period)*	_ _ , _ _ _
	17	**Total Project Cost** *(sum of lines 15 and 16)*	$ _ _ _ , _ _ _

Figure 7.1 The 17-line format.

- Special systems
  Conduit and wire management systems for telecommunications
  Cabling for telecommunications
  Conduit and wire management systems for security systems
  Cabling for security systems
  Conduit and wire management systems for computer systems
  Cabling for computer systems

- Taxes on labor and materials

- Permit costs

- Labor and material bonds and completion bonds

- Equipment hookup
- Attic stock

The items listed above under "special systems" are a gray area; sometimes they are in the building cost; convention normally excludes them from the contract and places them as part of the project cost on either line 11 or 12. In addition to the costs noted above, it is most useful to put any construction manager's fee in the building cost rather than on line 9. This is because the construction manager (CM) normally replaces the general contractor and awards subcontracts separately, replacing the general contractor's fee and markup with that fee. Indeed, many general contractors now have adopted the appellation of *construction manager* and offer their services for a fixed fee generally equivalent to the previously common general contractor's markup. Most often historical costs will be compiled to include the CM cost as part of the construction cost; if you are using a specific building as a model, however, it is best to ask if a CM was utilized and where the fee is in the data that you are using. If the CM was acting as a consultant only with a separate general contractor, the fee could be excluded from the historical cost. If this project will utilize a CM in a similar and separate consultant capacity, the fee should be added to line 9 rather than being included in line 1.

Line 2: Site

This is an evaluation of the present cost of the proposed site improvements, often a combination of cost per acre for various functions (grading, parking, landscaping, etc.) added to the best estimate of utilities. Utilization of a rule of thumb (a percentage of the building cost) as related to similar projects or the model can work as a last resort if combined with a premium analysis.

This usually includes all development from a line 5 ft outside the building to the property line or, for the large site, the agreed contract limit line. Site costs include required utility connections at the property line:

- Site demolition, landscape, paving, grading, site lighting and electrical systems, utilities and utility structures, drainage structures and storm water systems, retention ponds, septic fields and sanitary structures, and other physical improvements
- Taxes on labor and materials

In addition, environmental restrictions and requirements may require extensive modification of the subsoil (due to contaminants).

Protection of features such as wetlands and natural habitat can often add significant premiums to the project cost. These potentially fatal flaws are addressed in the cost evaluation workbook.

Line 3: Equipment

The best resource is the chosen model or an average of past projects of a similar type that will generate a percentage of the construction cost number. Special equipment or additions can be developed as premiums. These costs are normally defined as fixed equipment that will be purchased and installed as part of this contract and do not include portable equipment, disposables, consumables, or maintenance equipment:

- Prefabricated storage and shelf units
- Built-in coolers, refrigerators, or constant temperature rooms
- Laboratory benches
- Fume hoods, biosafety cabinets, and exhaust hoods
- Kitchen and food service equipment
- Conveyor equipment
- Lockers
- Dust collectors, dust collection, and disposal
- Automobile lifts and garage equipment
- Installation of owner-purchased equipment
- Library equipment and shelving
- Washers, sterilizers, laundry equipment, and fixed hospital equipment
- Built-in safes, vaults, and bank equipment
- Audiovisual (AV) equipment and theatrical equipment (except that many of the AV terminal devices are often included in line 11)

Line 4: Premiums and reductions

The identification, tabulation, and evaluation of these are done in the cost analysis workbook, a copy of which is to be found in Appendix E. The premiums and reductions are divided into seven categories: site, off-site utilities and improvements, building program, construction operations, construction market, client, and time. How to identify and determine these is discussed in step 4 of the cost evaluation process given on p. 150.

Line 5: Contingency on construction

See the discussion in step 5 above to determine this figure.

Line 6: Construction cost today

This line is self-explanatory (although see the discussion for line 7 below; this is only a true figure if the model building on line 1 has been escalated from the midpoint of its construction).

Line 7: Escalation

This determination requires that a rough schedule of construction start and duration be determined and that an estimate of inflation of construction cost be assessed. There has been little thought given regarding how escalation should be assessed at this phase. It is most often calculated to the proposed midpoint of construction when estimates are being made based on take-offs of material and labor during the preparation of design and construction documents. This practice, however, is not appropriate for a program estimate based on the historical cost of comparable structures, and this conventional application is one of the primary reasons for initial estimate shortfalls.

There is a subtlety here. If your calculation on line 1 is based on a specific historical building cost, often the only data available is (1) the completion date and (2) the cost. The average cost of construction of this building, however, is based on the cost of construction at the midpoint of its construction, not the end point—a building completed 4 years ago that took 3 years to build would need to be escalated 5½ years to bring it up to today's cost. Most often, however, the construction duration is not available for the model and it is simpler just to *escalate the proposed building to the end point of construction on line 7.* See Fig. 7.2 for a graphic illustration of this. By using this method, you are assuming that your project is roughly the same size as the model project and that the construction duration is roughly similar (make suitable adjustments if this is not true). The figure illustrates that a project completed at a cost of $105/sq ft would cost $134 four years later if escalated properly; the conventional escalation to midpoint would understate the escalated cost as $128.

Historical escalation indexes of building costs related to general geographic areas are available from periodicals, and the current year's index is available in *Means'* yearly construction estimating publications. Projection of escalation should be based on current expectations in the construction market combined with your judgment on the increase of

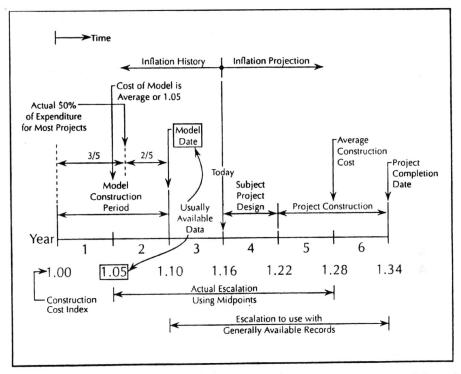

Figure 7.2 Escalation. Rule: *Escalation should be calculated to the proposed date of completion for the project, not to the start or the middle as is usually proposed.* The primary assumption upon which this rule is based is that the cost data on the historical project is related to its completion date, as this is generally the only information available. An ancillary, although less important assumption is that the construction period for both the historical project and the subject project are roughly similar. At later stages of design, when labor and material take-offs at current prices are the basis of the estimate, it is proper to use the midpoint of construction for escalation. The figure illustrates the principle and assumes that both projects are a year in construction. It shows that a project completed at a cost of $1.05 million would cost $1.34 million four years later, utilizing a compounded 5% rate of escalation.

The Consumer Price Index (CPI), excluding the volatile food component for the duration of design and construction.

Care needs to be taken not to escalate items that do not require escalation if they are large in relative value, e.g., a lump sum price for the installation of a sewer system extension provided by the utility for this project. In most instances, however, it is better to avoid the complication and just escalate the entire sum on line 6.

Line 8: Total construction cost

This is the evaluation of what the construction cost will be when the project is complete. It is a prediction of the bid price plus the cost of changes (not including the owner's additions to the project scope) during construction. The cost of changes is normally assumed to be 3 percent of the bid cost for new construction but could be considerably more for remodeling and retrofit work. It should be noted that the next project cost determination, the schematic design budget estimate, usually defines this figure differently as the cost at the bid table.

Other costs and project costs

Normally the costs below line 8, the total construction cost are of no concern to the programming team and are completed by the client. For many programs the information below line 8 is extremely confidential. The reason for the inclusion of the material below line 8 is to force the client who has not built frequently to allow for the cost of each of the line items and to confirm the exact definition of the terms *construction cost* and *project cost* for this project (see line 1 above for some gray areas related to lines 11 and 12). Often after going through the complete drill of completing the form the client may discover that the construction cost must be lowered to accommodate some of the project cost line items; it is unusual (but not unheard of) to have a naive client give the architect a program and the project cost instead of the construction cost, with disastrous consequences for the architect.

Line 9: Fees

This expense includes all design and consulting services necessary to bid and/or build the facility. It does not usually include construction management fees unless the construction manager is acting on a consulting or inspection services only basis and, in addition, there is a general contractor.

- Architectural and engineering services
- Legal services
- Survey services
- Geological testing and reports
- Cost consultant
- Programming consultant
- Specialty consultants (asbestos, acoustic, vibration, kitchen, theatrical, lighting, environmental, etc.)
- Financial services

Line 10: Off-site improvements and land cost

This would include all utilities and road improvements required by the local municipality. Often there are trade-offs required to obtain permits such as the deeding of easements or rights-of-way, the building of public facilities, and land for neighborhood schools or parks. The cost of these improvements should be included by the client to get a true picture of the project cost.

Line 11: Owner equipment, furnishings, and special systems

This category of cost is often not compared with line 1, allowing some things to slip through the crack. It is best to go over the list for each project with the client to be sure that you are estimating line 1 correctly and that the client will have a complete building when the project is finished. This category normally includes the following items:

- Computer and office equipment
- Connection and installation of portable and semiportable equipment
- Disposables and consumables
- Portable equipment (electrical plug or utility quick disconnect)
- Owner-purchased process, research, or factory equipment
- Furniture and furniture installation including open office partition systems and their wiring from a permanent electrical and data outlet
- File cabinets (even if built-in)
- Furnishings and loose accessories
- Indoor plants and containers
- Artwork
- Semiportable equipment (copy, telex, or facsimile machines)
- Printing or reproduction equipment
- Portable dishwasher, smallware, flatware, trays, and portable cooking and storage equipment
- Portable laboratory and library equipment
- Books
- Security system, telecommunication system, and data system wiring, including terminal devices (see line 1 for further discussion of these systems—they could be listed there)

- Devices that serve dedicated nonbuilding equipment even though permanently attached; examples would include machine controllers and regulators and electrical current modification devices
- Trash collection equipment including compactors, collection bins, and containers

Line 12: Miscellaneous

- Owner's insurance
- Owner's administrative costs
- Builder's risk insurance
- Training of operations personnel
- Interim and final financing
- Utility cost after permanent connection
- Moving and relocation costs

Lines 13 through 17: totaling the results

The operations to total the estimated project cost are self-explanatory with the exception of line 16, which is the contingency on the construction cost. In the proposed format, this line item is composed of two elements: (1) The first component of this amount should be the amount of money that the clients wish to have in their pockets as they walk away from the bid table; it is used to pay for errors, conflicts, and omissions in the architect's and engineer's documents, unforeseen site conditions, and minor changes or additions by the client. For new construction this should be in the 3 to 5 percent range, for renovation it should be no less than 7 percent, and for extremely old buildings with vague documentation it may be appropriate at 15 percent or more. (2) The second component is a contingency for any nagging doubts that cannot be quantified, an extra cushion if the project has an absolute and fixed cost limit, accommodation of a volatile construction market, and/or accommodation of a mandatory contingency policy.

Perform a Reality Check

After developing the unit costs, premiums, contingencies, and evaluation, it helps to stand back and review the bottom line.

- Does it make sense in the overall context of the project type and current costs?

- Is there more uncertainty calculated than is really necessary?
- Have I factored the contingencies to reflect that not everything will be either the best case or the worst case?
- Is there a large cost uncertainty that could be reduced or omitted by a small effort?
- Is there a single assumption or factor that, if false, might skew the entire evaluation?
- Is the economy or construction market so volatile as to upset the entire evaluation?
- Now that we have modified the model by premiums and contingencies, are we so different from the outset that the original model is no longer relevant and is a bad basis for cost evaluation?

Each project will have its own problems; take the opportunity to step back and apply some reflective thought before putting the final touches on the evaluation.

Describe the Evaluation and List Assumptions

To be useful, each assumption should be listed separately. It is assumed that contingencies have been developed to account for what will happen if they are not found to be fact as the project develops. The objective of including them is to support the numbers and reach agreement on what all believe to be a reasonable basis.

As the project develops, these assumptions will be confirmed, altered, or proven false and the contingencies modified to reflect a higher level of certainty. By treating them individually and prioritizing them related to potential impact on cost, the team will focus on the information that is important to the overall cost. When presenting the cost evaluation, it is best to draw attention to the largest uncertainties that need to be addressed and estimated.

Modifications Required for the Retrofit or Remodeling Project

The procedure described above is appropriate for the new construction project on a clear site. However, most of the steps can also be used for the remodeling or retrofit project. For this kind of project, however, the investigation of the site is replaced by the analysis of the building, and the cost evaluation is based on bridging the gap between what is present and what the program requires. The square foot cost for line 1, if a model is used, is the only gap that needs to be filled. To determine this number requires a great deal more work than figuring out new construction costs.

To arrive at the number in line 1 for the remodeling project requires a complete assessment of the building including all architectural and engineering systems and the subsequent identification of the money needed to bring it up to the quality of the model (which becomes only a reference number that indicates the quality level that is required and a top limit beyond which a new facility should be considered). Not only must the systems be investigated for adequacy, but a suitability assessment needs to be made relative to conversion for the future function; this would include structural adequacy, column spacing, platform size, floor to floor height, vertical transportation and exiting (the latter especially critical if the building function is to change), code compliance, etc. The only way to determine the cost and potential program fit is to do the building investigation simultaneously with the programming analogous to the site evaluation, and with the results of both in hand, do a preliminary feasibility study (I call this top-down, bottom-up programming). This kind of effort must include the work of both architects and the engineering disciplines, and the feasibility study of the project will often become more voluminous than the program itself.

Another variation of top-down, bottom-up retrofit programming is the program with a fixed budget and a list of improvement costs that are discovered to exceed the budget. This approach includes all of the requirements in the above paragraph but also requires that priorities be set as part of the mission statement. The total project is first broken down into discrete packages related to priorities and the cost of each package estimated. The projects are then included in order of priority and when the tabulation reaches the budget limit, the project is defined.

As an example of the latter variation, at Atlantic Community College in Mays Landing, N.J., a retrofit laboratory project with a fixed budget was determined along the lines of the procedures described above. An initial program of needs was established concurrently with an inspection of the building. An Assessment and Budget Development Report was issued that contained both the program and the existing building analysis. Accompanying this report (which included a complete estimate) was a Cost Estimating Workbook, which contained a detailed (albeit scribbled) cost breakdown for each discrete identified project. The total of all projects exceeded the funds available by about 35 percent. In a four hour work session with the client team, utilizing the priorities developed in the mission statement and the workbook as a rough guide, the final affordable project was defined. The dean sorted out what few conflicts remained with various faculty members. In the end, the program achieved its final objective as a consensus-supported prescription for the design and construction.

Language of Area

Moving from a leased building to their first new owned facility, the Chief Operating Officer of Chevron Geosciences found it difficult to understand why the new building would be only 65 percent efficient when the leased building they were leaving was "at least 85 percent efficient." In a 1985 corporate office building for ARCO in Houston, two future occupants of the facility, armed with tape measures, were chagrined to find that their 5 × 10 ft offices only measured 14 ft 9 in × 9 ft 7 in. Both of these incidents related to a lack of definition and communication of the language of area during the programming phase of the project.

The two quantitative building blocks of a project are its size and cost. Cost is driven by both quality (unit cost) and quantity (size). Developing a unit cost is the subject of Chap. 7. Size, the other quantitative component, and a standardized method of expressing it is the subject of this chapter. Size is one of the critical components to determine correctly if the program is to be a valid prescription for the design and construction to come. Yet the method of area calculation for most programs is often casually applied. To do it correctly (and be able to defend the results) you need a defined, sufficient, and consistent vocabulary that is appropriate to the task at hand. As you will see in this chapter, none of the existing universal measurement standards is usable for facility programming without modification.

This chapter will review the various contemporary systems that are available and describe a flexible system of measurement that can be adopted as a standard for programming and preliminary design. Since the simplest and most effective way to document the terminology you are using is to include the standard as an appendix to your program, the proposed *Standard Method of Area Calculation for Programming Facilities* should be copied and appended to your program document. Should you choose to use one of the alternative universal systems, I have identified where they may be obtained.

The first step in deciding which system to use is to determine if there is a mandated or implied language for the program in hand. This is often the situation if the task is doing tenant layouts in an office building and your language has to be consistent with the lessor's. Other common examples include public institutions for which the language must relate to various formulas for funding, area per student or teacher, or for a specific functional purpose. If there is a mandated system or a functional program language with which you must work, often the standards are very vague or simplified; you may need to add terminology to complete the program in a usable and organized format. If there is no mandated or implicit format, it is suggested that you use one of the universal standards listed below (with suitable modifications) or the format proposed in this text.

The second step in choosing a system or terminology is to determine the purposes to which the information is addressed. In addition to programming these purposes may include cost estimating, efficiency calculations, design manipulation and communication, comparisons between departments, calculation for revenue production or rent payments, etc. These requirements may suggest a shift in emphasis or additional terms and calculations. If done with some thought, the right choices can make the program a more useful document without the expenditure of much additional effort.

The third step in choosing a system is a consideration of the complexity required—there is little merit in having a system with an extensive vocabulary for a simple, owner occupied, single-use structure when just a simple net and gross area definition will probably do the job. In the interest of simplification and ease of communication, you should only incorporate the vocabulary needed for the project at hand and no more.

Universal Systems

In the United States, the first attempt at a universal standard was a single-page document by the AIA, *The Architectural Area and Volume of Buildings* AIA Document D101 (1953) in which, with four paragraphs and one hand-drawn section, the architectural area and volume of buildings were described. Since that time, four more or less universal standards have evolved.

1. *AIA Document D101:* The Architectural Area and Volume of Buildings, Jan. 1980 ed. The latest edition of the original document, it is two pages in length and is the simplest and most universal of all the

systems. It defines both the area and volume of buildings and "standard net assignable area." With a multistory sectional diagram it defines how to calculate various types of spaces. Since it suggests that balconies and canopies should be calculated at half area and factors other spaces as a whole system, it should be used primarily as a method of calculating area for early design cost estimating done on an average square foot basis. With the elimination of covered outdoor areas from your calculations it can be used as a programming standard for calculations of net to gross, efficiencies, etc., for the less complex project of any kind. Copies of this standard can be obtained from The American Institute of Architects, 1735 New York Avenue, N.W., Washington D.C. 20006, or any local office or bookstore of the organization.

2. Classification of Building Areas: Report No. 50 for the Federal Construction Council by Task Group T-56, *Publication 1235,* National Academy of Sciences–National Research Council, Washington, D.C. (1964). A now out of print publication by an organization that no longer exists, but it is perhaps the most comprehensive of all documents on this subject; it was originally prepared for adoption as a common language for federal agencies, and it is used today by many of them. The National Center for Education Statistics recently published the definitions contained in this report as the basis for their building definitions and data elements (in *Postsecondary Education Facilities Inventory and Classification Manual:* NCES 92-165, 1992, 27). The definitions contained in both reports are focused toward the needs of the institutional facility but are widely applicable. Many of the definitions in the proposed standard method of area calculation for programming facilities in this text are similar to the definitions in the original 1964 report. The later issued *Classification Manual,* which contains some of the material from the original report, is available from the U.S. Government Printing Office, Superintendent of Documents, Mail Stop: SSOP, Washington, D.C. 20402-9328.

3. Standard Method for Measuring Floor Area in Office Buildings: *American National Standards Institute ANSI Z65.1-1980 (reaffirmed 1989), Building Owners and Manager Association International (1991).* Arising from the initial work in the early 1950s by Sectional Committee Z-65 of the American Standards Association, this is the third and most current revision of a standard originally published in 1972; it focuses on the definition of terms for leased office buildings. It is available from the Building Owners and Managers Association International (BOMA), Suite 300, 1201 New York Ave. N.W., Washington, D.C. 20003.

4. *Proposed New Standard Classification for Building Floor Area Measurements, IFMA.* A fourth addition to these universal standards,

the IFMA Space Measurement Standard, is soon to be released by the International Facility Management Association (IFMA). Its draft form is being formulated to be consistent with the BOMA-ANSI standard listed above and, although it is focused primarily on office buildings, the standards are suggested as applicable for research, laboratory, and manufacturing buildings, but not for health care, education, or retail spaces. The work has been done in conjunction with the American Society for Testing and Materials (ASTM) Subcommittee E06.25 and its goal is to have this become the standard for IFMA, ASTM, ANSI, and International Organization for Standardization (ISO).

In addition to the universal standards there are many local and regional standards and many industry standards. Each major city will have its own methodology of tabulating leased space used by local developers and rental agents, and many states and public agencies have their own preferences. Your institution or area of practice may demand a specific language. Yet, despite the existence of all these standards, the programmer will most often find that the client has no requirements or preferences in this regard, and it will be the programmer's task to suggest an appropriate language and methodology.

Area Calculation for Programming Facilities

There are no existing standards that focus on the preliminary stages of programming and planning. All of the standards listed above, with the exception of the AIA D101, are designed primarily to measure existing buildings for calculating rent or obtaining statistical information. The AIA standard is designed principally to make area take-offs of preliminary design for the purposes of cost estimating. It is for this reason that this proposed standard is included in this text. Wherever possible, the definitions are those that are generally understood, agreed upon, and used by design professionals, facility managers, and programmers for these early phases of planning. Because there have been no standards, some details have not been explicitly addressed; they are added here in the hope of achieving a standard system of measurement.

Most programming projects will require little more than a simple net area tabulation along with an efficiency factor (see Chap. 4) and a resultant gross area. The extended terminology presented in the following schedule (which includes references to other common standards) will furnish the programmer with a selection of additional terms to describe, control, and communicate the intent of the program to the design team. In addition, the client or the landlord might wish to have the spatial requirements relate to other facilities or the calculation of a standard method. Often the facility that is being used as the cost and quality model for the new program will be expressed in an alternative system of measurement that then must be modified to get a valid comparison.

The standard method of area calculation for programming facilities presented here is designed to be included as an appendix to the program or design document, or alternatively, the format allows the editing of the terms and their associated diagrams. Most of the terms utilized in the three universal systems described above and others have been listed for comparison to the standard method. The terms are referenced by number to these standards. Surprisingly they are not the Tower of Babel one would expect. No system or individual program will require the use of all the terms, but they are defined to be consistent with each other. It is suggested that, should you choose to use one of the alternative universal standards as a reference, you should get a copy of that standard and include it as an appendix in your program.

Standard Method of Area Calculation for Programming Facilities

This standard describes a method of measurement and a standard terminology for use during the programming and preliminary design phase of a project. The symbols adjacent to the terms below are used in the formulas for conversion and definition. If terms are comparable to other universal standards, they are referred to by number. The four universal standards that are compared to the *Standard Method of Area Calculation for Programming Facilities* are (1) AIA Standard D101 (1982), (2a) FCC *Classification of Building Areas* (1964) and (2b) (1992), (3) ANSI Standard Z65.1 (1980) (BOMA), and (4) IFMA (1994) (draft).

The two basic measurements for programming are *gross area* and *net area*; they should be used for all programming projects.

Gross Area (G)

Building Gross Area (G) in standard (4) seems comparable

Construction Area (CoA) in standard (3) seems comparable

Definition. The sum of all floor areas enclosed within the outside faces of the exterior walls for all areas that have floor surfaces.

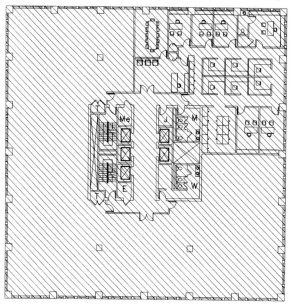

Figure 8.1 Gross Area.

Useful formulas.   For programming:

$$G = N + T, G = N/\text{efficiency}$$

For preliminary design cost analysis:

$$G + FA = AA$$

Basis for measurement. Measured from the outside face of exterior walls disregarding cornices, pilasters, buttresses, and other projections. For exterior common walls separating buildings, measurement is to the centerline of the wall except that measurement is to the property line when the property line occurs within the wall.

Details.   For programming, *Gross Area* (G) is derived by determining the overall efficiency of the facility related to the programmed *Net Area* (N) (see Fig. 4.4 for representative efficiencies of various building types).

For completed designs, *Gross Area* (G) includes basements, balconies, mezzanines, enclosed garages, enclosed porches, mechanical space, penthouses, and mechanical spaces over 6 ft 6 in in clear height. It does not include any exterior spaces or covered, but not enclosed, exterior spaces such as balconies, nor any mechanical spaces such as pipe trenches or duct space less than 6 ft 6 in high. Interstitial space containing only structure and service systems should not be included; if it contains equipment that would otherwise require dedicated floor space and a complete structural floor deck, it should be calculated at full area. When the calculation is for cost estimating purposes, interstitial space should be factored to reflect comparative cost. Light wells and shafts over 50 sq ft in area, atria, and multistory rooms should be calculated once only at the lowest floor level. Stairwells, elevator shafts, small utility and service shafts, pipe chases, etc., should be calculated at each floor level as part of gross area.

Utilization.   For all building types for the tabulation of the overall area during programming and early design. Note that for the tabulation of area related to the calculation of cost on a square foot basis after a preliminary design is established, you should use *Architectural Area* (AA), which adds factored exterior covered areas and mechanical spaces.

Net Area (N)

Definition.   The *Net Area* is the total of all the primary occupied and functional areas that are required to perform or provide operational support to the prescribed mission of the facility.

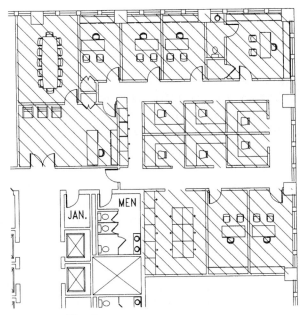

Figure 8.2 Net Area.

Useful formula

$$G - T = N$$

Basis for measurement. For rooms on an exterior wall, *Net Area* is measured from the dominant inside finished surface of the exterior wall (not including interior pilasters or minor projections) to the centerline of the opposite interior partition. All other measurements are to the centerline of the wall that separates the room from an adjoining room or space. *Dominant* as used above is defined to be more than 50 percent of the vertical surface between the wall and the ceiling or, in the case of sloping walls, where the wall intersects the floor.

Details. For programming and preliminary design, Net Area (N) is the total of all programmed spaces. Net Area includes assigned and primary functional spaces such as offices, laboratories, conference rooms, classrooms, workrooms, etc., along with operational supporting spaces such as lounges, mail rooms, enclosed loading docks, kitchens, dining rooms and serving lines, lobbies, and storerooms. It does not include intra- or interdepartmental circulation, corridors, toilets, stairs, custodial spaces (except for large storage rooms), mechanical and electrical spaces, or service spaces. Atria, lobbies, and foyers should be considered net area only to the extent that they exceed the circulation or exiting requirement. Freestanding structural elements are not considered in the calculation. Figure 4.3 lists many operational spaces and their conventional assignment to either net or gross area.

Utilization. A measurement used primarily for programming and for the measurement and analysis of the preliminary design related to the program. It is the basis for calculating the efficiency of the building. After the completion of the preliminary design phase, this measurement is rarely used except for comparative purposes. It is the measurement, however, that should be utilized in any comparative database, as it is the most useful for comparative design and program analysis. Note that it differs from standards (2) and (3), which measure to the inside finished face of the wall opposite the exterior wall; measuring to the centerline of the wall is recommended in this system to simplify the initial layout of modular rooms on a planning grid.

Additional terms

In addition to the two basic terms, there are other terms and definitions in common use that may be useful and appropriate for a specific program. Most of them, however, will be more useful for other purposes such as cost take-offs or rental tabulation and comparison. They are listed here so that the programmer may relate them to the language that is used in the program. Where the definition is related to a specific standard or document it is referenced and comparisons are noted.

Of the many terms below, the concept of departmental gross area (DGA) is especially useful for the designer who uses the program as it reduces the variables, allows a comprehensive and hierarchical view of the quantitative aspects of the program, and facilitates the manipulation of large blocks of space. Including this factor in the program will control the distribution of circulation space; to allow the maximum freedom for the design team it is best expressed in a range of values. Tare (T) is a term that may be new to many readers—it identifies the gap between gross and net (which to my knowledge has no other name) and is an expansion of a term commonly used to define the weight of the wrapper, container, or waste that is deducted to determine the weight of the goods.

AIA Standard Net Assignable Area [standard (1)]

Same as *Usable Area* (UA)

Architectural Area [standard (1)]

Definition. The addition of factored areas, including unenclosed areas, to the sum of all floor areas included within the outside faces of the exterior walls for all areas that have floor surfaces.

Useful formula

$$G + \text{factored areas} = AA$$

Basis for measurement. To the Gross Area (G) are added factored areas that are measured from the outside face of exterior walls disregarding cornices, pilasters, buttresses, and other projections. For exterior common walls separating buildings, measurement is to the centerline of the wall except that measurement is to the property line if the property line occurs within the wall.

Details. This calculation adds various factored areas to the gross area. It is the standard AIA area calculation. This term is defined in standard (1) above to include, in addition to the Gross Area (G) as defined above, the following areas: covered walkways, open roofed over areas that are

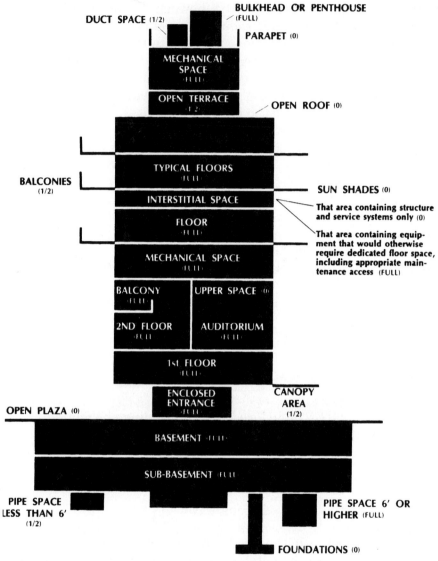

Figure 8.3 Architectural Area (AA). From AIA standard D101 (1980). (*Reproduced with the permission of The American Institute of Architects under license #94096. This license expires November 30, 1995.* Further reproduction is prohibited.)

paved, porches and similar spaces, spaces below canopies, balconies, and humanly accessible spaces for mechanical equipment or other services that are under 6 ft 0 in in height, including pipe spaces and tunnels, are to be factored at 0.50. Not included are open (and unroofed) terraces and plazas, open roofs, mechanical trenches, and void but unaccessible cavities.

Utilization. A standard calculation, the primary utility of which is in doing preliminary take-offs in early design phases to which you can apply square foot costs. It should not be used for programming or analyses of building efficiencies as it distorts the data. Regrettably, this system, because it is so widely used, is the basis for much of the data about buildings that we now use for comparative analyses and model development.

Assignable Area [standard (2)]

Same as *Net Assignable* (NA)

Seems similar to *Assignable Area* [standard (4)]

Building Service Area (BSA) [standard (2b)]

Definition. The same as *Custodial Area* (CuA) except that public toilets are added to the custodial spaces.

Useful formula

$$CuA + public\ toilets = BSA$$

Circulation Area [standards (2a) and (2b)]

Definition. The portion of the *Gross Area*, whether or not enclosed by partitions, that is required for physical access to some subdivision of space.

Useful formula

$$PC + SC + vertical\ circulation = CiA$$

Basis for measurement. From the centerline of the partition, or if the circulation is not enclosed, measurements should be taken from imaginary lines that conform as nearly as possible to the established circulation pattern of the building.

Details. Includes corridors (including phantom corridors through large unpartitioned areas), vertical circulation including stairs and stair halls, elevator shafts, escalators, lobbies, and tunnels and bridges for utilization by people. For lobbies, atria, foyers, prefunction spaces, etc., that are larger than required for passage through, the area for circulation should be defined as in the basis for measurement above and the balance relegated to net area.

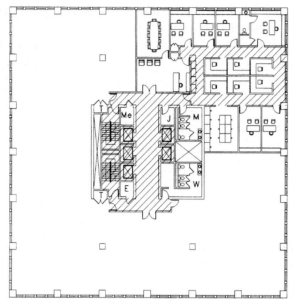

Figure 8.4   Circulation Area (CiA).

Note that this definition in standard (2b) differs slightly from standard (2a), which measures to the inside face of circulation spaces. The (2a) definition leaves the area of the partition as unaccounted space even within their own system.

Utilization.   Determination of building efficiency during design phases.

Construction Area [standard (2a), first definition]

Not similar to *Construction Area* of standard (3); see *Gross Area*

Definition.   The portion of the *Gross Area* that cannot be put to use or otherwise classified because of the presence of structural features of the building.

Useful formula

$$CoA = G - N - CiA - CuA - MA$$
$$CoA = G - UA$$

Basis for measurement.   The residual that remains after all other areas have been deducted from the Gross Area.

Details.   Not a precise computation, as many of the other computations such as net area include freestanding structural members and projections.

Utilization.   The measure of a designed structure; it is rarely used in programming or preliminary design.

Custodial Area [standard (2a)]

Definition.   The sum of all areas on all floors of a building used for building protection, care, maintenance, and operation.

Basis for measurement.   From the centerline of enclosing partitions.

Details.   Includes guardrooms, locker rooms, shops, janitor's closets, and maintenance storerooms. Deductions should not be made for columns and structural projections. Note that standard (2) measures area from the inside face of demising partitions. Normally, during the programming and preliminary design phase of the project, all these spaces except for incidental storage areas and janitor's closets would be programmed as net area. If the client wishes to utilize standard (2) as the basis of program measurement, these spaces must be removed from the net area and suitable adjustments made in the net area calculations.

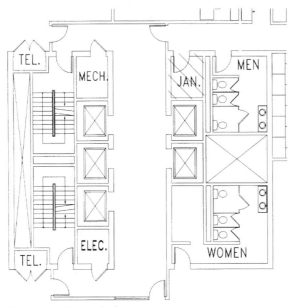

Figure 8.5   Custodial Area.

Utilization.   Analysis of building efficiency during design.

Departmental Gross Area

Definition.   The sum of all net areas within a subgroup and intradepartmental circulation for access to these areas.

Useful formula

$$N + SC = DGA$$

Basis for measurement.   From the centerline of all interior partitions and predominant inside face of exterior wall.

Details.   Generally the corridors or passageways that access areas within a department added to the net areas for that group of spaces. Major circulation that passes through a group of functionally related spaces, even though access may be gained from that circulation, is primary circulation and not part of DGA.

Utilization.   For programming and schematic design. This is a very useful calculation for the design team to have as it allows the manipulation of large groups of spaces. Indeed, if the calculation is not suggested by

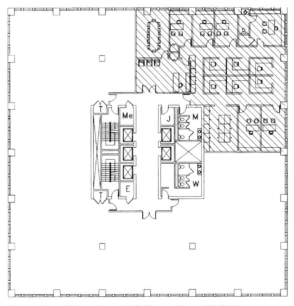

Figure 8.6   Departmental Gross Area (DGA).

the programmer, it is the first assessment that the designer must make to create space groupings. In addition, specifying this factor in the program is a means to control the distribution of circulation area and tare area within the building. For example, the designer might wish to use minimal corridors within the departments in order to have a grand lobby or vice versa; the designer can stay within the stipulated net to gross ratio with both approaches. It is up to the client to decide whether or not to be prescriptive about this detail. If the client wishes to include this factor in the program, it is best expressed as a range of percentage values to give the designer some latitude. In a typical office building, this factor will be from 15 to 25 percent depending on the size and depth of the accessed spaces. In a classroom or laboratory building this secondary circulation may not exist.

Floor Circulation Area (FCiA)

Same as *Circulation Area* (CiA)

Mechanical Area [standards (2a) and (2b)]

Definition.   The sum of all areas on all floors of a building designed to house mechanical equipment, utility services, and shafts.

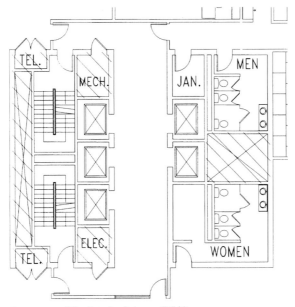

Figure 8.7   Mechanical Area (MA).

Basis for measurement.   Measure from inner faces of walls that enclose such areas. *Correction for programming:* measure from the predominant inside face of the outside wall and the centerline of all other partitions.

Details.   Note that the primary definition is that of *The Postsecondary Education Facilities Inventory and Classification Manual* (1992), described under standard (2a) above; the original standard (2a) (1964), included public toilet facilities. In standard (2b) (1992) public toilets are excluded from the building service area. Included in the mechanical area are air duct shafts, boiler rooms, central utility plants, mechanical and electrical equipment rooms, service shafts, meter rooms and communications closets, service chutes, transformer vaults, and emergency generator rooms—all for the building as a whole. If the equipment is dedicated to serving a single piece of equipment such as chillers to cool water to increase conductivity in a computer, the area should be designated as *Assignable Area* and not *Mechanical Area*.

Utilization.   For area take-offs of a finished design to determine efficiency or amount of area devoted to such spaces for statistical purposes.

Net Assignable Area (NAsA) [standard (2a)]

Definition.   The sum of all areas of all floors of a building assigned to an occupant or function related to the mission of the institution.

Basis for measurement.   Measure from the inside faces of inclosing walls or partitions [standard (2a)]. *Correction for programming*: measure from the predominant inside face of the outside wall and the centerline of all other partitions.

Details.   The same as net (N) with the exception of the basis of measurement above. Do not use this term in programming, because it forces the designers to add a factor for partition width (a 5 ft × 10 ft office must be a 5 ft 4 in × 10 ft 4 in office to avoid the wrath of the future occupant armed with a tape measure), which makes spaces and modules difficult to manipulate. In standard (2b) assignable area, which is equivalent, is the total of the "10 assignable room use categories," i.e., primary functional spaces.

Utilization.   The statistical analysis of a design or completed building.

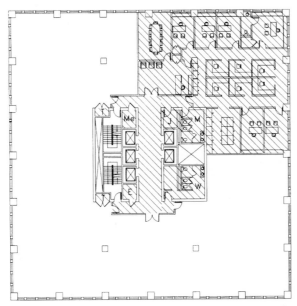

Figure 8.8 Net Usable Area (NUA). Note that only one developed tenant area is illustrated as the "designated area" along with circulation and general spaces.

Net Usable Area (NUA) [standard (2b)]

Definition. The sum of all areas on all floors of a building either assigned to or available for assignment to a specific use, or necessary for the general operation of the building.

Useful formula

$$NUA = NAsA + NA$$

Basis for measurement. Computed from the inside faces of the surfaces that form the boundaries of the designated areas. Excludes areas less than 6 ft 6 in high clear, unless the area is a separate structure. *Correction for programming:* measure from the predominant inside face of the outside wall and the centerline of all other partitions.

Utilization. The measurement of a design or existing structure.

Nonassignable Area (NAsA) [standard (2b)]

Definition. The sum of all areas on all floors of a building not available for assignment to an occupant or for specific use, but necessary for the general operation of a building.

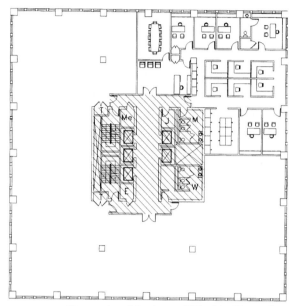

Figure 8.9 Nonassignable Area (NAsA). Note that standard 2a does not recognize what might be assigned to a tenant should an entire floor be occupied.

Basis for measurement.   Computed from the inside faces of the surfaces that form the boundaries of the designated areas. Excludes areas less than 6 ft 6 in high clear, unless the area is a separate structure. *Correction for programming:* measure from the predominant inside face of the outside wall and the centerline of all other partitions.

Details.   Includes *Building Service Area* (BSA), *Circulation Area* (CiA), and *Mechanical Area* (MA).

Utilization.   For calculation of building efficiency or statistical analysis of a designed or completed facility.

Primary Circulation Area (PCA)

Seems equivalent to *Primary Circulation Area* [standard (4)]

Definition.   The part of a facility devoted to circulation that must be maintained for use by the public and/or all the occupants on a floor. It includes minimum code or functional circulation between vertical circulation, elevators, public toilets, building entrances, and required exits.

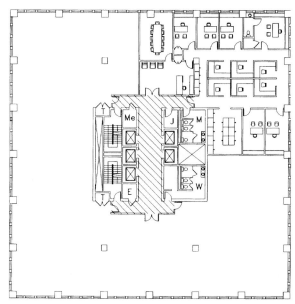

Figure 8.10 Primary Circulation Area (PCA).

Useful formula

$$CiA = PCA + SCA$$

Basis for measurement. See *Circulation Area* (CiA) above.

Details. Generally the connections between functions that require access by all occupants, it is also the circulation (interdepartmental) between departments. Includes corridors, bridges, and common passageways through spaces even if not partitioned. It does not include secondary circulation area (SCA).

Utilization. Can be useful for analyzing circulation area as a ratio of net to gross area on a comparative basis for early design alternatives. Not a useful calculation for programming as it is too prescriptive.

Rentable Area (RA) [standard (2a)]

Seems similar to *Rentable Area*, standards (3) and (4) except for calculation of elevator lobbies

Same as *Single Occupant Net Assignable Area* [standard (1)]

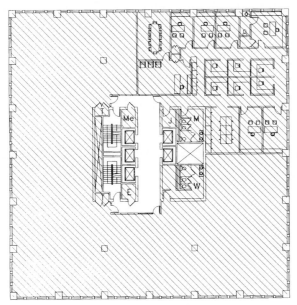

Figure 8.11 Rentable Area (RA).

Definition. The space occupied or that could be occupied by the tenant that occupies an entire floor. It includes corridors, utility and mechanical rooms, and public toilets but excludes major penetrations such as elevator shafts, major mechanical shafts, and stairs.

Basis for measurement. Measured to the inside finished surface of the permanent outer building walls, to the face of the walls of major vertical penetrations.

Details. This measurement by both standards (3) and (4) seems to include the elevator lobby as part of the *Rentable Area*; the AIA [standard (1)] *Single Occupant Net Assignable Area* is basically the same except that elevator lobbies are excluded in the AIA document. The AIA measurement is the best of the three as it reflects current fire codes that consider the occupant of the elevator lobby who accidentally gets off the elevator as trapped without a stair or exit; therefore the occupant requires access through the lobby to a stair which is then, by definition, always a public lobby and cannot be rented.

Utilization. Calculations related to the rental of a floor occupied by a single tenant. Since this is invariable, it is often used in early design to calculate the potential revenue of a floor plan. For programming, the rentable area can be a specified efficiency or floor requirement.

Secondary Circulation Area (SCA)

Similar to *Secondary Circulation Area* [standard (4)]

Definition.   The part of circulation that is within the individual tenant space and that is not required for access by all occupants of the floor.

Useful formula

$$SCA + N = DGA$$

Basis for measurement.   See *Circulation Area* (CiA) above for the recommended method of measurement and corrections.

Details.   See the discussion under *Departmental Gross Area* (DGA) for details.

Utilization.   A useful calculation for both programming and early design; for further discussion see *Departmental Gross Area* (DGA).

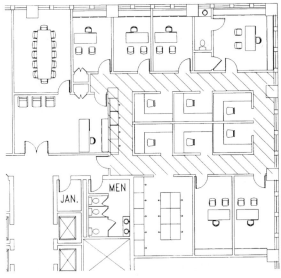

Figure 8.12   Secondary Circulation Area (SCA).

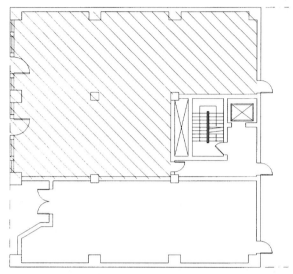

Figure 8.13 Store Net Assignable Area (SNAA).

Store Net Assignable Area [standard (1)]

Seems similar to store area standard (3) except that standard (1) measures to the exterior of both the exterior front and rear wall

Definition.   The area of a ground floor commercial space.

Basis for measurement.   Measured from the building line fronting the street, and from the outer surface of other outer building walls and from the center of partitions that separate the premises from adjoining rentable areas.

Details.   "No deduction shall be made for vestibules inside the building line of for columns or projections necessary to the building. No addition should be made for bay windows extending outside the building line." [standard (3)] Vertical penetrations such as elevator shafts, ducts, and stairs, should be deducted. The AIA store net assignable area is the same except that it is not as specific about secondary elements.

Utilization.   For calculating commercial rentable areas, rarely used in either programming or early design.

Structural Area (SA) [standard (2b)]

Same as *Construction Area* (CoA)

Tare (T)

Definition. The remainder after the Net (N) is subtracted from the *Gross* (G).

Useful formula

$$G - N = T$$

Details. Normally not calculated except as a remainder, it includes all circulation, mechanical, construction, and nonassigned spaces required to support the primary mission net space.

Utilization. Useful in both programming and early design; rarely used subsequent to these phases.

Usable Area (UA) [standard (2a)]

Same as *AIA Standard Net Assignable Area*

Seems similar to *Usable Area* in standards (3) and (4)

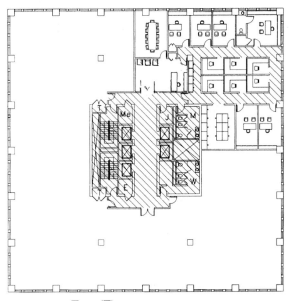

Figure 8.14 Tare (T).

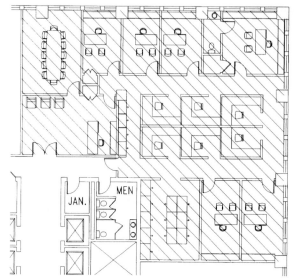

Figure 8.15 Usable Area (UA).

Definition. Measures the total area occupied by a tenant in a leased building.

Useful formula

$$UA = N + CiA$$

Basis for measurement. The *Usable Area* shall be measured to the finished surface of the office side of corridor and other permanent walls, to the center of partitions that separate the office from adjoining usable areas, and to the inside surface of the permanent outer building walls. *Correction for programming*: measure from the inside face of the outside wall and the centerline of all other partitions.

Details. This calculation is of interest to both the tenant and the landlord as it defines the extent of rental space. The usable area on a floor of a building will change in response to the reconfiguration of common corridors.

Utilization. Predominantly for the analysis of tenant areas in office buildings.

9

Epilogue

Facts, information, and beliefs are aggregated over time and a world view is constructed from all the information available at the given moment. As a new piece of information becomes available and accepted, the totality of all the facts that preceded it must be adjusted to accommodate this new understanding so as to improve the fit of all the facts to this improved perception of reality. It is an asymptotic process that gets ever closer but is never complete. An example of this insight restructuring would be relativity theory as an improvement over classical physic's Cartesian conception of the universe.

The rearrangement or restructuring of a given body of facts will always happen. It can happen as a natural realization—the facts become so overwhelming that there must be another explanation for reality—or facts can be consciously restructured. The natural method of restructuring without insight is simply reactive and always comes too late to create positive change; it is tantamount to being in the buggy whip business in 1910 and not seeing the effect that the automobile might have on future sales.

Programming as a process of discovery reveals new information and patterns; sometimes these discoveries are significant enough to require a new and adjusted reality for a company or institution. Historical patterns of operation, interaction, or teaching adjust to the physical environment in which they exist. A new facility will change this environment. By adjusting how the organization works internally and thereby how it reacts to the changing external environment in which it exists, the programming process can act as a lever to create insights and to change the basic fabric of the organization that will occupy the facility. Sometimes the idea for the creation of a new facility is the result of a new insight at the strategic level that precedes the programming process; sometimes the insight is revealed during the process.

Examples are many: A master plan for a new community college might accommodate the information and communication revolution by planning a series of remote distance learning centers or offering courses by individual interactive programming—both these approaches have a significant effect on the traditional approach of creating, phasing, and programming an individual campus.

In 1989, I programmed a new research facility for a private high-technology company in an extremely competitive global market that was then scattered in four locations. An insight realized halfway through the workshop was that we were programming four separate facilities instead of one building and not taking advantage of the possibilities of gathering in one location. In the end, the large and expensive machines became "the turf" (use of the creative analogy), owned and maintained by one group or another, but shared by all. This sharing realized a desired program objective for interaction between the various individual groups and their diverse technologies, leading to more productive research and ideas.

The programmer always needs to be alert to the possibilities of restructuring the entire program at the highest level of abstraction to achieve the true mission of the facility. Programming at this level is a very creative and exciting process for both you and your client.

Finally, the goal of this text is to help you program your projects better and thereby start off on the solid footing of a good client relationship. With this kind of beginning, satisfied clients, responsive design, and better architecture are natural consequences.

Recurrent Design Issues, Program Objectives, and Program Concepts

Introduction

There are many texts on programming with lists of topics that bear the names *facts, objectives, goals, issues, needs,* and similar terms. A list of "facts" (I would call them facts, objectives, goals, issues, and needs) is the essence of the programming system by White (1972). Other lists are to be found in Peña et al. (1987), Duerk (1993, pp. 24 and 25), Palmer (1981, p. 19), Cotts (1992), and others. All these lists are different in some way because they list the topics from a different viewpoint or according to a different hierarchy of thought. Their function is to provide a checklist of all the information that might be useful in a facility program.

From the examples given in Chap. 6 it is obvious that the words that have been chosen for this text—design issues, program objectives, program concepts, and design concepts—and also all of the ideas that could be expressed in terms of the words above (facts, objectives, etc.) are a continuum of ideas from the abstract to the concrete. Adjacent terms can often be substituted one for another by the manipulation of syntax and grammar. The organizing structure for the list below relates to the hierarchical organization structure *design issue–program objective–program concept,* outlined in Chap. 6, and it is best used as a checklist to stimulate the client and evoke responses on topics that the programmer believes are relevant to the project.

To use this list most effectively, the programmer should edit the list based on the needs of the program and then select the relevant design issues from column 1, one at a time, and discuss them with the client.

Using analysis cards, each printed with a topic from the list is a convenient and flexible way of doing this. The discussion should address some of the recurring objectives and concepts that are commonly used to define and implement these issues (column 2). Each project type, of course, will have its individual recurring issues that will need to be addressed; this is where the programmer's experience with the building type becomes important. The goal is to discover the client's objectives, constraints, thoughts, and ideas related to the wide variety of issues that comprise the comprehensive program. It is obviously good practice to publish an agenda before any meeting, and as an alternative approach this list can be sent to the client and distributed as part of the agenda.

If the client has no input on an issue and there are no patterns or insights to be contributed by the programmer, it is up to the design team—not the programming team—to address the issue by the design of the facility. Although the second column in the list mixes two hierarchical quantities, it does this by intention as many of the ideas can be expressed as either program objectives or program concepts. The programmer, however, should try to elicit and distill a more abstract program objective prior to developing a program concept (an objective must obviously exist if the concept is addressing an objective), although in practice often the program concept is stated first and then the program objective is defined when you ask: "Why is that a good idea?" The final format should be that suggested in Chap. 4. Note that many of the topics in the second column that are used to create program objectives and/or program concepts could be applicable to each of the issues in the first column.

Listing of Recurrent Design Issues, Program Objectives, and Program Concepts

Issue	Objective or Concept topics
Access	
Site	Employees
	Visitors' vendors
Building	Services
	Control (see Security)
	Hierarchy of access
	Restrictions
	Handicapped entry
	Image (see Image)

Issue	Objective or Concept topics

Accommodation

The details of accommodation are contained in the space lists, criteria sheets, etc. The purpose in including them in this list is to gather concepts related to their overall characteristics and to summarize in gross detail the quantitative material that is then developed in greater detail elsewhere. The information here is to be restricted to the future state to be attained.

Issue	Objective or Concept topics
Site	Number
	Requirements
Building	Time-related projections
	Nature of tasks
People	Grouping
	Relationship of elements
Vehicles	Location
Equipment	
Merchandise	
Activities	

Accommodation, Means of

Issue	Objective or Concept topics
Climate	HVAC
	Electrical power
Bias on systems	Water
	Sanitary sewer
Utility needs	Storm sewer
	Utilities
Utility source and cost	Control
	Intensity
Mechanical climate control	Source
	Reliability
Natural ventilation	Redundancy
	Emergency
Artificial lighting	Operation times and duration
	Different occupancy hours
Day lighting	Natural systems
	Energy conservation
	Existing resource utilization
	Building depth and platform size

Change and Flexibility

Issue	Objective or Concept topics
Adaptability	Occupancy strategies
	Leasing

Issue	Objective or Concept topics
Change and Flexibility (cont.)	
Expandability	Growth rate
	Churn rate
Versatility	Organization changes
	People changes
Time	Technology changes
	Rate of change
	Capacity at occupancy
	Occupancy five and ten years later
	Shared use
	Staggered use
	Platform size and configuration
Circulation	
Site	Convergent paths
	Divergent paths
Building	Speed and elapsed time
	Sequential flow
Pedestrian	Separated flow
	Mixed flow
Vehicular	Volume, number, or capacity
	Location
Emergency Vehicle	Space required
	Encounters
Visitor	Conflict
	Arrival
Employee	Wayfinding
	Site constraints and opportunities
Service	Orientation
	Meeting
Material Shipping/Receiving	Avoiding
	Origin
Parking	Destination
	Storage, holding, and delay
	Vertical circulation
	Horizontal circulation
	Mechanical devices
Comfort	
Physical	Confining space
	Open space
Psychological	Visual contrast and glare
	Lighting levels
	Climate control
	Outdoors connection—windows
	Scale
	Ambience

Issue	Objective or Concept topics
Comfort (cont.)	
	Building height
	Views
	Colors and textures
	Weather protection
	Isolation or togetherness
Convenience	
Efficiency	Path length
	Path characteristics
Time saving	Distance between functions
	Adjacencies
Energy saving	Time between destinations
	Toilets
	Employee amenities
	Food service
	Parking
	Circulation and access
	Technical systems
	People-moving systems
	Weather protection
	Priorities
Durability and Maintenance	
Building	Duration of occupancy
	Life of building
Building systems	Life of systems
	Maintenance cost
Site	Repairability
	Availability of future replacements
Site landscape	Quality
	Appearance (see also Image)
	Staff or contract maintenance
	Quality of maintenance staff
Economy	
Capital cost	Payback calculation methodology
	Effect on building design
Continuing cost	Lending institution requirements
	Maximum capital cost
Operating cost	Maximum operating cost
	Construction cost
Debt and debt repayment	Project cost
Funding methods	Return on investment
	Life of systems

Issue	Objective or Concept topics
Economy (cont.)	
Phasing	Comparison with similar structures
	Alternate system evaluation
Quality versus cost	Cost-effectiveness
	Purchasing strategy
Profit	Bidding strategy
	Building efficiency and cost
Tax considerations	Priority determination
	Escalation
	Contingencies
	Budget flexibility
	Utility rebates and incentives
Environmental Impact	
Protection of site elements	Recycling accommodations
	Ecosystems
Restriction on site utilization	Neighbors
	Values of organization
Studies and reports required	Minimize impact
Process of review and	Preserve habitat
approval and likely	Wetlands
timetables	Storm runoff
	Sanitary sewer
	Sewage treatment
	Shadows
	Effect on microclimate
	Use-generated pollutants
	Concealment of elements
Image and Ambience	
Identity	Employee
	Visitor
Symbolism	Public
	Trespasser
Character	Vendor
	From outside the site
	High or low visibility
	Spirit of the place
	Spirit of the organization
	Status
	Cultural context
	Neighborhood context
	Change by projection of design

Issue	Objective or Concept topics
Interaction and Privacy	
With the outside world	Distance
	Pathways
Individual	Barriers
	Offices closed
Group	Offices open
	Shared offices
Social	Team grouping
	Hierarchical
Visual	Idea exchange
	Chance encounters
Acoustical	Strategies to achieve goals
Legibility	
Sequence	Nodes
	Entries
Orientation	Path simplicity or complexity
	Different goals for use groups
Plan Awareness	Signage and maps
	Wayfinding
	Impaired individuals
Olfactory	
Positive odors	Process-generated
	From neighbors
Negative odors	Fumes
	Fume dispersion
	Wind direction
	Isolation methods
	Smoking
	Dining
	Food preparation
	Outside air availability
	Natural ventilation
Operation	
Building	Mode of operation
	Central versus distributed control
Site	Control by occupant
	Cost of operation
	Cost-saving initiatives
	Quality of operating personnel
	Energy efficiency

Issue	Objective or Concept topics
Operation (cont.)	
Site (cont.)	Simplicity of systems
	Garbage and trash
	Mail and parcel
	Shipping and receiving
	Special services
	Telecommunications
	Emergency operation mode
Safety	
Hazards	Fire protection
	Fire suppression systems
Accidents	Laboratory safety
	Production line safety
	Hazardous materials handling
	Hazardous materials storage
	Hazardous materials disposal
	Exiting
	Explosions
	Isolation of hazards
	Toxic exposure
	Equipment accommodation
	Response methods
	Fumes
	Natural disaster
Security	
Site	Telecommunications
	Conversation
Building	Documentation
	Methods
Personal, employee, and visitor	Staffing
	Terrorist threats
Information	Criminal threats
	Special interest group threats
Work confidentiality	Lines of security
	Levels of security
Materials and goods	Restricted access
	Points of access
Security image	Security systems
	Visibility of security systems
	Security hardware
	Computers
	Special security problems

Issue	Objective or Concept topics
Site	
Legal	Landscape character
	Bias on utilization
Technical	Orientation of elements
	Development restrictions
Aesthetic	Neighbors
	Views in
Functional	Views out
	Opportunities or constraints
	Adjacent properties
Territoriality	
Group	Demarcation clarity
	By function
Individual	By status
	By department or organization
Building	
Site	

A Checklist of Programming Errors

Throughout this text there are cautions and proscriptions related to errors that are often made when programming. Some of these mistakes are fatal flaws, some are minor errors, and some are just lost opportunities. This appendix lists some of the most common of these errors. Although there is some material here that will amplify your understanding of the directions and concepts that are contained in the main body of the book, the list is designed primarily to be a quick checklist to be used throughout the programming process. For the novice programmer, it should be reviewed again before you complete the draft program document. You might also find it useful to go through the list before you start programming, considering it a map through a minefield. Many of the errors on the list can be applicable to more than one aspect of the programming process, but for convenience, they are listed in three categories: general errors, document errors, and cost errors.

General Errors

Lack of support from the stakeholders

If the program is prepared without the appropriate support of either the upper hierarchy of the organization or the people that will be administering the facility and using it, the program is just a piece of paper. On the other hand, if these people participate, guide, and thereby become champions of the program, the document will become *their document* and have a life of its own—the program will be the measuring stick for the entire design and construction process, and the tool used to evaluate its ultimate success or failure. (See Chap. 3 for the strategy to achieve this kind of support for the program.) Even if the occupants have no part in the programming process (which is unfortunately true for some public projects), every effort should be made to secure all possible contributions and thereby rally support and acceptance for the program and the project that everyone really wants.

Confusing needs and wants

When offered an opportunity to express their needs related to a new facility often the occupants will express their wants. Wants (as defined here) means all of the things the user could possibly think of having in a utopian world of plenty. It is up to the programmer to gauge the overall nature of the program: Is it spartan, average, or luxurious? Be certain that the needs of the occupants are uniformly expressed in terms of what is possible. Often it is useful to set priorities as part of the mission statement to help make these choices. This is an especially useful technique if the budget is limited. Firmly establishing the quality of the project will also help (see below).

Incompatible quality goals

There are two components that need to be balanced to make a program consistent and realistic: (1) quantity—number of square feet and (2) quality—the cost per square foot (the word *quality* is used here in the sense of higher to lower quality as a measure of desirability or favorable physical attributes, not in the philosophical sense that qualities are merely attributes). There is an overlapping of these two concepts in that one of the measures of quality is the number of square feet (quantity·) to perform a given function. The large and luxurious office and spacious lobby are two obvious examples of this. The most obvious measure of quality is the quality of materials and equipment. This, in fact, is what most people think of when you talk about cost. For this quality reference, the best way to communicate a standard is to choose an existing building as a model. For the larger project, a tour can be made of one or two existing facilities; the quality standard can then be quickly decided.

Less obvious are program requirements that mandate higher cost buildings. A simple example of this would be a greater ceiling height that would require more exterior wall and more mechanical equipment. More subtle would be a program objective that states "every office and secretarial space will have a window," which in a large building may mean narrower or smaller floor plates and thus mandate lower efficiencies, greater first cost (as the ratio of exterior wall to floor area increases), greater lifetime operating costs (due to more exterior wall), and greater average traveling distances for the employees of the facility. This might be acceptable for a corporate headquarters with an average to luxurious budget, but for the limited-budget operations facility, perhaps a more compact building would be appropriate.

In this example, if the budget and the efficiency requirements were average for the operations function kind of building, the quality goal stipulated above would not be consistent. To have the design team attempt to achieve both would perhaps result in an inappropriately low level of finishes, extremely narrow corridors, short-lived and high-maintenance engineering systems, other unexpected and inconsistent attributes, or a budget overrun. The programmer must be alert to these issues so that quality requirements, both obvious, implicit, and disguised, are consistent with the available resources, and that a building of perceived uniformity of quality is what is described in the program.

Unresolved issues unidentified

In any programming project there will always be issues discovered that cannot (or should not) be resolved by the program. Examples may include decisions by organizations outside the powers of the owner or programmer to bring to a conclusion (utility company decisions, county board rulings, etc.) or like decisions whose time frames exceed that of the program activity. Other examples include decisions that must wait until the project is moved further along by the design team. A typical example of this might be the following: "if the office building goes in the northwest corner of the site it must be no more than three stories tall." It is best to be explicit and list these issues in a separate part of the program (see Chap. 4). If some of these are so serious as to be considered a fatal flaw, then the program should address the various resulting scenarios, their program implications, and potential cost impacts (if known, if not an appropriate contingency should be agreed upon and put in the cost evaluation).

Client's unique culture not recognized

The essence of the program should reflect the basic philosophy and mode of operation of the organization and require the architect to do the same with the design of the building or the master plan. The mission statement is the basic footing for the program; it should reflect this basic philosophy and be included in the program document. Since the design issues are founded on this statement, if it is well conceived and expressed at an appropriate level of abstraction, the balance of the program should be consistent, meaningful, and easy to put together. To not be aware of the mission statement and construct the program without it will lead to inconsistencies and false priorities—therefore, always include the mission statement in the program and review the entire document for conformance to the statement.

Organization and functional needs not differentiated

Most often the way people work with one another and perform their functions has very little to do with an organization chart, status, or hierarchy of command. This was true even before the advent of teaming and self-management techniques pruned the branches and layers of management. It is now common in industry, for example, to have project-focused interdisciplinary work teams rather than functionally related departments. A department head's direct reports might not only be scattered throughout the building, but throughout the world. Often a program for a new building will be a tool to change communication patterns such as "let's get the vice presidents out with the troops and out of the executive suite." Therefore, it is important to relate functions to each other by how they should interact to fulfill the mission statement, and develop space needs based on functional requirements rather than status or hierarchy.

Lack of contextual fit

Every program is unique in that it has a different entry point and different content. Before deciding on content, the information available that determines the scope of the programming effort must be validated and its scope determined. Has a mission statement been formulated? Has a rough approximation of scope been made? What are the assumptions upon which it was made? are they current? Answers to these and other questions comprise the foundation upon which the facility program will be built. I call this kind of information a *functional program* to differentiate it from a *facility program*. There are no rules for these functional programs and they are all different in terms of content. In their minimal format they contain a mission statement, a personnel count or list of primary functional spaces, net and derived gross area, and a construction cost. The purpose of the functional program is to initiate the process and thereby secure funding and/or justify the project. For the public institution, the functional program is usually in a standard format.

In addition to the definition of the entry point, a scope of work must be determined to determine the end point—what is the appropriate scope of the document? This determination is usually more flexible because you are addressing the future rather than history and, to some extent, the next step will be to fill in where the program left off. The issue involved is the amount of control the owner wishes to exert on the architect, balanced against the need for creativity (see the section "Too prescriptive" below).

Documentation Errors

Insufficient gross area

If you have developed a program of net areas, verify that the net to gross area ratio is reasonable for the building type and that everyone's definition of net area is the same as yours. It is not unusual to see efficiencies of 80 to 90 percent assumed in programs for buildings that usually have 65 to 70 percent efficiency, accompanied by incompatible assumptions about quality and services. (See Fig. 4.2 for typical efficiencies of buildings, and Chap. 8 to check the language for consistency.)

It should be noted that if the efficiency must be higher than typical for the building type, the cost per square foot might go up in response to the higher intensity of use or personnel density. In addition, mechanical, electrical, and plumbing design proposals will be driven in response to these constraints towards solutions that achieve this goal, such as rooftop mechanical units and pad-mounted exterior transformers, switch gear, and emergency generators. These single-factor solutions might not be compatible with quality goals.

Inappropriate or inconsistent language

Often the use of inconsistent terminology is a problem in the calculation for departments or subdivisions of space. The circulation within a department is often one third or more of the total tare area of the project. Whereas it might be useful for the designers to have the program define the division of the tare area, often this leads to confusion and it needs to be clearly stated. Another common error is the inconsistent categorizing of "gray areas"—areas that could possibly be considered net or tare. Dedicated toilets, maintenance storage, and lobbies are good examples (see Fig. 4.3 for conventions of assignment). The cure for this is to agree on a published standard beforehand and use it consistently. You may wish to use the terminology used in this text, *The Standard Method of Area Calculation for Programming Facilities* (see Chap. 8).

Too prescriptive

A program commonly becomes too prescriptive for three reasons: (1) it has too many insufficiently abstract program concepts or subtlety disguised design concepts parading as program concepts (see Chap. 6 for details of how this is done so that you can avoid it) because the programming team is trying to design or steer the design of the building, (2) the client is using the program to design the building, and (3) both client and programmer are taking too narrow a view of the possibilities and stating the program too narrowly.

Telltale signs of the overly prescriptive program, in addition to those mentioned above, are the grouping of large numbers of program elements in specific configurations when many configurations are possible, or the presentation of a parti (an overall program organization) in spatial or material terms, e.g., "a three story building" or "a red brick building with square windows." I call this kind of program "a rifle shot program." It is inappropriate because by being too prescriptive it robs the owner of the creativity of the architect. I can only think of one instance in my experience where the overly prescriptive program was appropriate. On that occasion, my client was forced to use an architect whom he did not like and wanted the programming team to design the building by weaving the program into an extremely prescriptive net of requirements. The final program included both design guidelines, mandatory materials, and a layout of the program elements on the site.

Rather than be too prescriptive, it should be the programmer's objective to enlarge the scope of possible solutions as much as possible. Indeed, this is one of the primary purposes of the system proposed in this text.

Too vague

The opposite of too prescriptive: this program does not give enough information. In its most extreme manifestation, it is a functional program masquerading as a facility program with only the minimal quantitative information (see the section "Lack of contextual fit" above). Sometimes the functional program itself is too vague. One of my favorite examples (it is not apocryphal but actual) was when the president of a county college for whom we were doing a new campus master plan said that he "had a complete program...[he] needed a campus for 4000 FTE [full time equivalent] students and the chalkboards must be green." There were no other issues or objectives.

Another problem related to vagueness, although not as common as others, is creating issues and objectives that are too abstract and not accompanied by concepts that help explain their meaning. This is easily remedied by seeking out concepts with the client as examples of how the objectives might be realized.

Too much information

Information overload is one of the primary issues addressed by the organization of both thought and material suggested in this text. Faced with an overload, the first step is to prune the information so that only the level of detail pertinent at the program level remains. The next step is to prioritize and group the information related to the idea of the program content. This latter step is made easier by using Chap. 4 as a table of contents. Next, summarize and simplify the messages and save for later the unnecessary frills and detailed elaboration more appropriate for later phases. Finally, with an awareness of the limitations of the human mind to manipulate variables, structure the program so the design team receives the information in appropriately sized bites (see Chap. 6 for a discussion of these issues).

Lack of organization

Information is useless without an idea. People looking at the same data will see different things and reach entirely different conclusions. Data will be thought significant or ignored depending on perspective. The design team that implements the program and the client that uses it as a yardstick of success or failure will look at the program as a series of isolated hierarchical patterns. By choosing the appropriate data and organizing it in the way recommended in this text, you will have gone a long way towards achieving these kinds of patterns and making the document both comprehensive and comprehensible at the same time (see Chap. 6 for a further discussion of these issues).

Lack of information priority

Since the process of design may be looked on as a series of successive heuristic compromises, criteria on how to make these decisions is a crucial component of the facility program. This text recommends that the programmer establish priorities by the use of prioritized program objectives (see "section heading"). This prioritization of objectives, the lack of which is the cause of most unexpected and often unpleasant design surprises, is rarely addressed in most programs; as a result, in the usual state of affairs, the architect chooses by default. The text recommends three to ten top priority objectives be chosen by the owner so as to put this decision where it rightfully belongs; this number is within the manipulative capability of most professionals. In addition, all other objectives may be ranked if the programming team wishes to do so. In practice, however, this is rarely useful, and it becomes an unnecessary restraint on the designers. After all, if the top three to ten priorities are considered in the design of any component of the facility, most will be satisfied, and the final design, hopefully an elegant resolution of all the issues, will at least have addressed the most important factors.

Unnecessary complexity

The program document and the process by which it is constructed should be as simple as possible. Only in this way can the whole and its elemental parts be grasped and thereby manipulated by the design team. Many programming "systems" prescribe matrices or other two-layered categories of information (see Chap. 6 for examples of these) to assure the programmer that all the necessary information is retrieved. This is, at best, confusing. Whereas it is helpful to have a checklist to assure yourself that something has not been left out (and Chap. 4 is a good one), it is best to use it merely as a catalyst, to be discarded once used and not retained as an explicit part of the program. This text recommends that qualitative information be categorized by design issue and that quantitative information be documented in the simple and separate formats proposed in this text without an unnecessary second structure.

No qualitative data

This is an issue for the architect, designer, or engineer confronted with a basic and, what I would consider, an inadequate program. Many programs are conceived as adequate with a space list and cost estimate only, leaving all questions of priority and qualitative judgment to the architect. Proceeding into design on this basis for all but the simplest buildings is a risky voyage for both the architect and the owner and can result in many iterations, as what is omitted in program is discovered in design. As the owner you should be more explicit so that you get what you want; as the architect you should be interested in getting the project designed efficiently and without recrimination. Without more than this minimum information, the architect is likely as not to design a three story brick building in the Tudor style when the client really wanted a one story steel and glass replica of the building down the street. At worst he or she may be fired or resign; at best, a lot of time has been wasted.

When confronted with the abbreviated space list and budget only, common sense will tell the design professional to take the time to do more of a program. The process will offer you an opportunity to get to know your client, and by an understanding of the scope of the project you may be able to identify design opportunities that will turn the project into something more than you thought possible. For the small project with a single client, all the bells and whistles suggested in this text for the larger project are unnecessary. But by using the program document outline in Chap. 4 as a guide, a simple two-page letter with perhaps a sentence or two for each topic will give you enough of a program to give the schematic design the right direction.

Inaccurate data

The program document is the first general treatment in a heuristic process. Therefore, it might appear that the programmer can adopt a casual attitude towards the numbers, anticipating corrections as the project moves through design. Nothing could be further from the truth. You must be as accurate as you can be, not only in what assumptions you make, but how you make and apply them. The only difference in accuracy required between numbers in programming and numbers in estimating the number of bricks and nails is the contingencies. Because the program acts as a lever for information, mistakes or errors in judgment are multiplied—a 2 percent difference in assumed efficiency or 10 more square feet in each office multiplied by 100 offices can generate wide variations in area and consequent cost.

To a great degree, the catastrophic and fatal error can be avoided by being methodical and reasonable about your assumptions and providing contingencies when the unknown must remain unknown for now. By organizing the space lists, developing graphic space standards, going through the cost evaluation procedure outlined in Chap. 7, and following other proposals in this text, a more predictable outcome can be achieved.

Cost Errors

The program is unbalanced

There are four variables to be manipulated to achieve a balanced program: (1) quality, (2) quantity, (3) time, and (4) cost. As with any equation, if three of the factors are known, then the fourth is known also. Almost all programs are not balanced in their first iteration if one or more of the variables are fixed. This is usually the case with most programs. If the program is unbalanced, one or more of the variables must be changed. This is best done in the workshop by negotiation with the program team and participants utilizing some of the strategies and graphic tools discussed in Chaps. 3 and 5.

Fatal unresolved issues

Many of the common errors listed in this appendix can be fatal to a program. There are, however, three particularly fatal errors: (1) programs without cost evaluations, (2) ignoring site utilities, and (3) ignoring subsurface conditions. Programs without cost evaluation are not programs at all and proceeding into design without an agreement on budget (except in those rare instances in which budget is *really* no matter) is most often disastrous all around. In addition, for the new project, site utilities and subsurface conditions (both treated in more detail below) are ignored only at your peril—even at this early stage you should have *some* idea of both conditions before you come out of the program phase. The good news, however, is that most other issues at the program level of detail can usually be approximated or contained within a contingency (see Appendix E, Cost Evaluation Workbook).

Basic quality misunderstanding

A cost per square foot that is either too high or too low because the quality level has not been communicated correctly is another common error in programming. This cost per square foot assumption, and the calculation of gross area using a multiplier of net area (the only way to do it) are the two most critical assumptions that are made regarding the likely cost of the facility. Worse yet, as you proceed down the 17-line format of project cost (see Fig. 7.1), the assumptions are multiplied by the various contingencies, exacerbating any errors of judgment. These two assumptions, therefore, should be approached with great trepidation and only arrived at after sufficient focus. See the discussion above titled "Incompatible quality goals" and Chap. 7 for some of the issues involved in determining square foot cost. Figure 4.4 is a list of efficiency ranges for common building types.

Contingencies or square foot costs too low or too high

As you evaluate the cost for a facility, you will add contingencies. Some of these have been discussed in Chap. 7. Oftentimes, the sum total of all these contingencies will make the project cost unreasonably high. This is because contingencies are variations of cost either up or down; to assume they are all up will assume that everything that could go wrong will go wrong (a conservative but unlikely scenario) and the cost of the project will be prohibitive. It is more prudent to factor the possibilities of excess cost impact on the project. In normal circumstances I would assume a conservative factor of 65 to 75 percent. After you have made the decision, stand back and ask yourself "Is this reasonable?"

Escalation inappropriately calculated

Estimating the cost of a facility without having a facility to estimate is a different sort of art. Escalation, the increase of cost over time due to inflation, is also differently calculated at the program level. Because most estimators apply escalation to a project exactly the same way they would apply it to the take-off of a design, most program estimates underestimate inflation. For the appropriate method of calculating escalation for a program cost evaluation see Fig. 7.2 and the discussion in Chap. 7.

Utilities ignored

Both on-site and off-site utilities pose a constant threat to the best of estimates at any phase. Even when they seem to be close by and adequate according to survey, many times they are found to be overloaded and without sufficient capacity to service the building. It is best to make a list of all that is required along with capacities and develop best- and worst-case scenarios for each along with associated costs. Often, you yourself will have the best information on availability and cost. Usually, the improvements off-site must be done by the utility and/or municipal employees and are extremely expensive. Retention, disposal, and treatment of storm water and sewage can also add a significant premium to site development costs.

Subsurface conditions ignored

Subsurface conditions can have a profound impact on the cost and configuration of a building. This early in the process, the goal is simply to eliminate the extremes: unsuitable or unstable soil, loose fill, high water table, extremely low or uneven bearing, subsurface rock, sink holes, and cavities. A preliminary geological report is best, but reviewing reports from adjacent sites or talking with local drilling companies or geologists might be helpful until the report is available.

If the site history leads you to suspect soil contamination, buried toxic waste, subsurface asbestos pipe insulation, or similar problems, it is prudent to obtain a preliminary report. Many sites are now considered unbuildable due to the cost of correcting these kinds of problems.

Regulatory requirements

Besides the usual requirements of zoning, rights-of-way, and building codes, most states, counties, and municipalities now impose many environmental requirements on a site. These may include floodplain and watershed protection, storm water retention, wetlands protection, resident animal or bird species protection, and other restrictions. Usually there are access and curb cut restrictions, protection of adjacent property owner's views, and in some jurisdictions noise and shadow restrictions. All of these regulations are often administered by completely different agencies at different governmental levels and on different and often lengthy timetables that may have a profound influence on the construction schedule and cost. It is rare nowadays, for a new building project of any size, to complete a program and site analysis without a civil engineer on the team to identify and quantify all of these issues. The program should list these issues and discuss their likely impact on the project; the required process for obtaining permits should be incorporated in the schedule.

Existing building analysis assumptions

When the project is a retrofit, remodeling, or leasing of an existing building, the analysis of the site is replaced by an analysis of the building. For the leased office space, usually all the information is readily available from the landlord. The building that is to be purchased and remodeled, however, presents a different kind of problem. On the one hand, if the building is currently occupied, you can get a good idea about the capacity and reliability of the utilities serving the building by asking questions. In addition, often drawings and specifications are available to tell you about the features of the building. If no documents are available and the building is not occupied, the potential for unexpected costs and problems is greatly increased. As regards programming for the retrofit project, it is always necessary to do a building evaluation simultaneously with the programming. It is impossible to arrive at a cost without it, and a program without cost is not a program. I call this top-down bottom-up programming, and some details of this process are outlined in Chap. 3. In regard to errors, the analysis of existing buildings related to retrofit for a specific program is an art that requires high levels of skill and experience in all architectural and engineering disciplines; it is replete with pitfalls for the unwary and inexperienced.

Equipment Data Form

EQUIPMENT	PROJECT NAME:
DATA	FORM COMPLETED BY:
FORM	DATE:

PLEASE READ INSTRUCTION ON BACK OF FORM BEFORE FILLING OUT:

1. Department or room name where equipment is to be located:	

2. Equipment name:	3. No. Req:

4. Equipment Function:	5. Who uses this equipment/How many at one time:

6. Location in room and/or adjacency to other equipment:

7. Equipment is: ☐ Existing ☐ New ☐ Used	8. If equipment is existing to be reused, where is it located presently:

9. If new, estimated cost: $	10. If existing, estimated cost to move & repair: $

11. If equipment is to be purchased new, list manufacturer & model number here, & attach manufacturers data & specifications:

12. If equipment is exisiting to be reutilized, purchased used equipment, new equipment w/o mfgr. data or custom built, please furnish the information below as applicable:

13. Size: Length ___Ft. ___ In.   Width ___Ft. ___ In.   Height ___Ft. ___In.

14. Mounting height:	15. Weight:

16. Access, operation, maintenance or ventilation clearance requirement:

Top ___Ft. ___ In.	Left side ___ Ft. ___ In	Right side ___ Ft. ___In.
Rear ___Ft. ___ In.	Bottom ___Ft. ___In.	Front ___Ft ___In

17. Special characteristics or requirements, including operating environment:

18. Utility Requirements (direct attachment to equipment only):

☐ Water Cold	☐ Gas (Combustion)
☐ Water Hot	☐ Compressed Air
☐ Vent Air	☐ Electrical
☐ Exhaust Air	☐ Other
☐ Waste	

19. Special Notes:

20. Equipment sketch or diagram:.

GUIDE FOR COMPLETING THE EQUIPMENT DATA FORM

The purpose of this form is to help the Architects and Engineers furnish appropriate space for required equipment and its proper arrangement, and to provide proper utility and system connections for its operation.

EQUIPMENT TO BE LISTED ON THIS FORM

List all fixed and movable equipment, especially those pieces that have an impact on the space layout, physical facilities and utilities the building must provide, and are generally to be installed in a stationary location. Include machines of all types, special motors and power devices, sinks and specialized plumbing equipment, and equipment of all types including; food service, medical, laboratory, vending, commercial process, specialized handling, conveyor, testing, special water treatment, etc.

BUT DO NOT TABULATE

Furnishings - Including desks, chairs, tables, ash trays, plants, etc.

Incidental Equipment - Silverware, linens, dishes, utensils, pencil sharpeners, table lamps, mops, ladders or other extremely portable equipment subject to frequent movement, relocation, and/or replacement.

Fixed Architectural Built-In Equipment or Building Mechanical Equipment - Countertops, built-in storage closets or cabinets, lavatories, toilets, lockers (except specialty lockers), etc.

ITEM

1. Please indicate where the equipment is to be located in the completed project or space.
2. Common name or usual designation i.e. "Convection Oven".
3. List the number required of this piece of equipment in this space; use another sheet for similar equipment going in other spaces.
4. Complete if the function is not obvious from the name or usage is not common knowledge.
5. List all users, by type, i.e. "All Biochemists", "Students", etc., and how many will be using it simultaneously.
6. List especially devices with sequential or serial functions related to this piece, and/or how close or how critical the relationship; if a critical adjacency exits, please show in the space below for the diagram or on an attached separate sheet.
9. Include cost of shipping and installation; indicate certainty (i.e. + 10% etc.); price should reflect timing of intended purchase.
11. If more than one manufacturer is acceptable, and purchase is likely because of competitive bidding, please list all potential manufacturers and model numbers.
12. It is not required that you fill out the rest of this form for new equipment if manufacturers data is available and complete. Please review, however, the listed requirements and indicate any requirements you are aware of that are not listed in the data.
14. If equipment is to be mounted above the floor, give the height required, i.e. "30 inches from the floor to the control top", and the required method of support.
15. Furnish only if extremely heavy (over 40 lbs./sq.ft. of plan area), or to be placed on a countertop or other surface where support might be a problem.
16. Include space for operating the piece of equipment.
17. Note here any special features of the equipment that the building and its systems must accommodate such as:
    a. Special mounting or structural support, vibration isolation, leveling, etc.
    b. Noise generation characteristics.
    c. Noise isolation requirements and tolerances.
    d. Special lighting intensity for use.
    e. Special environmental atmosphere, including temperature and humidity range and special ventilation requirements.
    f. Heat and light generation characteristics.
18. **Utility Requirements**
    Water Cold - Min. required pressure GPM, min/max temp., size of pipe connection.
    Water Hot - Min. required pressure GPM, min/max temp., size of pipe connection.
    Ventilation Air - Is fan in unit? if not, what is the static pressure required? Size of connection?
    Exhaust Air - Is fan in unit? if not, what is the static pressure required? Size of connection?
    Waste - Size; is trap in equipment?
    Gas - Required flow, type of gas required, min/max pressure, size of connection.
    Compressed Air - Size of pipe, pressure required.
    Electrical - Power requirements, voltage and phase.
    Other - List here special systems connections including: computer or communications, warning, control, or security systems attachments, special gases, vacuum lines and pneumatic tubes, etc.
19. Use to amplify nos. 1-18 above or to add other requirements or call attention to some special aspects of the equipment.
20. Please designate on this drawing which is front and top, show basic dimensions as listed in #13 above, and show measured locations for utility connections. If in addition, a photo is available, please attach.

D

AEC Form

Completed sample of a simple method to tabulate room requirements at the program level; this level of data will be sufficient for the preliminary calculations of all system loads and will allow a more accurate cost evaluation of the program and early design. For simple projects such as an office building only three or four columns may be needed.

Space name	Biology laboratory	Anatomy laboratory	Faculty office	Biology preparation	Classroom (future laboratory)	Computer equipment
Architectural						
Ceiling height (ft, min.)	10	10	8	8.5	10	8.5
Raised floor/ht. (in)					8	12
Noise level (dB, max.)	40	40	40	45	40	50
HVAC						
Temp. max., min.	78, 72	78, 72	78, 72	78, 72	78, 72	75, 72
Rel. humidity max., min.	60, 30	60, 30	60, 30	60, 30	60, 30	60, 40
OA (outside air), ft^3/min per person	20	20	20	20	20	0.5 ft^3/min per sq ft
ACPH (air changes per hour)	6	6	6	6	6	6
Systems						
Cooling	×	×	×	×	×	Special
Heating	×	×	×	×	×	×
Ventilation						
Humidity						
Special			1-fume hood		Man, purge	Special
Control	Individual	Zoned	Individual	Individual	Individual	Individual
Plumbing and Fire Protection						
Sprinkler type	Wet	Wet	Wet	Wet	Wet	Dry
Water, cold potable	×		×	×	× (future)	
Water, hot potable	×		×	×	× (future)	
Water, other						
Waste	×		×	×	× (future)	
Waste, special						
Gas 1	Natural		Natural	Natural	Natural (future)	
Gas 2			Oxygen			
Vacuum			Oil free			
Compressed air						
Other						
Lighting						
Foot candle, work surface	75	50	75	50	50	25,50
Type	Fluor.	Fluor.	Fluor.	Fluor.	Fluor.	Fluor.
Voice and Data	×	×	×	×	×	Special
Operating schedule	8–22:00	8–22:00	8–22:00	8–22:00	8–22:00	24 h
Reliability						
HVAC						High
Equipment						High
Lighting						High, 25

E

Cost Evaluation Workbook

This workbook was originally developed for TKLP in Philadelphia. With their kind permission, copyright for the workbook has been released to the author and it is reproduced here.

Program
Cost Evaluation
Work Book

Date

_____

Project No.

_____

Project Name

_____

Program Cost Evaluation

Evaluation of Construction Cost and

Project Cost Summary

The 17-Line Format

Construction Cost

Line			
	1	Building (............... SF X $ _ _ _ /SF)	$ _ _ , _ _ _
	2	Site	_ _ , _ _ _
	3	Equipment	_ _ , _ _ _
	4	Premiums/Reductions	_ _ , _ _ _
	5	*Contingency (on Construction, Lines 1 through 4)*	_ _ , _ _ _
	6	Construction Cost Today *(sum of Lines 1 through 5)*	$ _ _ _ , _ _ _
	7	Escalation	
		[..... % per year X ..... years (endpoint of construction) X Line 6]	$ _ _ _ , _ _ _
	8	*Total Construction Cost*	
		[(Completion Date: ....); Sum of Lines 6 and 7]	$ _ _ _ , _ _ _

Other Costs/Project Cost

Line			
	9	Fees	$ _ _ , _ _ _
	10	Off-site Improvements/Land Cost	_ _ , _ _ _
	11	Owner Equipment/Furnishings/Special Systems	_ _ , _ _ _
	12	Miscellaneous	_ _ , _ _ _
	13	*Contingency (on Other Costs, Lines 9 through 12)*	_ _ , _ _ _
	14	Other Costs *(sum of Lines 9 through 13)*	$ _ _ _ , _ _ _
	15	Project Cost *(sum of Lines 8 and 14)*	$ _ _ _ , _ _ _
	16	*Owner's Contingency (for Line 8 during the construction period)*	_ _ , _ _ _
	17	*Total Project Cost (sum of lines 15 and 16)*	$ _ _ _ , _ _ _

Program Cost Evaluation

Model Comparison Checklist

COST EVALUATION (+ / – / 0) $	DESCRIPTION	NOTES
	Site	
(.....) $	• steep slope or dead flat topography	....
(.....) $	• thick trees and vegetation for removal or preservation; environmental restrictions: protection, maintenance, operations	....
(.....) $	• demolition of structures & improvements required	....
(.....) $	• unfavorable subsoil characteristics: rock, fill, and debris; peat or loam; toxic waste needing removal; ground water, surface water, or flooding; building in flood plain; unstable, variable or low bearing	....
(.....) $	• seismic, including unfavorable soil type	....
(.....) $	• high wind stresses; including microclimatic analysis	....
(.....) $	• small or irregular site requiring higher number of stories, uneconomic configuration, or structured parking	....

Program Cost Evaluation

Model Comparison Checklist

COST EVALUATION (+ / – / 0) $	DESCRIPTION	NOTES
(.....) $	• storm water detention and/or retention requirements	....
(.....) $	• unfavorable political climate or approval process	....
(.....) $	• site location macro/micro climate	....
(.....) $	• unfavorable local zoning, land use restrictions, or code requirements	....
(.....) $	• traffic requirements on-site	....
(.....) $	• other	....
(.....) $	*Total Site Premiums/Reductions*	

2

Program Cost Evaluation

Model Comparison Checklist

COST EVALUATION (+ / – / 0) $	DESCRIPTION	NOTES
	Off-Site Utilities/Improvements	
(.....) $	• lack of adjacent sewer & water supply, requiring wells, tanks, treatment systems, pumping systems, or long extensions	....
(.....) $	• electrical power substation or transformers for high voltage supply not provided by electric utility	....
(.....) $	• gas service	....
(.....) $	• local assessments for community improvements	....
(.....) $	• road improvements required (signals, widening, bridges, etc.)	....
(.....) $	• other	....
(.....) $	*Total Off-Site Utilities/Improvements Premiums/Reductions*	

3

Program Cost Evaluation

Model Comparison Checklist

COST EVALUATION (+ / – / 0) $	DESCRIPTION	NOTES
	Building Program	
(.....) $	• high ratio of exterior envelope to enclosed area; large glass areas required	....
(.....) $	• mandated uneconomic systems and performance criteria	....
(.....) $	• special finishes	....
(.....) $	• underwriter requirements that exceed code	....
(.....) $	• increased hours of operation	....
(.....) $	• higher personnel density	....
(.....) $	• higher quality than model	....
(.....) $	• requirements for special systems (fire protection, audio/visual, security/telecommunications)	....

4

Program Cost Evaluation

Model Comparison Checklist

COST EVALUATION (+ / – / 0) $	DESCRIPTION	NOTES
(.....) $	• flexibility/convertibility requirements	....
(.....) $	• higher MEP system capacity requirements: 100% fresh air; high fume hood density; clean rooms; standby & backup for reliability; high level of controls and monitoring; corrosive or hazardous chemicals or agents with filtration, isolation, & disposal requirements; emergency power; clean power	....
(.....) $	• greater structural requirements, including heavy floor loads, long spans, or vibration sensitivity	....
(.....) $	• specific design requirements	....
(.....) $	• other	....
(.....) $	*Total Building Program Premiums/Reductions*	

Program Cost Evaluation

Model Comparison Checklist

COST EVALUATION (+ / – / 0) $	DESCRIPTION	NOTES
	Construction Operations	
(.....) $	• remote location or access difficulty	....
(.....) $	• limited site area for construction operations	....
(.....) $	• controlled access or limited time access	....
(.....) $	• high crime and security problem	....
(.....) $	• noise or construction procedures restrictions	....
(.....) $	• existing building: interface, protection, maintenance, demolition, continuous operation during construction	....
(.....) $	• rights of way maintenance and/or utility protection	....
(.....) $	• phased construction	....

6

Program Cost Evaluation

Model Comparison Checklist

COST EVALUATION (+ / − / 0) $	DESCRIPTION	NOTES
(.....) $	• other	....
(.....) $	*Total Construction Operations Premiums/ Reductions*	

7

Program Cost Evaluation

Model Comparison Checklist

COST EVALUATION (+ / − / 0) $	DESCRIPTION	NOTES
	Construction Market	
(.....) $	• few contractors for job size	....
(.....) $	• low interest because of high volume of work	....
(.....) $	• bid timing related to other work	....
(.....) $	• few qualified subcontractors for major por- tions of the work available	....
(.....) $	• unavailability of skilled labor	....
(.....) $	• upcoming union contract settlements and/or strikes	....
(.....) $	• single project client with little leverage in contracting market	....

8

Program Cost Evaluation

Model Comparison Checklist

COST EVALUATION (+ / − / 0) $	DESCRIPTION	NOTES
(.....) $	• other	....
(.....) $	*Total Construction Market Premiums/ Reductions*	

Program Cost Evaluation

Model Comparison Checklist

COST EVALUATION (+ / − / 0) $	DESCRIPTION	NOTES
	Client	
(.....) $	• questionable capitalization ability or credit	....
(.....) $	• reputation for late payment or slow payment	....
(.....) $	• union labor contract requirements in open shop area	....
(.....) $	• paper work and approval requirements	....
(.....) $	• minority hiring requirements (%) or other restrictions on labor	....
(.....) $	• prevailing labor rate requirements	....
(.....) $	• special contract requirements; terms and added requirements for service	....
(.....) $	• lack of clear organization and decision-making power	....

10

Program Cost Evaluation

Model Comparison Checklist

COST EVALUATION (+ / – / 0) $	DESCRIPTION	NOTES
(.....) $	• high risk contract provisions (liquidated damages, contingent liability)	....
(.....) $	• unusual insurance and bonding requirements or limits	....
(.....) $	• requirement for separate prime contractors to perform portions of the work	....
(.....) $	• other	....
(.....) $	*Total Client Premiums/Reductions*	

11

Program Cost Evaluation

Model Comparison Checklist

COST EVALUATION (+ / − / 0) $	DESCRIPTION	NOTES
	Time	
(.....) $	• schedule that is compressed or lengthened beyond optimum times	....
(.....) $	• bidding period too short	....
(.....) $	• schedule related to seasonal problems (cold weather concrete & masonry, etc.)	....
(.....) $	• penalties for late completion	....
(.....) $	• other	....
(.....) $	*Total Time Premiums/Reductions*	

Glossary

This list contains terms that are used most frequently throughout this text. The list is short because the text assumes a reader who is conversant with most of the common terms utilized in the world of design and construction, which are thus not included. The definitions here are quite brief so the list can be quickly scanned by the reader. If the meaning of a term is more fully explained in the text, a page reference is given parenthetically after the description for the primary location of the expanded definition. Secondary references are included in the index.

construction cost   The costs of the physical improvements. Includes the building, fixed equipment, and site improvement costs (p. 159).

design concept   A single design idea derived from a *program concept*. The design concept suggests a way that the program concept can be implemented).

design issue   A programming term that describes one of the factors by which the *mission statement* will be realized. A list of these issues is paired with *program concepts* and *program objectives* in Appendix A (p. 125).

facility program   The program that is prepared as a prelude to the design process for a building. It is normally followed by the schematic design phase (p. 26).

functional program   The basic requirements for a facility, usually prepared by the client to secure funds or provide information for a strategic plan. It precedes the *facility program* and is often the basis upon which it is built. Usually contains basic quantitative parameters such as population, function, and project cost.

gross area   The total area of the project that is obtained by the division of the project *net area* by the efficiency factor (p. 171).

mission statement   A statement that succinctly describes the mission of the organization and the relationship of this statement to the project.

net area   The area that is assigned to a single function and supports the mission of the organization. The total of all these areas is the *project net area* (p. 173).

priority statement A ranked list of the four to ten highest priority *program objectives* (p. 53).

program concept A single idea at the lowest level of abstraction for a program. It is the bridge between the *program objective* and the *design concept* (p. 129).

program objective A single idea that describes the objectives of the client related to a single design issue. It may generate one or more *program concepts* (p. 129).

project cost The construction cost and the addition of all other costs including equipment and furnishings and soft costs such as fees, land cost, and financing (p. 160).

wall display The display of information in the programming workshop. It usually consists of analysis cards, graphical area charts, budget tabulations, and other graphics mounted on the wall (pp. 98–107).

workshop The interactive interviewing process to gather program information. These activities usually take place on the client's premises and last from one to two weeks on average. This term also refers to the principal room in which these interviews take place (pp. 35–40).

Bibliography

Abbott, Edwin (1884) *Flatland: A Romance of Many Dimensions,* 2d ed. New York: Dover.

Adams, James L. (1979), *Conceptual Blockbusting.* New York: Norton. An excellent short text on problem solving when confronted with an impasse in logical thinking. Includes chapters on perceptual, emotional, cultural, environmental, intellectual, and expressive blocks and how to get around them. The chapters titled "Alternate Thinking Languages" and "Blockbusters" are a good overview of techniques related to nonlinear and lateral thinking.

Alexander, Christopher (1964), *Notes on the Synthesis of Form.* Cambridge, Mass: Harvard University Press. An attempt to systematize the process of design and avoid the problem of the "self-conscious designer," which Alexander concluded was the cause of so much of the bad architecture of the 1950s and 1960s. The system is too rigorous for most designers, but an understanding of the approach will help the programmer develop program and design concepts. An extensive discussion of this work and its relationship to the theory of programming suggested in this text is to be found in Chap. 6.

Alexander, Christopher et al. (1977), *A Pattern Language.* New York: Oxford University Press. A rich source of design ideas. It addresses issues such as story height, building circulation, and privacy. Many of the patterns can be exposed to the client to generate program concepts. See Chap. 6 for a further discussion of this text.

Allen, Thomas J. (1977), *Managing the Flow of Technology: Technology Transfer and the Dissemination of Information Within the R & D Organization.* Cambridge, Mass: The MIT Press.

Allen, Thomas J., and Fustfield, A. R. (1975), "Research Laboratory Architecture and the Structuring of Communications," *R & D Management,* Vol. 5, No. 2, pp. 153–163. Allen has devoted an entire career to the study of the effect on distance related to communication. This article looks at the laboratory and has much to say about parameters for physical distance related to behavior and interaction. The book listed immediately above is a more detailed development of the subject and is still in print.

American Institute of Architects (1966), *Emerging Techniques of Architectural Practice.* Washington, D.C.: The AIA Press. A small booklet that was among the first to address programming as a special topic.

American Institute of Architects (1980), AIA Standard D101, *The Architectural Area and Volume of Buildings.* Washington, D.C. A basic measurement standard cited in Chap. 8. It is the one most familiar to architects although its usefulness is limited to cost estimating take-offs in schematic design.

American Institute of Architects (1987), AIA-B141, *Standard Form of Agreement between Owner and Architect,* 14th ed. Washington, D.C. This is the latest edition of a flagship document that describes the contractual relationship between architect and client. Although now supplemented with a host of other forms utilized for special circumstances, this agreement continues to be the accepted standard that defines the scope of architect's professional services in the United States.

Arnheim, Rudolph (1969), *Visual Thinking.* London: Faler and Faler.

Barker, Roger G. (1968), *Ecological Psychology: Concepts and Methods for Studying the Environment of Human Behavior.* Stanford, Calif: Stanford University Press. A basic text on behavior and the environment. It is the last word on behavioral studies of the sort that would interest the facility programmer but often is quite opaque for the uninitiated; it is not for the casual social scientist.

Barron, Robert A. (1985), *Understanding Human Relations.* New York: Allyn and Bacon.

Brauer, Roger L. (1992), *Facilities Planning,* 2d ed. New York: Amacom. An excellent all-around reference for the facilities manager; it includes chapters on the programming process and how it fits into the process of design from the facility manager's viewpoint. Available from IFMA.

Burger, Dionys, translated by Cornelie J. R. Heinbolt (1965), *Sphereland: A Fantasy About Curved Spaces and an Expanding Universe.* New York: Crowell.

Camp, Robert C. (1989), *Benchmarking: The Search for Industry Best Practices that Lead to Superior Performance.* Milwaukee, Wis: ASQC Quality.

Campbell, Donald T., and Stanley, J. C. (1963), *Experimental and Quasi-Experimental Designs for Research.* Chicago: Rand McNally College Publishing. A useful book for the researcher interested in setting up behavioral studies.

Classification of Building Areas: Report No. 50 for The Federal Construction Council by Task Group T-56, Publication 1235, Washington, D.C. National Academy of Sciences–National Research Council (1964). A standard reference but now out of print. Most of the contents are reproduced in the *Postsecondary Education Facilities Inventory and Classification Manual* (1992).

Cotts, David G. (1992), *The Facility Management Handbook.* New York: Amacon. Presents alternative ways of financial analysis and examples of how facility managers operate and their concerns. Appendix A is an excellent example of a midrange business plan, which is the kind of private enterprise functional program into which the facilities program must tie.

Dalkey, N. D. (1967), *Delphi.* Chicago: Rand Corporation.

Debono, Edward (1971), *Lateral Thinking for Management.* UK: McGraw-Hill. Starting with *The Use of Lateral Thinking* (1967), Debono has written over 25 books on thinking and related issues. The facts that he is English, lives in the United Kingdom, and his books have been translated into 20 languages have made his name more familiar overseas than in the United States. He has lectured widely and completed two television series. The text recommended here will give you an overview; the original 1967 book and two more recent ones, *Six Thinking Hats* (1985) and *The Master Thinkers Handbook* (1985), are also instructive. The concept of *lateral thinking* and the many methods to stimulate it are key arrows in the advanced programmer's quiver.

Delbecq, Van de Ven, and Gustafson (1986), *Group Techniques for Program Planning: A Guide to Nominal Group and Delphi Processes.* Middleton, Wis: Green Brier.

Deutsch, Morton (1949), "An Experimental Study of the Effects of Cooperation and Competition Upon Group Process," *Human Relations II.*

Duerk, Donna P. (1993), *Architectural Programming: Information Management for Design.* New York: Van Nostrand Reinhold. A good student text that begins to bridge the gap between the behavioral scientists and the practitioner. She builds on the work of Peña, White, Brill, and others and contributes the idea of design issues as a way of structuring the programming process [Verger also utilizes this device in *Connective Planning,* (1993)]. In addition, she introduces an "algorithm for developing performance requirements for each issue/goal area and creating concepts for each performance requirement" (p. 5). This is expressed as a hierarchical tree. Chapter 6 of this book contains some discussion of the theoretical aspects of her approach.

Dunn, John A., Jr., Schaw, Walter A., and Harris, Caspa L., Jr. (1989), *Financial Planning Guidelines for Facility Renewal and Adaption.* Ann Arbor, Mich.: The Society for College and University Planning (SCUP), The National Association of College and University Business Officers (NACUBO), The Association of Physical Plant Administrators of Universities and Colleges, (APPA), and Coopers and Lybrand. A joint effort under the support of The Lilly Endowment focuses on a system to anticipate and fund adequately the postsecondary institution's needs related to the maintenance and renewal of physical facilities. The facilities audit and the facilities program enter into this conceptual system, which is now utilized by many institutions to identify and justify funding. It is available through SCUP.

Environmental Design Research Association (EDRA) (1968–1994), various editors, *Annual Conference Proceedings,* Vols. 1–26. Oklahoma City, Okla. All the volumes are still in print and available; they are a rich source of specific data related to the environment. Although academics outnumber practicing professionals in this organization and much of the material is opaque, the programmer who is willing to dig through the papers will find much useful data. EDRA is an interdisciplinary organization of design professionals, social and behavioral scientists, educators, and facility managers dedicated to improving the quality of human environments through research-based design.

Evans, B. H. and Wheeler, C. H. (1969). *Emerging Techniques 2: Architectural Programming.* Washington, D.C.: The American Institute of Architects. An early, 70-page, booklet of the AIA devoted entirely to programming. It was a catalog of the ways particular architectural firms programmed and was a response to the interest in the 1966 AIA publication cited above. This compilation was the first to hint at the difference between a *functional program* and a *facility program.*

Farbstein, Jay (1993), "The Impact of the Client Organization on the Programming Process," in *Professional Practice in Facility Programming,* edited by Wolfgang Preiser. New York: Van Nostrand Reinhold.

Fisher, Roger, and Ury, William (1981), *Getting to Yes: Negotiating Agreement Without Giving In.* Boston: Houghton Mifflin. A landmark text on how to deal with people's differences. Much of the programming process is negotiation and compromise; this book's principles and techniques will help the programmer reach amicable and reasoned settlement (its principles are handy in negotiations with your landlord, boss, and auto mechanic also).

Fobes, Richard (1993), *The Creative Problem Solver's Toolbox.* Corvallis, OR: Solutions Through Innovation. A goal-oriented approach to problem solving with many "tools" to use. Gives over 200 examples of creative solutions and relates them to the tools described in the book. Well organized and illustrated.

Gordon, William J. J. (1961), *Synectics.* New York: Harper and Row. Synectics is both a technique and philosophy. Its interest to the programmer is in its emphasis on metaphorical thinking and how it allows criticism without allowing the ego and affiliation needs of the participants to interfere with the process. During the 1960s this technique was tried by many large corporations as a problem-solving tool. A good description of its use as a group technique (developed by Synectics, Inc., a split-off of the original Synectics Group) is to be found in Adams, *Conceptual Blockbusting,* (1979), pp. 137–139.

Hall, Edward T. (1969), *The Hidden Dimension.* Garden City, N.Y.: Doubleday. Further develops the language of proxemics, or personal distances, which he first described in *Silent Language* in 1959. Distances for communication and personal space boundaries for various cultures are defined along with their relationship to the designed environment. These works are basic building blocks for the programmer.

Heise, G. A., and Miller, G. A. (1958), "Problem Solving by Small Groups Using Various Communication Nets," *Journal of Abnormal and Social Psychology, XLVI.* Reprinted in *Small Groups, Studies in Social Interaction,* edited by A. P. Hare, E. F. Borgatta, and R. F. Bales (1955). New York: Knopf.

Interaction Associates, Inc. (1972), *Strategy Notebook: Tools for Change.* San Francisco, Calif: Interaction Associates. A list of the 66 strategies is reprinted in Chap. 5 with the kind permission of the corporation. The original text (regrettably just now out of print) devoted a single page to each technique and addressed its power and limitations along with a simple exercise. Worth finding in a used bookstore for its simple and useful format.

Janis, Irving L. (1982), *Groupthink: Psychological Studies of Policy Decisions and Fiascoes.* Boston: Houghton Mifflin.

John-Steiner, Vera (1985), *Notebooks of the Mind.* Albuquerque, N.M.: University of New Mexico Press. Uses sources from literature and history to explain how we think; includes chapters on visual, verbal, and scientific thinking along with a chapter on the language of emotion. Based in part on interviews with creative people. It has an excellent bibliography on the creative thought process.

Kaderland, Norman (1994), "The Profession Expanded Services: It's Still a Design Firm—Or Is It?" *Architectural Record* (March). A contemporary overview of initiatives by architects to expand their services; reviews independent consultants as well as some of the larger firms. The knowledge-based services, including programming and the programming process, are the keys to offering many of these services.

Kaiser, Harvey H. (1989), *The Facility Managers Reference.* Kingston, Mass.: R. S. Means. An excellent reference especially for the financial aspects of analysis prior to the decision to build. Chapter 12 on estimating capital renewal and replacement is especially useful as are the references to the facility audit.

Kaiser, Harvey H. (1993), *The Facilities Audit.* Kingston, Mass.: R. S. Means. Has excellent forms that can be used for the facilities audit. Available through IFMA.

Koberg, Don (1974), *The Universal Traveller,* 3d ed. Los Altos, Calif: William Kaufmann. An enjoyable, disorganized, and idiosyncratic romp through the subjects of problem solving and creativity related to design, accompanied by "Pythonesque" humorous graphics and drawings. Subjects interesting to the student programmer include a "Guide to Measurable Objectives" and many checklists.

Korobkin, Barry J. (1975), *Images for Design: Communicating Social Science Research to Architects.* Washington, D.C.: American Institute of Architects. The core of this work is "Theory of Imaging in Architecture," which speaks to the "interior images" of the architect and how he or she relates to specific concepts. Builds upon the earlier work of Hillier and Leaman. Useful for understanding the reaction of the potential designer to the manner in which program concepts are expressed.

Kumlin, Robert R. (1990), "Program Cost Evaluation," *Critical Issues in Facilities Management, Vol. 7, Planning Design and Construction.* Alexandria, Va. APPA (Association of Physical Plant Administrators of Universities and Colleges).

Larson, Carl (1969), "Forms of Analysis and Small Group Problem Solving," *Speech Monographs,* Vol. 36.

Maier, Norman R. F. (1963), *Problem Solving Discussion and Conferences.* New York: McGraw-Hill.

McLaughlin, Herbert (1979), "Programming, Predilections and Design," *Architectural Record* (January). An article on the problem of preconceptions of the owner and architect while programming. He adopts a position opposite of Peña and states that "programming is design." His strategy of making the architect's biases explicit as part of the programming process is not possible if the architect has not yet been selected and a potentially embarrassing exercise in self-flagellation if he or she has. Usually, the architect is chosen for his or her bias rather than in spite of it and the job of the programmer is to provide a document that allows the architect's unique creativity to be encouraged and manifest in the final design, while simultaneously giving the client sufficient parameters to make rational judgments about its response to the requirements.

Michaelson, William, editor (1975), *Behavioral Research Methods in Environmental Design*. Stroudsburg, Pa.: Hutchinson Ross. A collection of seven essays on various methods including how to go about choosing the appropriate one for a particular problem; includes photodocumentation.

Miller, George A. (1956), "The Magical Number Seven Plus or Minus Two: Some Limits on Our Capacity for Processing Information," *Psychological Review,* Vol. 63, pp. 81–97. This article and the later research of Yntema and Meuser (1960) cited below are the theoretical basis of the priority statement numerical limitations advocated in this text.

Mills, Theodore M. (1967), *The Sociology of Small Groups*. Englewood Cliffs, N.J.: Prentice-Hall.

Mosvik, Roger K., Nelson, Robert B. (1987), *We've Got to Start Meeting Like This! A Guide to Successful Business Meeting Management*. Glenview, Ill.: Scott, Foresman.

Mumford, Lewis (1955), *The Brown Decades*. New York: Dover.

Osborn, Alex (1953), *Applied Imagination*. New York: Charles Scribner. The man who coined the phrase *brainstorming* and the book that stimulated what was to become a great volume of literature on creativity in the 1950s.

Pagonis, William G., and Cruikshank, Jeffery L. (1992), *Moving Mountains: Lessons in Leadership and Logistics from the Gulf War*. Cambridge, Mass.: Harvard Business Press.

Palmer, Mickey A. (1981), *The Architect's Guide to Facility Programming,* Washington, D.C.: The American Institute of Architects. One of the first complete surveys of the then current programming practices by architectural firms. Palmer also presents his own information matrix system. Much of the book is devoted to case studies. Now out of print.

Pearce, Joseph Chilton (1971), *The Crack in the Cosmic Egg: Changing Constructs of Mind and Reality*. New York: Washington Square Press. An extremely stimulating book that challenges our perceptions of reality. It is included here because it at once speaks to both nonlinear thinking and how we interpret and see data. It (correctly, I think) theorizes that reality is a product of the observers expectations'—"mythos leads logos." It weaves a relationship among the ideas of Jesus, Castenada, Tillich, Teilhard, Polyani, and others related to our conception and interpretation of the universe. It develops the concept that perception *is* reality beyond where most are willing to go, but along the way the reader will develop many insights as to how our personal perception may differ from both the person standing next to us and the real (and perhaps unknowable) universe.

Peña, William M., Parshall, Stephen A., and Kelly, Kevin A. (1987), *Problem Seeking: An Architectural Programming Primer*. 3d ed. Washington, D.C.: AIA Press. Certainly the most widely known book on architectural programming. First published in 1969, it has been the basis for CRSS's practice for more than 20 years. It was originally developed to program schools and midsize projects of moderate complexity. Its strengths are in its process and in some of the unique tools (analysis cards and brown sheets) that were developed by Peña and Folke. The weaknesses of the approach lie in its origins—the system is not effective without significant addition and modification for large projects, projects with complex clients, or projects of great complexity.

Petronis, John P. (1993), "Strategic Asset Management: An Expanded Role for Facility Programmers," *Programming the Built Environment*. New York: Van Nostrand Reinhold. Addresses the issue of how the facility program fits into the asset management plan of the institutional facility manager.

Phillips, Donald (1948), Report on Discussion, *Adult Education Journal,* Vol. 7 (October).

Phillips, G. M. (1966), *Communication and the Small Group*. Indianapolis, Ind.: Bobbs Merrill.

Postsecondary Education Facilities Inventory and Classification Manual, Washington, D.C.: National Center for Education Statistics–U.S. Department of Education (1992).

A basic manual that provides definitions of area classification; its use should be encouraged in the creation of a database of postsecondary institutions for comparison between institutions.

Preiser, Wolfgang, F. E., editor (1978), *Facility Programming.* Stroudsburg, Pa.: Dowden, Hutchinson & Ross.

Preiser, Wolfgang, F. E., editor (1985), *Programming the Built Environment.* New York: Van Nostrand Reinhold.

Preiser, Wolfgang, F. E., editor (1993), *Professional Practice in Facility Programming.* New York: Van Nostrand Reinhold. Preiser, along with Joanna W. Looye and David G. Saile, present in the introduction a detailed survey of current developments in the field (albeit recommending that the reader look to the 1978 and 1985 volumes for earlier history) and project how facility programming will evolve. Other chapters are by practitioners and educators; some of these are included in this bibliography.

Pugh, D. S., editor (1971), *Organization Theory.* Harmondsworth, U.K.: Penguin.

Rand, Ayn (1952), *The Fountainhead.* New York: NAL-Dutton.

Rosenthal, D., and Cofer, C. N. (1948), "The Effect on Group Performance of an Indifferent and Neglectful Attitude Shown by One Group Member," *Journal of Experimental Psychology,* Vol. XXXVIII.

Ruys, Theodore, editor (1990), *Handbook of Facilities Planning: Vol. 1, Laboratory Facilities.* New York: Van Nostrand Reinhold. A good reference for the programmer of the general academic or industrial laboratory. Chapter 2 includes contents for the POR (program of requirements), techniques and tools to gather data, historical space guidelines, and a good checklist to evaluate an existing building's potential for conversion to a laboratory.

Ruys, Theodore, editor (1991), *Handbook of Facilities Planning: Vol. 2, Laboratory Animal Facilities.* New York: Van Nostrand Reinhold. In the same format as the earlier and more general book but focused specifically on animals. Has less information devoted to programming than the 1990 volume, but it is an essential reference for this kind of building. The programmer should be cautious about having the most up-to-date information in this field, as good practice is driven by an ever changing regulatory and legal environment.

Sanoff, Henry (1977), *Methods of Architectural Programming.* Stroudsburg, Pa.: Dowden, Hutchinson and Ross. Presents methods of research for architectural programming. Henry Sanoff has been a Professor of Architecture at the North Carolina State University School of Design since 1966. He was the founder of EDRA; he has received many grants and awards, lectures widely, and has written many books related to architectural programming.

Sanoff, Henry (1991), *Visual Research Methods in Design.* New York: Van Nostrand Reinhold. A text that focuses on research methodology in programming. Contents include topics such as environmental measurement, imageability, environmental mapping, visual notation, environmental simulation (including some discussion of virtual reality), and planning and design. Develops Hall's *Proxemics* and Lynch's concepts of *identity, structure,* and *meaning* related to wayfinding and notation. Has an excellent bibliography for sources related to behavioral research.

Selltiz, Wrightsman, and Cook, (1981), *Research Methods in Social Relations,* 4th ed., edited by Louise Kidder, for the Society for the Psychological Study of Social Issues. New York: Holt Reinhart and Winston. A text on research methodology that covers most issues including research design and measurement, preparation of questionnaires and surveys, and the measurement of reliability and validity. Of interest to the programmer who wants to develop these ancillary tools.

Slater, Phillip E. (1958), "Contrasting Correlates of Group Size," *Sociometry* Vol. XXI.

Sommer, R. (1969), *Personal Space: The Behavioral Basis of Design.* Englewood Cliffs, N.J.: Prentice-Hall.

Standard Method for Measuring Floor Area in Office Buildings: American National Standard ANSI Z65.1 (1980) (reaffirmed 1989). Washington, D.C.: Building Owner's and Manager's Association International (1991). A measurement standard that is most useful for the office designer. Some comparisons of the terminology of this system with others is in Chap. 8.

Stephan, Frederick F., and Mishler, Elliot G. (1952), "The Distribution of Participation in Small Groups: An Exponential Approximation," *American Sociological Review,* Vol. XVII; reprinted in *Small Groups, Studies in Social Interaction,* edited by A. P. Hare, E. F. Borgatta, and R. F. Bales (1955). New York: Knopf.

Studer, Raymond G., and Stea, David (1966), "Architectural Programming, Environmental Design, and Human Behavior," *Journal of Social Issues,* Vol. XXII, No. 4.

Tversky, A., and Kahneman, D. (1980), *Normative and Descriptive Analysis be Reconciled.* College Park, Md.: Institute for Philosophy and Public Policy, a division of The University of Maryland.

Verger, Morris, and Kaderland, Norman (1993), *Connective Planning.* New York: McGraw-Hill. One of the few how-to-do-it books on architectural programming for the professional. The principal focus of the text describes an interactive interviewing process called *multiple channel communication* to get at the soft qualitative issues so often missed in the programming process. The "dynamic clustering" of analysis cards ("Delographs") related to issues is similar to the system proposed herein (except that the clustering is completely reactive to the flow of information in the workshop) as is the meeting of a "core group" to set quantitative parameters (I call it a strategy meeting) as a prelude to the process. A key concept of the method is to separate the connective planning (soft and qualitative) from the programming (hard and quantitative). This approach may be useful for the professional concerned about compensation.

Watson, Gregory H. (1993), *Strategic Benchmarking: How to Rate Your Company's Performance against the World's Best.* New York: Wiley.

Watzlawick, Paul, Weakland, John, and Fisch, Richard (1974), *Change: Principles of Problem Formation and Problem Resolution.* New York: Norton. An outgrowth of the author's joint work at The Brief Therapy Center of The Mental Research Institute in Palo Alto. It is a key text for an understanding of the basis of nonlinear and nonlogical problem solving, the mechanics of which are developed by Osborn, Debono, and others (see references) for group settings.

White, Edward T. (1972), *Introduction to Architectural Programming.* Tucson, Ariz.: Architectural Media. A short (84-page) primer on architectural programming. The often reproduced "Traditional Facts" list from this text suffers from the lack of any hierarchical ordering of topics.

White, Edward T. (1983), *Site Analysis: Diagramming Information for Architectural Design.* Tucson, Ariz.: Architectural Media. This is the best available text on how to display site information at the program level and should be in every programmer's library. White tells you how to separate the information by category and addresses the making, refinement, and organization of site diagrams in great detail.

White, Edward T. (1986), *Space Adjacency Analysis: Diagramming Information for Architectural Design.* Tucson, Ariz.: Architectural Media. The same excellent treatment for the affinity diagram as he did with site analysis in his earlier work; this text should also be in the programmer's library.

Whitehead, A. N., and Russell, B. (1927), *Principia Mathematica.* Cambridge, England: Cambridge University Press.

Wright, D. W. (1975), *Small Group Communication: An Introduction.* Dubuque, Iowa: Kendall/Hunt.

Yntema, D. B., and Meuser, G. E. (1960), "Remembering the Present States of a Number of Variables," *Journal of Experimental Psychology,* Vol. 60 (July), pp. 18–22.

Index

ABOUT THE AUTHOR

Robert R. Kumlin is the founder and director of Facility
Programming Consultants and a principal of Duca/Huder & Kumlin,
an architectural firm in Moorestown, New Jersey. He has had more
than 25 years of experience with such notable architectural firms as
Perkins & Will, Ellerbe Beckett, and VOA. He has served as director
of projects for The Kling Lindquist Partnership in Philadelphia, Pa.,
and as vice president and project director for CRSS in Houston,
Texas. He has worked with AT&T, ARCO, Glaxo Inc., Chevron,
Merck, the University of Georgia, Cornell, and others—helping each
to plan and program facilities. He has written and lectured widely
about the architectural programming process and is licensed to
practice architecture in five states.